The Brain-Friendly Museum

The Brain-Friendly Museum proposes an innovative approach to experiencing and enjoying the museum environment in new ways, based on the systematic application of cognitive psychology and neuroscience.

Providing practical guidance on navigating and thinking about museums in different ways, the book is designed to help develop more fulfilling visitor experiences. It explores our cognitive processes and emotions, and how they can be used to engage with and enjoy the museum environment, regardless of the visitor's background, language, or culture. The book considers core cognitive processes, including memory, attention, and perception, and how they can successfully be applied to the museum environment, for example, in creating more effective displays. Using evidence-based examples throughout, the book advocates for a wellbeing approach improving visitor experience, and one that is grounded in research from psychology and neuroscience.

This book is a must-read for all museum practitioners and psychologists interested in the relationship between cultural heritage, psychology, and neuroscience. It will also be of great interest to art therapists, neuroscientists, university students, museum stakeholders, and museum lovers.

Annalisa Banzi is an art historian and researcher at CESPEB with a Ph.D. in psychology applied to museum studies. She has an interdisciplinary specialisation in museum studies, psychology, and neuroscience which aims to improve the dissemination of museum contents and to develop visitors' mental wellbeing and satisfaction.

The Brain-Friendly Museum

Using Psychology and Neuroscience to Improve the Visitor Experience

Edited by Annalisa Banzi

Routledge
Taylor & Francis Group
LONDON AND NEW YORK

Cover image: Getty

First published 2023
by Routledge
4 Park Square, Milton Park, Abingdon, Oxon OX14 4RN

and by Routledge
605 Third Avenue, New York, NY 10158

Routledge is an imprint of the Taylor & Francis Group, an informa business

British Library Cataloguing-in-Publication Data
A catalogue record for this book is available from the British Library

Library of Congress Cataloging-in-Publication Data
A catalog record has been requested for this book

ISBN: 978-1-032-30330-7 (hbk)
ISBN: 978-1-032-30329-1 (pbk)
ISBN: 978-1-003-30453-1 (ebk)

DOI: 10.4324/9781003304531

Typeset in Bembo
by MPS Limited, Dehradun

To Giacomo

(A.B.)

Contents

Contributors

Annalisa Banzi Ph.D., Position and affiliation: Researcher–CESPEB

Vincenza Ferrara, Position and affiliation: Director of Art and Medical Humanities Lab - Pharmacy and Medicine Faculty – Sapienza University of Rome. Autobiographical note: Vincenza Ferrara. Art historian. Director of Art and medical humanities lab – Sapienza University of Rome. Her research topic is the promotion of the cultural heritage in the School and Medical Education field in order to improve learning and promote museums. She is an expert and trainer of Visual Thinking Strategies.

Maurizio Forte Ph.D., Position and affiliation: Distinguished Professor of Classical Studies, Art, Art History and Visual Studies, Duke University. Autobiographical note: Maurizio Forte, professor of Classical Studies, Art History and Visual Studies, is director of the Dig@Lab at Duke University. He was a pioneer in digital technologies applied to heritage and archaeology and he published several books and over 200 scientific papers.

Stephen Legari MA, MSc(A), Position and affiliation: Program Officer, Art Therapy, Montreal Museum of Fine Arts. Autobiographical note: Stephen Legari is a registered Canadian Art Therapist and licensed couple and family therapist. He has worked extensively in both community and clinical settings. Since 2017, Stephen has been Program Officer for Art Therapy at the Montreal Museum of Fine Arts.

Eva Pietroni, Position and affiliation: Senior Researcher at CNR Institute of Heritage Sciences (ISPC). Autobiographical note: Eva Pietroni is a Senior Researcher at CNR ISPC, Conservator of BB.CC., art historian and musician. Her research concerns virtual museums and museum technologies, digitisation, virtual reconstruction, new forms of narration, and interaction based on the hybridisation of media, user experience design. In this domain, she coordinates national and international projects.

Robert Sadleir, Position and affiliation: Co-founder, QWB Lab Ltd. Autobiographical note: Robert Sadleir is a Co-founder of QWB Lab Ltd., a firm unlocking the value of the cultural sector by measuring wellbeing. He is a technical expert for British Standards on sustainable communities and SMART cities. He has a Bachelor of Economics University of Sydney, MA University of Geneva, and a MTS Harvard University.

Kate Straneva, Position and affiliation: Undergraduate Student majoring in Computer Science and Biology. Autobiographical note: Kate Straneva is a recent graduate of Duke University where she majored in Computer Science and Biology. Kate is interested in a career in the biotechnology space.

Leonard White Ph.D., Position and affiliation: Associate Professor in Neurology, Duke University School of Medicine. Autobiographical note: Leonard E. White is a neuroscientist and educator at Duke University who studies human and non-human neuroanatomy and the relationships between the structure and function of neural circuits in the brain.

Sean Woytowitz, Position and affiliation: Undergraduate Researcher, Duke University (Trinity College of Arts and Sciences). Autobiographical note: Sean Woytowitz is a senior at Duke University majoring in psychology and preparing to attend medical school next year. He is from San Diego, California and is currently studying mental health and how it relates to diversity and the human condition.

Cristian A. Zaelzer-Pérez Ph.D., Position and affiliation: Founder & President of the Convergence Initiative. Autobiographical note: Cristian Zaelzer-Perez is a Chilean-Canadian neuroscientist, artist, graphic designer, educator & science communicator that explores new ways to engage (neuro)science with different communities. In 2016, he founded the Convergence Initiative to create bridges between neuroscience and art, connecting institutions that work and research those fields and the students they teach.

Foreword

As public institutions go these days, museums are relatively old, having been around in some form or another for hundreds of years. However, the appearance and focus of today's museum bear only a passing resemblance to its ancestors. The collection, preservation and study of precious objects and ideas remain a central activity of most museums, but increasingly these activities have become mere means to a greater end, the goal of supporting the public's learning and enjoyment. Reflective of this growing commitment to the public, museum professionals have become increasingly focused on learning how best to improve the quality of their offerings; how best to enhance the experience of the millions of people who annually engage with museums. In response to this growing interest in improving the museum, experience has been development of an expanding number of resources on the subject. Every year, dozens of new books and hundreds of journal articles are written about the museum experience. Every year, scores of researchers and practitioners deliver conference presentations on the latest and greatest approaches for improving the public's museum experience. I confess to being one of those adding to this growing pile of resources. In fact, I probably am one of the most prolific generators of such books, articles and talks, having been at this task for nearly half a century. Year after year, I have strived to better understand why people visit museums, what they do there, and what they take away from their museum experiences. In pursuit of this objective, I have conducted many hundreds of studies, written more than a dozen books, several hundred articles and given many hundreds of talks on the museum experience; all in an effort to turn my understandings into better museum practice.

Thus, it is from this perspective, the perspective of someone who has long toiled in the trenches of thinking long and hard about how best to analyse the public's museum experiences and convert those analyses into useful ideas for museum practice, that I came to know Annalisa Banzi. Dr. Banzi reached out to me to talk about her work and mine. I was delighted to make her acquaintance, to "talk shop" with her about studying visitors. Ultimately, she asked, and I agreed to write the Foreword for this book: The brain-friendly museum. Using psychology and neurosicnece to improve the visitor experience.

I was happy to discover that in this new book, Dr. Banzi makes an important contribution to the growing museums studies literature. Hers, as suggested above, is far from the first book seeking to apply insights from the field of psychology to the topic of museum visitor experiences, but her focus on the latest insights and tools from the brain sciences are quite unique. It is fair to say, largely due to the work of the brain sciences, we have discovered more in just the past couple of decades about how the mind works than was known in all the previous decades combined. The insights and understandings of human thinking and behaving being developed by these investigations continues to grow at a rapid pace. Thus, this volume can only begin to provide a foundation, an initial sense of how to create a brain-friendly museum. Like all complex edifices, and the museum experience certainly represents a complex edifice, a sound and strong foundation is essential. The foundational understandings about the museum experience presented in this book will provide museum professionals with the secure launch pad they need in order to re-think their practices and create new approaches and innovations for today's and tomorrow's visitors. Dr. Banzi covers a lot of ground in her book, touching on a vast array of cognitive psychology and neuroscience topics. Included are discussions about perception, attention, memory and learning. Also covered are current understandings of the nature of language and communication, problem solving, decision-making, judgement, reasoning and creativity. But what I most appreciate and applaud her for, is that she begins by focusing on emotions, and ends by focusing on wellbeing. If I had to summarise what I have learned about the museum experience over my decades-long research career, I would say the visitor's museum experience always begins with emotions, and always ends with wellbeing.

As stated by Dr. Banzi, the brain-friendly museum must be an institution that respects the importance of human emotions. For years, cognitive psychologists essentially ignored emotions, assuming they were only marginally relevant for understanding how people think, learn and make decisions. Thanks in large part to advances in the neurosciences, it is now apparent that virtually everything going on in the brain, including awareness and perception, learning and decision-making, all involve the emotions. As a consequence, it is now widely accepted, that far from being marginally important, emotions are actually a consistent and central feature of all human cognition. To understand why people use museums, what they do there, and what they learn, requires understanding something about the role emotions play in all of these different stages of the museum experience. Unfortunately, as a consequence of their long neglect as a topic of study, and despite the current appreciation of their importance, emotions remain poorly understood and largely under-studied; including within the museum context. This is likely to be an area of ever-increasing investigation in the coming decades and we can look forward to significant improvements in museum practice as greater understanding develops for how to most effectively harness the power of user's emotions.

In a similar way, the other major "new frontier" for understanding museum experiences is wellbeing. As I discuss at length in my latest writings, I now believe that the fundamental reason people use museums, as well as the fundamental benefit they derive from those experiences is wellbeing. Like emotions, it is only recently that brain scientists have come to appreciate just how fundamental a process the pursuit of well-being is for humans. As I have argued, wellbeing is so fundamental that it cannot be understood through an exclusively psychological lens. Well-being is a basic biological process, a mechanism for achieving balance with one's world. In fact, the need to achieve well-being balance is at the core of what it means to be alive, and the pursuit of wellbeing underlies everything people do. As researchers, and museum professionals, come to more fully understand the fundamental importance of well-being, it too is likely to become an area of ever-more intensive focus. As my research has shown, humans are strongly drawn to museum experiences because they believe these experiences support and enhance some aspect of their wellbeing. Thus, the question for museum professionals will increasingly become, not if it is possible to create museum experiences that support wellbeing, but rather in what form, in what ways, and to what degree can we create museum experiences that maximally achieve this outcome?

In conclusion, this is a book well worth reading. The brain-friendly museum. Using psychology and neurosicnece to improve the visitor experience. is rich in detail and enriched by numerous real-world examples. It will serve as a handy reference for years to come and I look forward to having it in an easily accessible place on my bookcase for just that purpose.

John H. Falk, Ph.D.
Institute for Learning Innovation
Author of: The Value of Museum: Enhancing Societal Well-Being
Born to Choose: Evolution, Self and Well-Being
Learning from Museums
The Museum Experience
Identity and the Museum Visitor Experience

Acknowledgements

I would like to wholeheartedly thank all the people who have been very important in the creation and writing of this book. None of this would have been possible without the invaluable advice or contributions of: my family, Andrew Mashigo, Annalisa Ferroni Bismut, Annelise Ream, Attilio Maranzano, Brita Köhler, Catterina Seia, Ceri McLardy, Christian Cataldo, Clelia Valdesi Valeri, Cristian Perez-Zaelzer PhD, Daniele Monti, Danny Meadows, Emilie Coin, Eva Pietroni, Flora Santorelli, Giuliano Gaia, Hakan Johansson, Johanna Bokedal, Kate Straneva, Khyati Sanger, Laura Vigo, Lauren Ellis, Marco Toscano, Marko Daniel, Michelle Harrell, Nicolò Scialanga, Nivedita Menon, Paola Azzola, Patrizia Vaccaro, Phil Terry, Pietro Nozza, Prof. Francesca Pazzaglia, Prof. John H. Falk, Prof. Leonard White, Prof. Maurizio Forte, Prof. Michael W. Eysenck, Prof. Riccardo Manzotti, Prof. Vincenzo G. Dovì, Prof. Vincenza Ferrara, Radhika Bhartari, Riccardo Betti, Robert Sadleir, Rosanna and Nicola Labianca, Sabine Doolin, Sean Woytowitz, Sonia D'Arcargelo, Stefano Verri, Stephen Legari, Susan Comber, and Zhisheng Wang.

Annalisa Banzi

1 The Brain-Friendly Museum

How Psychology and Neuroscience Can Help Museums to be Brain-Friendly and Promote Wellbeing

Annalisa Banzi

Imagine a couple of friends visiting a museum. As soon as they *look* at the displayed objects, they pay *attention to* and *read* the captions as well. They will likely compare these objects with others previously seen, recalling the information stored in *long-term memory*. They will use their *language* skills to share thoughts on what they are *learning*, which may be affected by their *emotional state*. They will also *decide* how much time to spend on the tour, and maybe they will have to *solve some problems* (e.g., being thirsty, being tired, and needing a restroom) while walking through the galleries.

The mental processes described above represent major aspects of human cognition. They are interdependent, meaning that each of them depends on other processes and structures. Cognitive psychology aims at analysing these internal processes by observing the behaviour of individuals who perform several cognitive tasks. It has also recently begun to investigate emotions and their relationship to cognition. It is one of the main approaches to understanding human cognition along with cognitive neuropsychology (an approach that studies patients with brain damage), computational cognitive science (an approach that develops computational models of human cognition), and cognitive neuroscience (an approach that takes into account both behaviour and brain activity). In this book, the term cognitive psychology is used in the broadest sense proposed by Eysenck and Keane (2020), which encompasses all of these approaches. However, I will not explicitly mention notions and findings related to brain-damaged patients to avoid overloading the reader.

Every aspect studied by cognitive psychology is important in the museum experience. Once the needs of the brain are met, visitors will have a better chance of appreciating our heritage. Taking cognitive processes and emotions into consideration saves us from designing inadequate museum experiences. For instance, as we know, the crowding of objects in the exhibition rooms is harmful to the perception of an individual object for various reasons: perceptual aspects (the objects are too close), attention-related aspects (too many stimuli can be distracting), semantic satiety (too many experiences of the same type), and memory difficulties in remembering the objects seen (Antinucci, 2006).

DOI: 10.4324/9781003304531-1

What Is a Brain-Friendly Museum?

The brain-friendly museum (BFM) is an institution based on the respect of human beings' cognitive processes and emotions as well as on the protection, preservation, dissemination, and appreciation of our tangible and intangible heritage for the purposes of education, study, and enjoyment. The specific tasks and mission of museums have already been addressed by museum experts. However, I believe that the definition of the museum should include respecting the needs of our brains. It is a fundamental condition for a greater appreciation by visitors of our heritage.

While I was attending university, I often worked as a museum guide. It was a job that helped me to delve into some topics related to art history from different standpoints. I am mentioning this because in that period I realised that there were visitors who were very interested in the topics and contents introduced in the exhibitions, and they wanted to learn about them but they couldn't "absorb" all the information. Even if they were interested and enthusiastic about the displayed objects, and even if I was doing my best to share with them some information about these artworks, I noted that their memories of the contents were vivid for a short period of time. After a few museum halls and new concepts were added, the previous information was "blurred". The groups of visitors who were not familiar with the content of the exhibition were the most disadvantaged. During that period I started thinking how I could have been of help to these museumgoers. The literature (e.g., Antinucci, 2007) remarks that this problem exists and we should take it into consideration. That's why my first interest, which started during the Ph.D. programme, was devoted to studying how to adapt the psychology knowledge and techniques to foster visitors' memory. My first concern was to give some support to help them remember better what they wanted to learn. Of course, emotions are great allies to memorise contents; however, there are other aspects that can help this process. Psychology over time has developed many techniques and methods that could be applied to the museum environment.

In recent years, I enlarged this objective by introducing the idea that all cognitive processes and emotions can be of help to a meaningful museum experience. This is why I am developing the BFM approach which aims at embracing all these processes.

The role that psychology (in particular the cognitive branch) can play in the museum environment has already been mentioned above. Together with neuroscience, it is one of the main disciplines involved in the BFM approach. Let's now introduce the role of the latter and its contribution to the achievement of meaningful visitors' experiences. As we will see, we can take into account the findings collected by neuroscience and also we can use its tools (chapter 7) to assess museumgoers' skills once psychological concepts have been applied to the museum setting. In this regard, note that the Peabody Essex Museum (USA) is mentioned several times in this book as it is the first institution that officially introduced neuroscience into its strategy. However, the BFM approach emphasises the beneficial impact that could also be brought by the systematic application of psychology to the museum environment.

Museums already promote their own research; however, they could expand their capabilities by collaborating with universities and other institutions to carry out experiments that increase knowledge of our cognitive processes and emotions. It is a key service that museums could offer to society. The BFM's philosophy encourages a collaborative approach between museum practitioners and experts from other fields to develop fulfilling museum experiences.

In a provocative way, I believe that museums can be considered as "ecologically valid laboratories". What is ecological validity? As explained by Eysenck and Keane (2020), it is the applicability or otherwise of the results of laboratory studies to everyday life. Therefore, ecological validity is the applicability to real life and has two aspects: *representativeness*, which is the naturalness of the experimental situation and the task to be performed, and *generalisability*, which is the extent to which the results of a study apply to the real world (Eysenck & Keane, 2020). To some extent, museums, which are part of the real world, can control and isolate the factors that are involved in a cognitive process as if carried out in a laboratory and can count on a huge potential sample of participants in experiments (their visitors).

Of course, the experiments carried out by psychologists and neuroscientists that are introduced in the first 7 chapters are different from each other in terms of "grain-size". They need to be adapted to the museum environment while respecting the ecological validity.

The first 7 chapters are intended to be an introduction to different psychological concepts and theories that could be adapted and tested in museums based on the specific needs of each institution. This means that there is no single ideal psychological content that could be used in all types of museums. Each institution requires a specific analysis of the audiences, collections and so forth to choose the right means to engage and satisfy their public.

Psychologists and neuroscientists are used to investigating cultural heritage to draw insight into how the brain works. I think it is also very important for museum practitioners to become more interested in psychology and neuroscience in order to develop even more meaningful museum experiences. Learning about our brain helps us to communicate with psychologists and neuroscientists to design more effective exhibitions and educational activities. My wish is that we can develop a smooth and fruitful dialogue.

It took me years to develop this book, and I hope this will just be the beginning. It can be a starting point if we install a permanent and systematic collaboration between experts from different fields. The experiences of other researchers and museum experts can be the "follow up" of this book. Psychologists and neuroscientists are still in the process of understanding completely how our brain works but we can take advantage of the numerous findings collected up to now. This is a very fascinating journey, the theories proposed by psychology have yet to be perfected, and neuroscience is still looking for numerous answers which can clearly explain how our brain functions. In other words, there is often no simple and direct relationship between what we understand about the brain and what it implies for practice. However, combining these disciplines with the research into museumgoers' needs can contribute and advantage each of these fields.

This book is an invitation to carry out experiments which will make it possible to compare and integrate the theories derived from different disciplines (i.e., psychology and the analysis of museum visitors' needs). In order to reach this goal, experts from different fields are encouraged to collaborate. It is intended to be an introduction to these complex topics which will be examined in depth in further publications using this collaborative approach.

What is discussed in this book? It is an attempt to fill a gap in the museum field. Each of the first 7 chapters matches a cognitive process with a specific museum topic. They introduce numerous examples and proposals that try to adapt the contents of psychology and neuroscience to the museum environment. Chapter 8 focuses on examples of wellbeing initiatives in which museums are involved. Mental wellbeing is one of the main objectives that the BFM approach would like to achieve.

Note that the book opens with an introduction to emotions which I consider the first connection to our heritage and that the section "Practical application of psychology and neuroscience in the museum environment" (chapter 4) describes a concrete application of these disciplines to the museum setting. Also, in the section "How to involve visitors in museum experiments. Some practical advice" (chapter 7), I share some ideas that could help to involve and interest visitors in museum experiments.

It is the first and promising attempt to combine psychology, neuroscience, and the museumgoers' needs. Of course, the connection between them is not explicitly evident. It is a work in progress. It requires experiments to collect data that could be used to define effective and proven strategies. We will have the great opportunity to *compare* these experiments and data, collected from *different* museums, to improve the BFM approach for the benefit of visitors.

Since there are no experimental and statistical reports yet on the BFM approach, I also took advantage of brainstorming techniques to propose ideas. Obviously, they will need to be verified in the museum environment.

The following contributions (chapters 9–13) to this book are based on the valuable experiences of museum practitioners and university researchers who share their projects, pilot studies, and ideas. These may be inspirational and adaptable to the BFM approach.

The selection of the part related to cognitive psychology content and papers mentioned in this book is based on that proposed by Michael W. Eysenck and Mark T. Keane (2020) in their cognitive psychology handbook. The concepts and theories have been chosen considering the needs of museums, hence for a broad and comprehensive analysis of cognitive processes and emotions one should refer to the seminal work of Eysenck and Keane. The BFM approach wants to encourage the collaboration between experts with different mindsets and expertise.

Writing these chapters and editing the Brain-Friendly Museum book, alias the BFM book has been a passionate, many times challenging, and hard-fought journey for me into the worlds of psychology and neuroscience. It deals with complex and vast disciplines and topics. Of course, it does not claim to be a comprehensive essay of all of them. The overall goal of the book is to develop "more brain-friendly" museums, sharing some ideas and food for thought in order to start thinking from a different perspective which could enhance the museum experience. Every time I read again what I have written, I get very excited thinking about the numerous applications of these disciplines. We could develop all these together as a community of experts from different fields. As I said, we are only at the beginning!

References

Antinucci, F. (2006). *Comunicare nel museo*. Roma-Bari: Edizioni Laterza.

Antinucci, F. (2007). *Musei virtuali. Come non fare innovazione tecnologica*. Roma-Bari: Laterza.

Eysenck, M. W., & Keane, M. T. (2020). *Cognitive psychology. A student's handbook*. Oxon-New York: Routledge.

2 Emotions

The First Connection to Our Cultural Heritage

Annalisa Banzi

Emotions are introduced at the beginning of this book because, in my opinion, they are the first element which connects us to our cultural heritage and museums. The emotional relationship between visitor and object can develop in at least two directions. First, even if a person does not know the meaning of a museum object, they can establish an initial contact with this exhibit thanks to the emotions that the object elicits. Additionally, as we will see shortly, emotions have a strong connection with our cognition. This means that they can improve the visitor-exhibit relationship because they can facilitate processes such as memory and learning (e.g., we can better remember an object which gives us a strong emotion). Second, a museum object can help us to explore our emotions. Sometimes people are not aware of their emotions or deny them because they are too intense or traumatic. The encounter with museum objects can be a soft and gentle way to get in touch with these emotions (e.g., art therapy). Especially due to the psychological consequences of Covid-19, taking care of emotions is becoming increasingly important for our wellbeing.

The intimate emotional dialogue between museumgoers and exhibits relies on a very delicate balance; any educational support that aims to improve this dialogue should be based on the maieutic principle of bringing out the visitors' emotions. Maieutic in general is the search for truth, consisting in soliciting the thinking subject to find it in themselves. It is a method based on the active participation of the subject and can also be used to bring out the emotions of visitors.

Since the encounter with the exhibits typically generates emotions, in my opinion, means such as technology (if necessary) should not produce *additional* emotions. Instead, these means should highlight and promote the emotional message of museum objects. For example, there is no need to animate a portrait to give emotions, rather, we need to encourage visitors to get in touch with *their* emotions while looking at this portrait (less technology and more maieutic).

Feldman Barrett (2018) explains that there is a traditional approach to emotions which considers them universal. It proposes that emotions are innate, are very clear-cut and recognisable phenomena, and are expressed

DOI: 10.4324/9781003304531-2

through our voice, posture, and face. This approach suggests that since we feel anger, happiness, and other emotions clearly, it seems reasonable to assume that each emotion follows a precise pattern in the brain and body. Emotions are products of evolution, they survived because they were convenient for our survival, and thus they became part of our biological nature. This approach has been around for millennia and has invaded our culture. For example, happiness is matched with a smile while surprise is paired with an open mouth (this means that emotions should be recognised through body language). However, Feldman Barrett claims there is scientific evidence nowadays that this view cannot be true. Emotions are not universal and vary from culture to culture. They are not caused by external stimuli but are produced by ourselves; we are active creators of them. They are the result of the combination of physical properties of our body, the flexibility of our brain, culture, and past experiences. Electromyography (EMG) is an objective technique which detects the electrical signals that allow facial muscles to move; it shows how the movements of these muscles do not reliably reveal when a person is angry, scared, or sad. In the last decades, experiments have been carried out in remote places of the world to demonstrate that emotions are not universal. People, who have had very little contact with the Western culture, perceive emotions in a way that is different from our stereotypes. Thus, emotions are not correlated with a specific and unique facial expression or a body reaction. For example, the heartbeat can be faster in the presence of different emotions. Moreover, to be able to communicate and perceive an emotion, a group of people is needed to agree on the existence of this affect (e.g., if you want to tell a friend you are happy, both of you have to agree on the concept of happiness).

Learning about emotions and how they work allows us to be more aware of how we can foster the spontaneous emotional reactions of museumgoers. The following sections of this chapter briefly introduce emotions from the psychological standpoint. Some notions of neuroscience are also mentioned.

Emotion in Cognitive Psychology

As stated by Owen (2021) it is almost by definition that a museum exists thanks to emotions. Conversely, many cognitive psychologists in the past neglected the effects of emotion on cognition by trying to make sure that participants in experiments were in a neutral emotional state. Recently the situation has changed, the relationship between emotion and cognition has been investigated in cognitive psychology. Research is currently oriented in two directions: exploring the influence of our cognition on emotional states, and analysing the impact of emotional factors on attention, perception, memory, language, judgement, and decision-making (i.e., effects of emotion on cognition).

Psychologists have identified numerous emotions and mood states. Emotion is an affective state of short duration which is usually provoked by a specific event (Eysenck & Keane, 2020). *Mood* differs from emotion because it is generally longer lasting, less intense, and the cause is often unclear. *Affect* includes both emotions and moods. There are positive affect (i.e., positive emotions and moods) and negative affect (i.e., negative emotions and moods). The positive or negative nature of the emotional experience is called *valence*.

So far the brain mechanisms related to emotions have not yet been fully identified. It is generally accepted that large-scale brain networks are associated with most emotions.

It is useful to start mentioning right away some contents proposed by the Peabody Essex Museum – PEM (USA), which is the first museum to announce that it is making use of neuroscience. I will report their suggestions throughout the first 7 chapters. For example, according to the PEM's analysis, emotion has two dimensions: *arousal* and valence. The first refers to the intensity of the emotional experience and is measured physiologically using biometric tools. The latter refers to the pleasantness of a given experience and has to be reported by an individual (it cannot be measured biometrically).

Emotional experience relies on complex interactions between bottom-up processes (i.e., the processing is directly influenced by environmental stimuli) and top-down processes (i.e., the processing is affected by the individual's expectations and past experience). According to the PEM's analysis, bottom-up influences are the physical features of an object or scene (e.g., the sounds and smells that make their way into our brain via our sensory pathways) while top-down influences can be the background knowledge that we bring to our interpretation of an artwork or a memory elicited by a particular experience. While most people will react similarly to bottom-up factors (e.g., colour contrast), top-down factors (e.g., knowledge base) will vary considerably from individual to individual and from culture to culture[1].

Effects of Cognition on Emotion

Our cognitive appraisals (i.e., interpretations) of a given situation influence our emotional experience. By and large, cognitive processes affect *when* we feel emotions and *what* type of emotional state we experience.

There are *appraisal theories* which claim that emotional responses are aroused when the organism assesses the relevance of environmental changes to its own wellbeing (Brosch, 2013)[2]. These theories are based on the assumption that cognitive appraisals of a specific situation mostly determined emotional state.

People can have a spontaneous emotional response to a given situation (called *emotion generation*), or they can use explicit or implicit processes[3] to change their spontaneous emotional response, generally a negative one, to a given situation (called *emotion regulation*). For example, I once visited an exhibition whose works were explicitly related to sexual violence against children. The impact of these exhibits was unmediated. No educational support was provided, with the exception of the "standard" explanation of the works. At the entrance to the exhibition, there was only a sign informing the parents of the content of the exhibition and of an album with photos of the works for a preview. Indeed, it was a challenging exhibition! I still wonder what the reaction of the families who visited the exhibition might have been. Did they inhibit their anxiety and fear and act as if everything was fine? If the answer is *yes, they did* (sadly we will never know) this is a case of emotion regulation.

Regarding explicit emotion regulation, most strategies involve attention deployment (e.g., *distraction*, which is a strategy that allows individuals to shift attention from emotional processing to neutral information) or cognitive change (e.g., *reappraisal*, which is a strategy based on the elaboration of the emotional response before changing its meaning). Conversely, implicit emotion regulation is automatically triggered by the stimuli themselves, can be accomplished and terminated without conscious monitoring, and can occur without intuition and awareness (Etkin et al., 2015)[4]. Compared to explicit emotion regulation, it has the advantage of using less cognitive resources. According to Doré et al. (2016)[5], the effectiveness of these strategies is determined by complex interactions between the individual, the situation, and the strategy itself.

Many effective emotion regulation strategies involve cognitive control processes that activate the *prefrontal cortex* and reduce the activation of the *amygdala*, which is an almond-shaped structure in the *temporal lobe* strongly associated with several emotions.

The notion of emotion regulation can be one of the take-home messages for museums, which could take advantage of this knowledge when designing an exhibition that introduces a challenging topic. Several episodes similar to the exhibition I described above come to mind. We cannot take for granted that people can successfully elaborate the emotions provoked by shocking exhibits. In terms of the educational mission of museums, *visitors who act as if everything is fine* cannot be a satisfactory result.

Effects of Emotion on Cognition

According to Blanchette and Richards (2010)[6], our emotional state affects many aspects of cognition. Some findings and theories related to the effects of emotion on attention, memory, judgement, and decision-making are briefly introduced below.

The attentional breadth is influenced by affect. Positive affect (i.e., positive mood or emotion) in many cases determines broadening of attention.

Conversely, negative affect (i.e., negative mood or emotion) often produces narrowing of attention[7]. However, according to the findings obtained in the research studies, attentional breadth mainly depends on the level of motivational intensity. Attentional narrowing can be triggered by positive or negative emotional states of high motivational intensity. In contrast, attentional broadening can occur with positive or negative emotional states of low motivational intensity (Gable et al., 2015)[8]. According to Huntsinger et al. (2014)[9], positive affect leads people to maintain their current attentional strategy, while negative affect leads them to change their attentional strategy.

As for memory, emotional events are typically remembered better than neutral ones. Research on flashbulb memories, which are vivid memories of dramatic events, provides evidence that emotional experiences are more lasting than neutral ones. Falk (2021) reported a study conducted with Katie Gillespie at the California Science Center, in which particularly emotional museum experiences produced the strongest and most lasting memories. By and large, the experiences most likely to be perceived as emotionally arousing were those involving moments where something was particularly inspiring, new, personally relevant, and reinforced the agenda.

From the anatomical point of view, the role of the amygdala is important in influencing the effects of emotion or mood on long-term memory. According to Dolcos et al. (2017)[10], there are two brain mechanisms concerned with memory-enhancing effects of emotions: one involves the *medial temporal lobes*, and the other activates several areas within the *prefrontal cortex*. Note that the amygdala plays an important role in both mechanisms.

Mood congruity is an example of how affect influences learning and memory. It usually occurs when people in a negative mood mostly recall unpleasant memories, and when high-spirited individuals generally recall good memories. *Mood-state-dependent memory* is another effect of mood on memory: the performance of memory is typically better when the mood state of a person is the same at learning and retrieval than when it is different.

Let's now turn to decision-making and judgement. Decision-making is the activity of selecting an option from a set of presented possibilities that can be trivial (e.g., what will I eat tonight?) or important (e.g., what job do I want to do?). Judgement is part of the decision-making process and is the capacity to calculate the probability of various possible events. In the case of a moral dilemma to be resolved, individuals can use *deontological judgements*, which are based on moral rules and obligations, or *utilitarian judgements*, which are based on pragmatic considerations.

In recent years, the impact of the affect on decision-making and judgement has been increasingly studied in research, which has focused mainly on anxiety, sadness, anger, and positive moods. According to Angie et al. (2011)[11], who reviewed the literature on this topic, mood states have different effects on decision-making and judgement and have a greater impact on decision-making than on judgement.

Lerner et al. (2015)[12] explained the effects of emotions on decision-making by stating that decisions can be seen as a channel through which emotions guide daily attempts to avoid negative feelings and enhance positive feelings.

There is an important distinction to keep in mind between *integral emotions* and *incidental emotions* (Lerner et al., 2015)[13]. Integral emotions are triggered by the current judgement or choice (e.g., when you spend a lot of money in a risky project you may experience anxiety). Conversely, incidental emotions are not connected to the current judgement or decision (e.g., the positive affect you experience from visiting an interesting exhibition may influence your subsequent judgements and decisions on entirely different issues). Integral emotions often have a stronger impact on judgement and decision-making than incidental emotions (whose effects on judgement can sometimes be easily removed).

As mentioned above, affect impacts decision-making and judgement. Let's focus on the four mood states investigated in cognitive psychology research studies (anxiety, sadness, anger, and positive moods):

- Anxiety is constantly linked to gloomy judgements about the future. Anxious people show a lower *optimism bias*[14] than calm and serene individuals. Additionally, anxious people are usually less likely to make risky decisions than non-anxious individuals.

  Anxiety can also impair our judgements and decisions in museums. As Hooper-Greenhill (1994) explained, when one arrives for the first time in an unfamiliar place, the immediate sensation is often that of not knowing what to do or where to go. For some individuals, this is a thrilling situation. For others, this situation generates a feeling of being out of control and confused, and so these people tend to avoid unfamiliar places as much as possible.
- Sadness, which can turn into depression if intense, is more strongly connected with the absence of positive affect than anxiety. Thus, sad people may be less optimistic than others.

  According to Raghunathan and Pham (1999)[15], sad people prefer a high-risk job to a low-risk job because they lack a fully rewarding environment, so they are highly motivated to get a prize.

  There is evidence that sad individuals show the *misery-is-not-miserly effect*, which is the tendency exhibited by sad people to be willing to pay more than others for a given good (Cryder et al., 2008)[16]. *Myopic misery* is another tendency shown by sad individuals, who feel a sense of loss and so are eager to get rewards that can compensate for this loss (Lerner et al., 2013)[17].
- Anger is generally considered a negative affect but is regarded as relatively pleasant when it leads people to believe they can control the situation or other people (Lerner & Tiedens, 2006)[18].

  Compared to anxiety and sadness, anger is linked with relatively optimistic judgements about the probability of negative events (Waters, 2008)[19]. Angry people think they are less at risk of dramatic life events than other individuals, even though they are actually more likely at risk (Lerner & Keltner, 2001)[20].

Anger in many cases leads people to make judgements and decisions based on relatively superficial or heuristic processing (i.e., rules of thumb). It can lead people to make risky decisions because angry individuals think they are in control of the situation.

- Positive moods were investigated by Campos et al. (2013)[21]. According to the researchers, there are at least eight positive mood states: awe, amusement, interest, pride, gratitude, joy, love, and contentment.

  Until recently, research has explored the effects of single negative affects (anxiety, sadness, and anger) on judgement and decision-making, but it has only analysed the effects of the broad category of positive affects on these forms of thinking. Research on positive affect has mainly focused on optimism bias. According to Lench and Levine (2005)[22], high-spirited individuals have a greater optimistic bias than anxious or scared people, but they are no more optimistic than neutral-minded people. High positive affect generally leads people to be risk-averse in decision-making, with the exception of excitement. Additionally, when individuals experience positive affect they tend to use heuristic processing instead of analytic processing in decision-making.

Admittedly, the effects of emotions on cognition as described above do not have a *direct* application in the museum environment. However, these dynamics, explained through concrete examples, bring out the extent of the impact of emotions on very important cognitive states such as attention, memory, judgement, and decision-making.

Museum experts have a great experience in dealing with emotions in museums. However, I would like to dwell on the environmental and cultural factors that impact emotions, before introducing perception. I report an experiment carried out by Wang et al. (2020) in which an environmental factor such as artificial lighting influences the emotions (i.e., comfort, clarity, preference, and warmth) of the participants in three museums. Three modes of illuminance and correlated colour temperature (CCT) combination were considered and analysed. Three Japanese art museums were involved:

- the National Museum of Western Art. The experiment was conducted in the painting exhibition room of the 19th–20th century, which has a *direct* illuminance – CCT = 2079 K

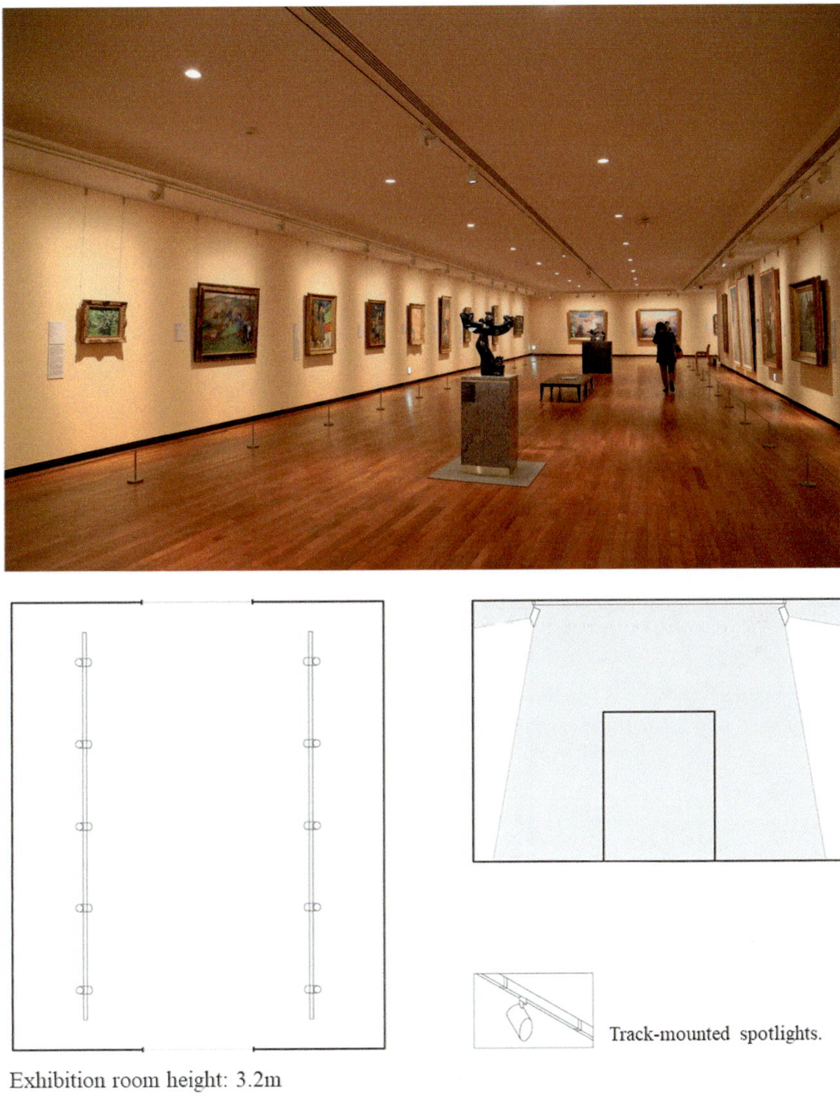

Figure 2.1 The National Museum of Western Art, Japan. Example of direct lighting. Courtesy of Dr. Zhisheng Wang.

- the Aichi Prefectural Museum of Art. The experiment was carried out in the permanent exhibition room, which has an *indirect* illuminance – CCT = 2960 K

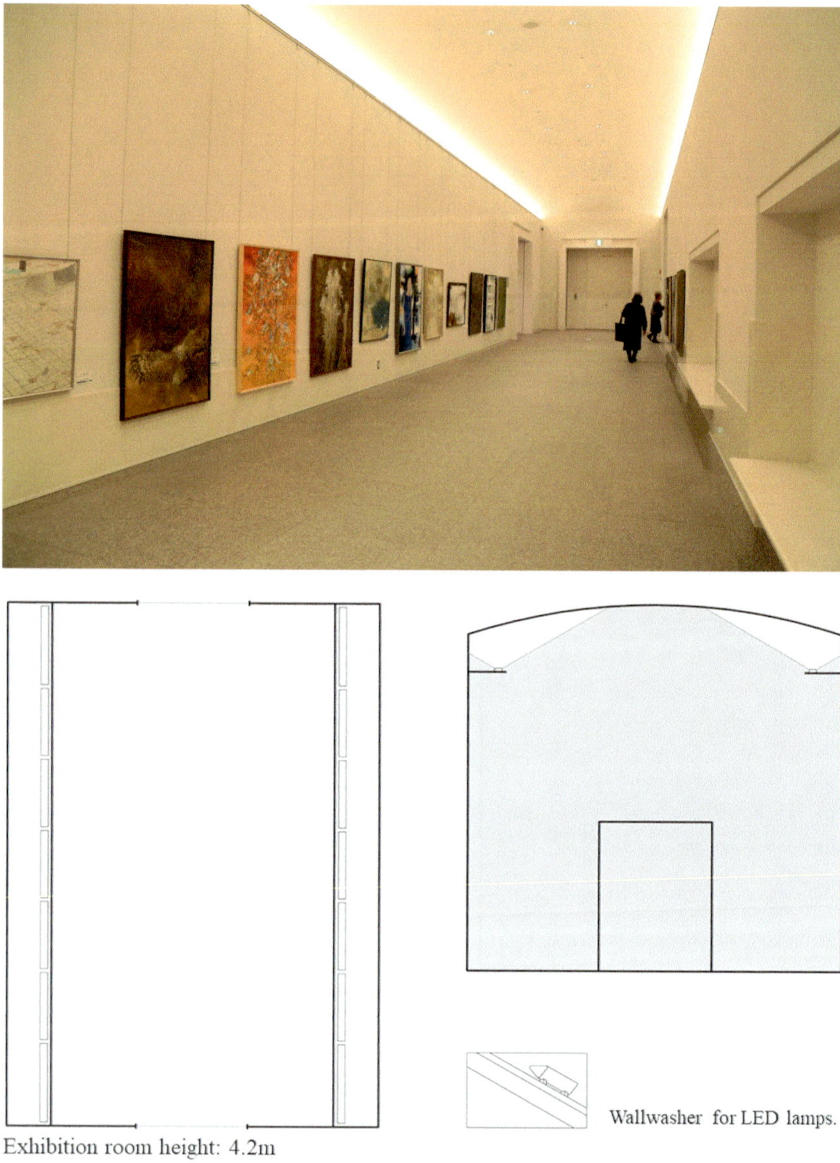

Figure 2.2 The Aichi Prefectural Museum of Art, Japan. Example of indirect lighting. Courtesy of Dr. Zhisheng Wang.

- the Yamazaki Mazak Museum of Art. The experiment was conducted in the painting exhibition room on the fifth floor, which has a *mixed lighting* – CCT = 3568 K

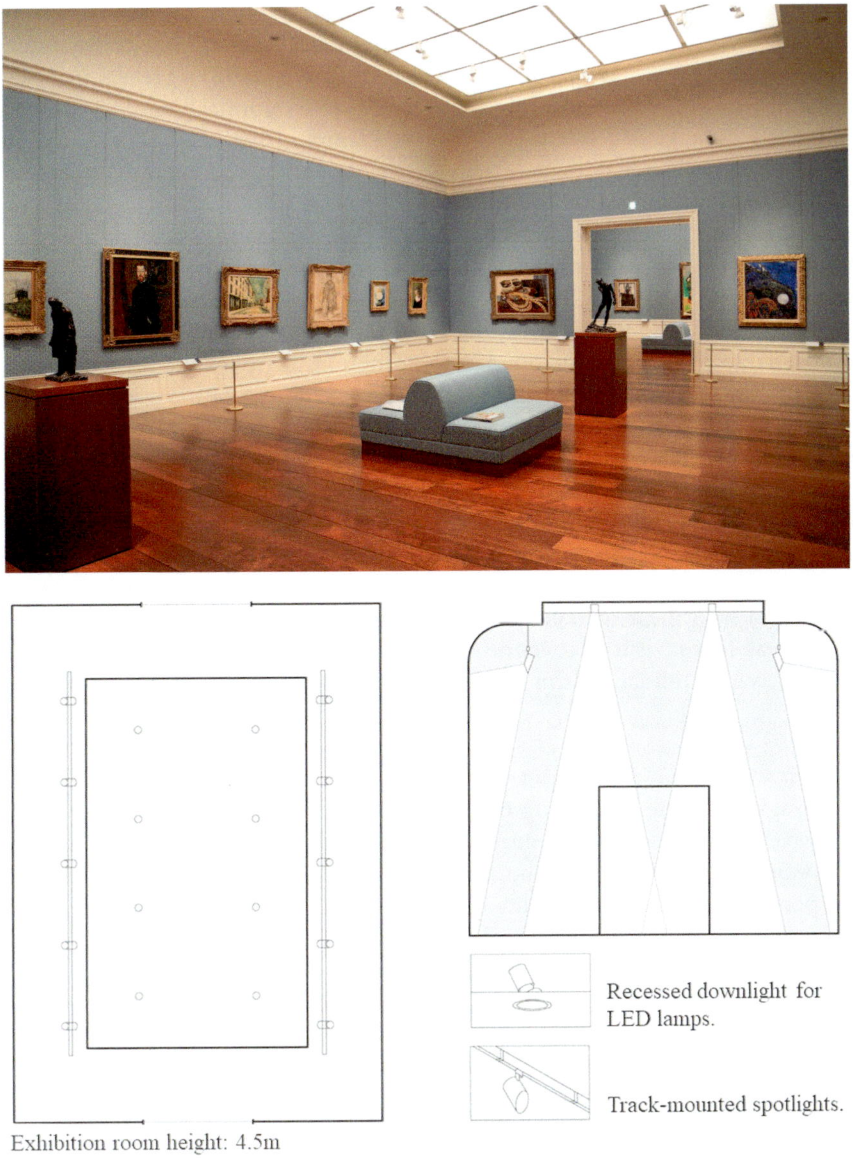

Figure 2.3 The Yamazaki Mazak Museum of Art, Japan. Example of mixed lighting. Courtesy of Dr. Zhisheng Wang.

The collected findings suggested that the lighting conditions in the Yamazaki Mazak Museum of Art were the most suitable. However, the National Museum of Western Art had the highest data feedback value for warmth due to the low CCT environment. Beyond the very technical aspects, the most significant result in this context is the comparison of the illuminance conditions which provides evidence of the different emotional impact of light on participants.

As for cultural factors, there is a compelling example that came to my mind after reading *Planning for emotions in museums* by Owen (2021). He claimed that hospitality is one of the most important factors in emotional planning. A good host plans their guests' needs in advance. Planning should consider ways to accommodate all audiences, especially first-time visitors and anyone unfamiliar with that specific museum or museums in general (Owen, 2021). This made me think about *omotenashi*, which is part of the Japanese culture meaning to wholeheartedly look after guests. It is a deep-rooted tradition which comes from *sado* (tea ceremony), and it represents the Japanese mindset of hospitality centred around *care rather than expectation*. Each culture has its forms and rituals of hospitality that can be included in the different phases of the museum visit. Omotenashi's philosophy works in the Japanese culture since it was born there and can be applied to Japanese museums. It is an example of a cultural factor (hospitality) which impacts emotions.

Owen (2021) also stated that probably the part of the museum experience that most justifies the emotional planning is the arrival experience. Especially first-time visitors may not know what to expect. They might be excited about the visit, but maybe they might be frustrated because of the long queues, discomfort from heat or cold, and from the trip fatigue. The organisation of the arrival helps visitors to cope uncertainty and generates a positive impression which influences the entire visit. Owen divided the arrival into four phases:

- *first engagement*, which can be an icon or another element that gives an insight into the interesting objects displayed in the museum
- *process*, which refers to security and ticketing
- *decompression*, which is the time needed to gather family or friends, personal items, and thoughts
- *realisation*, which means stepping into the moment

I think that decompression and realisation are not always considered by museums as important parts of arrival. Sometimes they are neglected. In these cases, they should be introduced and clearly communicated to visitors, giving them the chance to become aware of these two moments that can influence the museum experience.

Notes

1 https://www.pem.org/neuroscience-initiative/from-neuroscience-to-museum-practice, accessed 10.06.2021.
2 See reference in Eysenck & Keane, 2020, p. 719.
3 Explicit processes are intentional and require effort, whereas implicit processes are relatively automatic.
4 See reference in Eysenck & Keane, 2020, p. 725.

5 See reference in Eysenck & Keane, 2020, p. 730.
6 See reference in Eysenck & Keane, 2020, p. 730.
7 The hypothesis that negative affect narrow attentional breadth was proposed by Easterbrook (1959 – see reference in Eysenck & Keane, 2020, p. 731), whereas Fredrickson and Branigan (2005 – see reference in Eysenck & Keane, 2020, p. 731) put forward the prediction that positive affect broaden attention.
8 See reference in Eysenck & Keane, 2020, p. 731.
9 See reference in Eysenck & Keane, 2020, p. 734.
10 See reference in Eysenck & Keane, 2020, p. 736.
11 See reference in Eysenck & Keane, 2020, p. 743.
12 See reference in Eysenck & Keane, 2020, p. 743.
13 See reference in Eysenck & Keane, 2020, p. 744.
14 Optimism bias is the tendency of a person (compared to other people) to exaggerate the likelihood of experiencing positive events and to minimise the probability of experiencing negative events.
15 See reference in Eysenck & Keane, 2020, p. 745.
16 See reference in Eysenck & Keane, 2020, p. 746.
17 See reference in Eysenck & Keane, 2020, p. 746.
18 See reference in Eysenck & Keane, 2020, p. 747.
19 See reference in Eysenck & Keane, 2020, p. 747.
20 See reference in Eysenck & Keane, 2020, p. 747.
21 See reference in Eysenck & Keane, 2020, p. 748.
22 See reference in Eysenck & Keane, 2020, p. 749.

References

Angie, A. D., Connelly, S., Waples, E. P., & Kligyte, V. (2011). The influence of discrete emotions on judgement and decision-making: A meta-analytic review. *Cognition and Emotion*, 25, 1393–1422.

Blanchette, I., & Richards, A. (2010). The influence of affect on higher level cognition: A review of research on interpretation, judgement, decision making and reasoning. *Cognition and Emotion*, 24, 561–595.

Brosch, T. (2013). Comment: On the role of appraisal processes in the construction of emotion. *Emotion Review*, 5, 369–373.

Campos, B., Shiota, M., Keltner, D., Gonzaga, G. C., & Goetz, J. L. (2013). What is shared, what is different? Core relational themes and expressive displays of eight positive emotions. *Cognition and Emotion*, 27, 37–52.

Cryder, C. E., Lerner, J. S., Gross, J. J., & Dahl, R. E. (2008). Misery is not miserly: Sad and self-focused individuals spend more. *Psychological Science*, 19, 525–530.

Dolcos, F., Katsumi, Y., Weymar, M., Moore, M., Tsukiura, T., & Dolcos, S. (2017). Emerging directions in emotional episodic memory. *Frontiers in Psychology*, 8 (Article no. 1867).

Doré, B. P., Silvers, J. A., & Ochsner K. N. (2016). Toward a personalized science of emotion regulation. *Social and Personality Psychology Compass*, 10, 171–187.

Easterbrook, J. A. (1959). The effect of emotion on cue utilization and the organization of behavior. *Psychological Review*, 66, 183–201.

Etkin, A., Büchel, C., & Gross, J. J. (2015). The neural bases of emotion regulation. *Nature Review Neuroscience*, 16, 693–700.

Eysenck, M. W., & Keane, M. T. (2020). *Cognitive psychology. A Student's Handbook*. Oxon-New York: Routledge.

Falk, J. H. (2021). *The value of museums: Enhancing societal well-being*. Lanham, MD: Rowman & Littlefield.

Feldman Barrett, L. (2018). *How emotions are made: The secret life of the brain*. New York: Macmillan.

Fredrickson, B. L., & Branigan, C. (2005). Positive emotions broaden the scope of attention and thought-action repertoires. *Cognition and Emotion*, 19, 313–332.

Gable, P. A., Browning, L., & Harmon-Jones, E. (2015). Affect, motivation, and cognitive scope. In T. S. Braver (Ed.), *Motivation and Cognitive Control* (pp. 164–187). London: Routledge.

Hooper-Greenhill, E. (1994). *Museums and their visitors*. London: Routledge.

Huntsinger, J. R., Isbell, L. M., & Clore, G. L. (2014). The affective control of thought: Malleable, not fixed. *Psychological Review*, 121, 600–618.

Lench, H. C., & Levine, L. J. (2005). Effects of fear on risk and control judgements and memory: Implications for health promotion messages. *Cognition and Emotion*, 19, 1049–1069.

Lerner, J. S., & Keltner, D. (2001). Fear, anger, and risk. *Journal of Personality and Social Psychology*, 81, 146–159.

Lerner, J. S., & Tiedens, L. Z. (2006). Portrait of the angry decision maker: How appraisal tendencies shape Anger's influence on cognition. *Journal of Behavioral Decision Making*, 19, 115–137.

Lerner, J. S., Li, Y., & Weber, E. U. (2013). The financial costs of sadness. *Psychological Science*, 24, 72–79.

Lerner, J. S., Li, Y., Valdesolo, P., & Kassam, K. S. (2015). Emotion and decision making. *Annual Review of Psychology*, 66, 799–823.

Owen, T. (2021). Planning for emotions in museums. in *NEMO Emotions and learning in museums*, pp. 61–65.

Raghunathan, R., & Pham, M. T. (1999). All negative moods are not equal: Motivational influences of anxiety and sadness on decision making. *Organizational Behavior and Human Decision Processes*, 79, 56–77.

Wang, Z., Nagai, Y., Liu, J., Zou, N., & Liang, J. (2020). Artificial lighting environment evaluation of the japan museum of art based on the emotional response of observers. *Applied Science*, 10, 1121.

Waters, E. (2008). Feeling good, feeling bad, and feeling at-risk: A review of incidental affect's influence on likelihood estimates of health hazards and life events. *Journal of Risk Research*, 11, 569–595.

3 Perception and Museum Display

Annalisa Banzi

"It's not what you look at that matters, it's what you see," said Henry David Thoreau. What do you see in the following picture (Figure 3.1)?

Do you see a young girl or an old lady? Don't you see the old lady? The young woman's necklace is the old lady's mouth. Do you see her now?

The Rubin figure, the Ames room, and the Beuchet chair are some of the other famous illusions that you may have seen in books or in the Museum of illusions[1], which has several locations around the world (e.g., Milan, London, Boston, Doha, etc.). Reversible images are one of the topics mentioned in this chapter to explain how our brain interprets the visual stimuli of the environment around us. This visual interpretation is also vital in the museum display.

According to the PEM, the brain mechanisms that control visual processing affect how we see and what we perceive. For example, the purpose with which visitors look at an object influences their viewing behaviour, and therefore what they actually perceived of that exhibit. Likewise, a space that is too full of objects does not help museumgoers identify a specific goal. It is a distracting setting. The PEM staff stressed that it is important to take into account the numerous factors that influence the nature of our visual perceptions. Understanding how different factors affect our visual perception is key to designing exhibitions where visitors interact with desired elements and follow the embedded narrative[2].

Environmental psychology is a discipline that studies the effects of the physical environment on human behaviour, moods, and wellbeing. It studies factors such as aspects of design (e.g., lighting), environmental stressors (e.g., noise, crowding, air pollution, and temperature), and other qualities of the physical environment (e.g., floor plans, building size and location, and proximity to nature). It can help to understand the interaction between museum environments and the behaviour, interests, and motivations of visitors.

Many visitor studies adopt approaches and techniques similar to those of environmental psychology that allow exploring the visitor–environment interaction from a psychological standpoint. It analyses how museumgoers perceive, process, react, and respond to the exhibition environment, which has been intentionally designed and organised as part of the museum experience since the 1960s. The investigation of the museum experience has

DOI: 10.4324/9781003304531-3

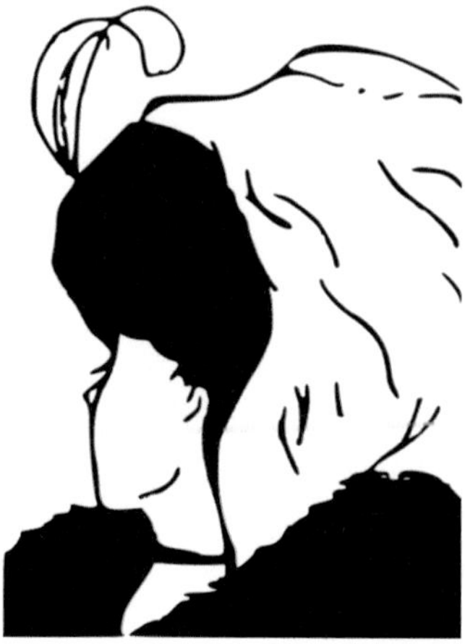

Figure 3.1 Ambiguous Image Known as "My Wife and My Mother-in-Law" (1915). It Is an Example of a Cognitive Illusion. It Was Made by the Cartoonist William Ely Hill.

traditionally been focused on the content of the exhibitions rather than on the physical nature of the environment in which they were proposed and on the reactions of visitors to the various environmental stimuli. However, at the beginning of this century, the physical space of the museum began to be studied and its effects on the visitor's experience were recognised. Recently, it has been proposed to study the interaction between the visitor and the museum in terms of motivation and evaluation. In the last few years, the concept of *atmospherics*, born in the design of sales environments, has also been applied to museums; it impacts the visitor through sensory and emotional mechanisms with even unconscious behavioural outcomes. Another important environmental property investigated in museums is the *regeneration process*, which is the quality of regenerating an individual from stress and cognitive fatigue; it has been studied based on two main theories: Ulrich's Stress Reduction Theory (1983) and Kaplan and Kaplan's Attention Restoration Theory (1989). By and large, the exhibition design can influence the flow of visitors, the quality of social interactions, attention, and affectivity, which can foster an open mind to discovery, exploration, and learning (e.g., Tizi et al., 2019).

In the following two parts of this chapter, some of the main cognitive psychology theories and notions on perception are analysed in order to develop more effective museum displays. The first part addresses the brain mechanisms of visual perception, the principal functions of the visual system, and the main aspects of visual perception (e.g., colour perception and depth perception). The second part focuses on understanding how our brain recognises 3D objects, and face recognition versus object recognition.

At the end of these two parts, the role of the visual imaginary is mentioned. Motion perception, which is part of the subject of perception, will not be tackled in this book, as explained at the end of this chapter. It will be the topic of further publications.

Let's now introduce perception, which allows us to interpret the stimuli in the world around us, such as the variety of an object's visual properties (e.g., colour) and the recognition of an object in different positions with different orientations.

Visual Perception Processes

Let's start with a brief introduction to the brain (Figure 3.2), alias the "magic box" as it is called by Cerasa and Tomaiuolo (2019). It is an organ made up of 100 billion neurons, and it is divided into two hemispheres (right and left), which are composed of four main lobes (*frontal*, *parietal*, *occipital*, and *temporal*). The *cerebral cortex*, the outer surface of the brain, is made up of convolutions (*gyri*) that are prominent elevated areas.

Brodmann identified 52 brain areas and produced a brain map based on these areas. For example, when neuroscientists mention *BA17 area*, they are referring to Brodmann Area 17 (commonly known as the *primary visual cortex*).

This section focuses on visual perception, which is a complex phenomenon involving several areas of the brain, at least 30, located throughout the *occipital cortex*, the *temporal lobe*, and the *parietal lobe*.

Perception processes begin in the *retina* of the eye, where the *cones* (used for colour vision and sharpness of vision) and the *rods* (specialised for vision in low light and movement) are located.

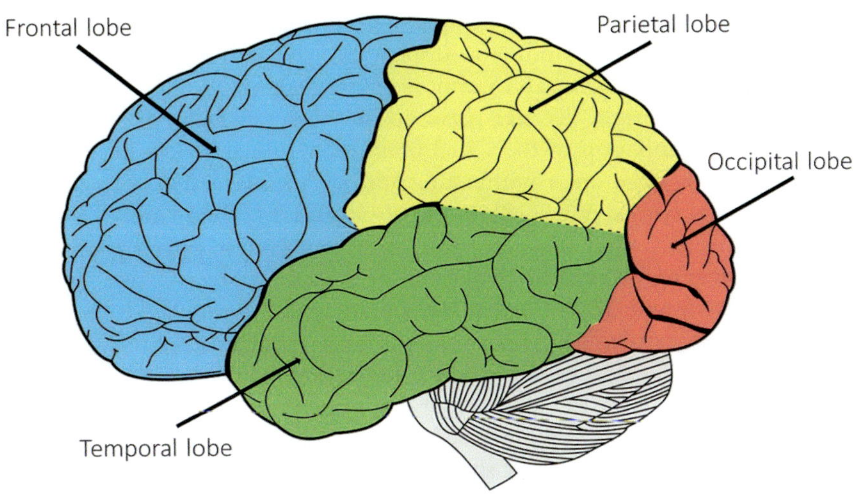

Figure 3.2 The Four Lobes of the Two Hemispheres in the Brain.

The *retina–geniculate–striate pathway* connects the retina (rods + cones input) to the primary visual cortex (V1) and *secondary visual cortex* (V2) via two channels:

- the *parvocellar (or P) pathway*, which receives most of its information from the cones, and is more sensitive to colour and fine details
- the *magnocellular (or M) pathway*, which receives most of its information from the rods, and is primarily sensitive to movement

These pathways are not completely independent as they have many interconnections. There is also a third channel called *koniocellular (or K) pathway* but its functions are not yet fully understood.

After reaching V1 and V2, the information is transmitted to:

- the *parietal cortex* through the *dorsal stream*, which is associated with the M pathway
- the *inferotemporal cortex* through the *ventral stream*, which is associated with the P pathway

The ventral stream is primarily concerned with shape and colour processing and object recognition, while the dorsal stream is primarily involved in motion processing. The ventral and dorsal streams are not completely separated; there are numerous interconnections between them. The types of information processed by these two streams are also not completely distinct.

It is important to keep in mind that *visual acuity*, which is the sharpness of vision, is stronger in the *fovea* (i.e., visual field centre) than in the peripheral vision, even though the latter covers most of the visual field. In the museum context, how can we use this information in the design of exhibitions? Are there particular object positions or light sources that can help visual acuity? What is the most effective museum display case for activating visual acuity? What kind of surface, font, and position of the caption (if any) help a clear vision? What is the right distance between the object and the visitor?

As for the organisation of the visual brain, early visual processing requires the activation of large areas within the primary visual cortex (V1) and the secondary visual cortex (V2). Cells in the visual area 3 (*V3*) are more involved in shape processing, while those in *V4* are more involved in colour processing. Motion processing is mainly associated with activity in *V5/MT* (medial temporal cortex) and *MST* (medial superior temporal cortex). According to the American Psychological Association (APA), a visual area is a region (there are many) of the cerebral cortex where neurons are mainly sensitive to visual stimulation. The visual areas, all together, compose the visual cortex. They can be distinguished from each other based on their anatomical connections (i.e., their cytoarchitecture) and their specific visual sensitivities. Each area is defined by "V" plus a number (V1; V2; V3; V4; V5), which roughly indicates the distance between the area and the striate cortex[3].

Zeki (1993, 2001)[4] presented a *functional specialisation theory* in which different cortical areas are specialised for different visual functions. It means that colour, shape, movement, etc., are processed in anatomically separate parts of the visual cortex. This theory is supported by findings from visually impaired patients. However, there is far less specialisation than Zeki claimed because most of the visual processing depends on a vast brain network rather than specific areas. In addition, visual perception generally depends on recurrent processing (i.e., the higher visual brain areas send feedback to the lower ones).

Zeki's approach also poses the still unsolved binding problem: how is information about an object integrated to produce a coherent perception?

One of the most influential theories on the major functions of the visual system is the *perception–action model* by Milner and Goodale (1995, 2008)[5]. It is based on two visual systems:

- the *vision for perception system*, which is mainly used to identify objects (e.g., when a visitor has to decide if the object is the exit door or a window), and is based on the ventral stream
- the *vision for action system*, which is used primarily for visually guided actions (e.g., when a visitor grabs the museum map at the entrance), and is mainly based on the dorsal stream

A task like grasping an object (vision for action), as stated by Milner and Goodale in 2008, in fact, requires some elaboration in the ventral stream as well as the dorsal stream. Ventral stream is of key importance in the visually guided actions, for example, when memory is involved. It is difficult to disentangle the contribution of each stream in most of the visual tasks.

However, Milner and Goodale's model is only partially correct. For example, brain imaging techniques have confirmed that the brain network involved in perception and action is more complex. Also, there is evidence that two partially separate dorsal streams are engaged in actions towards objects:

- the *dorso-dorsal stream*, which is activated when an object is quickly grabbed
- the *ventro-dorsal stream*, which exploits the knowledge of the memorised object, works more slowly than the dorso-dorsal stream

Furthermore, Haak and Beckmann (2018)[6] discovered a third stream, the lateral one, which could comprise aspects related to vision, action, and language.

Regarding the major aspects of visual perception, it is important to focus on colour vision and depth perception. Colour vision help us to recognise and classify objects, and to distinguish objects from the background. Any colour has three main qualities:

- *hue*: the colours (green, red, blue, etc.)
- *brightness*: the intensity of light in colours
- *saturation*: the vividness or paleness of colours depending on the amount of white

There are several theories describing colour vision, such as the *trichromatic theory*, the *opponent-process theory*, and the *dual process theory*. So far, there is no theory that fully explains the colour vision process.

Colour constancy is of key importance in everyday life. It is the tendency to perceive an object as having the same colour even when the wavelengths contained in the light source (called *illuminant*) change. It allows us to recognise objects rapidly and accurately as lighting conditions change. It also confirms colour vision does not rely only on the wavelengths of the light reflected from objects. For example, the wavelengths of light of Keith Haring's "Boxers" (1987; Figure 3.3) depend on the sculpture itself, the illuminant, and the reflections from other objects on the sculpture surface (the latter is called *mutual illumination*).

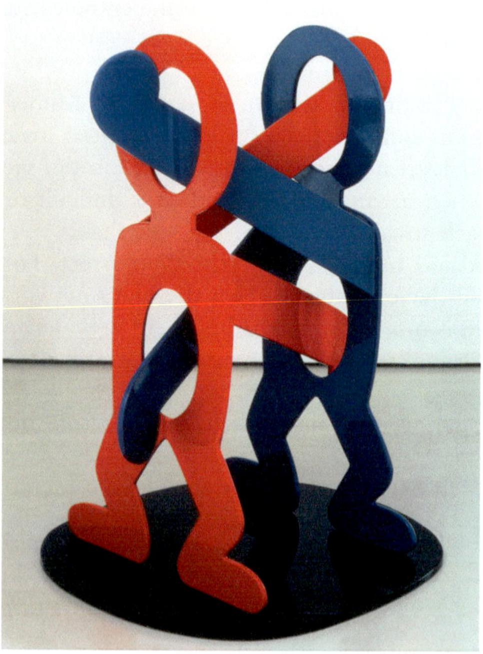

Figure 3.3 Keith Haring, Untitled (Boxers), 1987, Keith Haring artwork © Keith Haring Foundation. Courtesy of Keith Haring Foundation.

However, colour constancy is influenced by different factors:

- the familiarity with the colour of an object (i.e., we tend to perceive an item in its typical colour even when the real colour differs from the typical one)
- the chromatic adaptation (i.e., the visual sensitivity to a given light source decreases over time)
- the local colour contrast (i.e., the effect of one colour on another when viewed side by side)
- the ability to accurately assess the illuminant

As for the walls of the museum, how can we avoid the overwhelming influence of the background on the chromatic balance of objects (especially in a museum of fine arts)? Also, since there are 125 million rods in the outer regions of the retina, how can we support and promote the work of rods when designing a display for light-sensitive objects like manuscripts? What are the best sources of artificial light that preserve the different types of artefacts while triggering cones and rods? How can we avoid visual fatigue?

Our ability to perceive the 3D and the distance of an object is called *depth perception*. It relies on different cues which are any sensory information that provides sensory evaluation (Ernst & Bülthoff, 2004). There are non-visual depth cues (e.g., the sound of the alarm system when a visitor gets too close to a museum object) and visual depth cues. This section is mainly concerned with visual depth cues in a static environment (observers and objects are static, such as in museums when visitors stop to look at museum objects). There are three groups:

- *monocular cues* that involve only one eye, although they also work with both eyes open. They are also called *pictorial cues* because artists use them to create the illusion of a 3D space on a 2D canvas. An example of monocular cue is *interposition*, where a distant object is hidden by a nearer one
- *binocular cues* that involve the use of both eyes and include *binocular disparity*, which is based on the slight difference in the two retinal images as a person observes a scene; this phenomenon produces *stereopsis* (i.e., depth perception)
- *oculomotor cues* that are based on the eye muscle contractions. An example is *accommodation*, which relies on changes in optical power produced by thickening of the eye's lens when a person focuses on close items

The pending question is how we combine cues to estimate depth or distance. So far, we know there are two options (Bruno & Cutting, 1988)[7]: *additivity* (i.e., combining information from different cues), and *selection* (i.e., using information from a single reliable cue, e.g., when the cues are in strong conflict).

Visual perception can also be affected by *size constancy* (i.e., the tendency to perceive an item to have a given size regardless of the retinal image size), and partially by our own body perspective (our lifelong experience of seeing the world around us from a specific point of view, our body).

Tymkiw and Foulsham (2020), carried out a study in three UK museums examining the viewing behaviours of 51 participants, who were wheelchair (20%) and non-chair users (80%). The museums involved were the Firstsite in Colchester, the Victoria and Albert Museum in London, and the Essex Collection of Art from Latin America (ESCALA) on the campus of the University of Essex. The researchers used the eye tracker, which is a devise that records *fixations* (i.e., the eye gaze stops in a specific position), and *saccades* (i.e., the eye movement from one position to another). They collected interesting data on the spatial bias, which is the tendency to focus on specific regions of space when looking at an exhibit or a group of exhibits. They were cautious about making broad generalisations due to the small sample size of the participants. Based on the collected results, they suggested that the viewer's degree of mobility, viewing height, and other bodily characteristics have a considerable impact on spatial biases. For example, a different spatial bias between the two groups of participants involved the depth at which objects were displayed in two horizontal display cases at Firstsite. Most of the chair users' fixations (77%) were recorded on the front half of the display cases while non-chair users' fixations were distributed between the front (53%) and the back (47%) of the display cases. As reported in the responses to the qualitative questionnaire, this difference is likely due to the elements on the back which were difficult for wheelchair users to see: a problem that can be mitigated by placing objects and labels on a slope, as proposed by a participant.

Eye-tracking technology allows us to detect and correct (potential) visual perception mistakes in a museum display for the benefit of different types of visitors. It gives us the chance to collect numerous empirical data on how individuals look at objects on display. As stated by Tymkiw and Foulsham (2020), eye-tracking studies in museums have provided a wealth of insight into viewing patterns (e.g., showing to what extent viewing behaviour can be influenced by prior knowledge, or revealing some of the visual characteristics within an artwork that are likely to capture the viewer's attention).

Viewing behaviour was also explored by Reitstätter et al. (2020) in the Austrian Gallery Belvedere, which rearranged its permanent collection in 2018. The research team was composed of art historians, museologists, psychologists, and computer scientists. They investigated the viewing behaviour of 259 participants before and after the new display of specific artworks. From a statistical point of view, the larger sample sizes enabled them to reach more ecologically valid and generalisable findings. Their research approach was exploratory and led by the question: how does the display influence the way people see and experience art in a museum? They employed a mixed-method approach that combined quantitative and qualitative methods: the eye tracker, subjective mapping (i.e., a drawing task in combination with an open interview), and a questionnaire to connect gaze patterns with processes of meaning-making. This approach allowed them to evaluate the new arrangement in terms of viewing time of the artworks, reading time of the captions, and visitors engagement with the artworks. They also had the opportunity to ascertain that interest in specific works of art and preferences for art forms proved to be solid and independent of display methods. Note that at the end of the experiments, the participants were given a small, unannounced, gift from the museum shop. It is a nice gesture to thank visitors.

Both studies have been mentioned as examples of how we can design experiments in museums focused on viewing behaviour, within a single museum or in multiple institutions, and employing mixed-method approaches.

2D Patterns and 3D Objects

The second part of this chapter deals with the analysis of how 3D objects are recognised. In order to achieve this goal, it is first necessary to understand how 2D patterns are identified, and which parts of the visual world compose each object. Moreover, the differences between face recognition and object recognition are outlined.

Identifying 2D patterns, such as alphanumeric patterns, is a skill called *pattern recognition*. Each pattern consists of specific features as stated by Jain and Duin (2004)[8]. For example, number 1 is made up of a straight line and a sloping line. Pattern recognition is based on two processes: global processing and processing of specific features. As a rule of thumb, feature processing usually (but not always) occurs before global processing in the categorisation of 2D patterns.

The first systematic and influential attempt to study which parts of the visual world make up each object—a challenging task in an environment rich in so many elements—was made by Gestalt psychologists. According to APA, Gestalt psychology is an approach that focuses on the dynamic organisation of experience into patterns or configurations. It claims that experience is an organised whole of which the pieces are an integral part. The term "Gestalt" is a German word which means form, configuration, and totality. German psychologists Wolfgang Köhler, Kurt Koffka, and Max Wertheimer proposed this approach in the early 20th century to counter structuralism and behaviourism[9]. According to Gestaltists, perceptual organisation is innate. Their primary principle is the *law of Prägnanz* (also called the *law of simplicity*), which assumes that human beings perceive the simplest possible organisation of the visual field. They also proposed other organisational principles of perception:

- the *law of proximity*: visual elements that are close to each other tend to be grouped together
- the *law of similarity*: similar items tend to be perceived as a unified group
- the *law of good continuation*: elements in alignment tend to be considered as forming smooth and unbroken contours
- the *law of closure*: missing parts of a figure tend to be filled in to complete it

Gestaltists also stressed the importance of *figure-ground segregation* (i.e., the perceptual organisation of the visual field into a figure of central interest and the remainder, which is consider less important and so forms the background; the main difference between the figure and the background is that the former has a specific shape while the latter lacks form).

Gestalt approach has some limitations such as the marginal role played by past experience and learning in perceptual grouping and figure-ground segregation, while recent theories have confirmed their importance. Gestaltists described important perceptual phenomena but they did not explain them adequately. They did not discover several other principles, such as the *uniform connectedness principle* (Palmer & Rock, 1994)[10]: items are perceived as a single unit if they share uniform visual properties, like colour and lightness. Almost all the evidence gathered by Gestaltists to support their principles of perceptual organisation was based on 2D drawings involving only one law at a time. However, real-world scenes are often more complex to perceive due to the involvement of several laws operating simultaneously.

Identifying objects in the visual field (called *object recognition*) is vital to survive in the world around us. The visual process underlying object recognition typically begins with general processing followed by fine (detailed) processing. This means that we can perceive visual scenes at two levels (general level and/or fine level). The primary visual cortex is of major importance in object recognition because some of its cells respond to high spatial frequencies by capturing fine details, while other cells respond to low spatial frequencies by capturing general information. The speed transmission of these spatial frequencies to higher-order brain areas varies greatly:

- low spatial frequencies depend on the fast magnocellular (M) pathway and the dorsal stream
- high spatial frequencies are conveyed more slowly by the parvocellular (P) pathway and the ventral stream

This diversity in speed explains why general processing typically occurs before fine processing.

There are several object recognition theories. Marr (1982)[11] proposed the influential *computational theory* based on three levels of understanding:

- the first level is a 2D description of the main variations of light intensity in the visual input; it is *viewpoint-dependent*, meaning that the recognition of an object is easier when viewed from specific angles
- the second level collects information about the depth and orientation of visible surfaces with the help of binocular disparity, motion, etc. (it is viewpoint-dependent)
- the third level provides information about the shape and position of 3D objects; it is *viewpoint-invariant*, meaning that the recognition of an object is fast and easy regardless of the viewing angle

Marr's theory has some limitations such as the excessive emphasis on bottom-up processes (i.e., processing is directly influenced by environmental stimuli), the marginal role played by top-down processes (i.e., processing is affected by the individual's expectations and past experience) in visual perception, and the complexity of computational processes.

However, Marr's approach was very influential because he was one of the first to understand that object recognition is much more complex than previously thought. He proposed a clear explanation of the processes involved in object recognition through a computational model. The distinction of the two types of representations (viewpoint-dependent and viewpoint-invariant) inspired many researchers.

As shown before, viewpoint (viewpoint-dependent and viewpoint-invariant) influences the recognition of the object, which also takes into account *categorisation* (e.g., is the object a painting?) and *identification* that is a distinction within the category (e.g., is the object a still life?). When categorisation occurs, object recognition is often viewpoint-invariant (i.e., recognition does not depend on the viewing angle). When identification occurs, object recognition is usually viewpoint-dependent (i.e., recognition depends on the viewing angle).

Many theorists in the past, as in the case of Marr, have emphasised the importance of bottom-up processes. Lately, researchers have gathered evidence that top-down processes are involved in object recognition when bottom-up processes are not very informative. For example, top-down processes help us to recognise the couple when looking at a blurred image like Ferruccio Ferroni's "Dancers" (1954; Figure 3.4).

In conscious visual perception, recurrent processing from higher to lower brain areas is often required, which is a type of top-down processing. Although it is a difficult task to demonstrate a direct impact of top-down processes on perception, recently many studies have demonstrated this influence, especially when visual stimuli are degraded. For example, Goolkasian and Woodberry (2010)[12] carried out an experiment showing observers some ambiguous or reversible images after a picture (called *prime*) relevant to one interpretation[13]. The primes systematically influenced the interpretation of the ambiguous images, this means that top-down processes were triggered to recognise the object represented.

Summing up, many theorists have pointed out that object recognition is based on top-down processes as well as bottom-up processes.

Face recognition requires more holistic processing than object recognition. Holistic processing involves the integration of information from an entire object, and it is based on the analysis of the relationships among features as well as the features themselves (Watson & Robbins, 2014)[14]. Compared to feature processing, holistic processing is:

- faster because facial features are processed in parallel rather than separately
- more reliable because individual facial features (e.g., the shape of the eyes) change over time

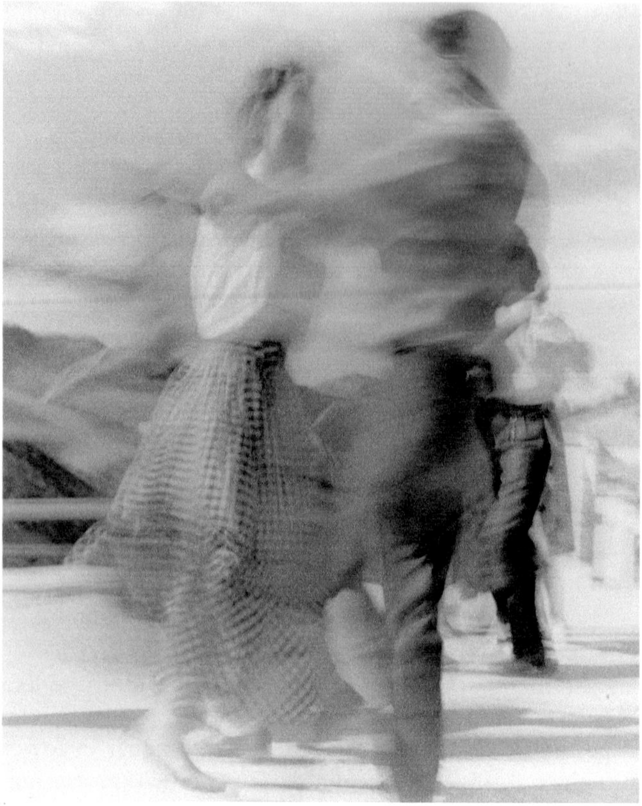

Figure 3.4 Ferrucio Ferroni, Dancers (1954). Museo Comunale d'Arte Moderna, dell'Informazione e della Fotografia, Senigallia (Italy). Courtesy of the Ferroni heirs.

The *face inversion effect* (i.e., the finding showing that it is more difficult to recognise faces when they are upside-down or inverted) and the *part-whole effect* (i.e., the finding that demonstrates that it is easier to recognise a part of the face when it is presented within a whole face rather than alone) provide some evidence that faces are processed holistically.

Anatomically, the *fusiform face area* (located in the *ventral temporal cortex*) and other regions of the brain, including the *occipital face area* and the *superior temporal sulcus*, are involved in face recognition. Therefore, face recognition likely engages one or more brain networks.

Note that the fusiform face area is of key importance in face recognition in the majority of individuals. This area is also activated when processing various types of objects other than faces.

Supporters of the *expertise hypothesis* (e.g., Wang et al., 2016)[15] argued that the brain and processing mechanisms activated for faces are also triggered in the recognition of any object category for which an individual possesses expertise.

Various theories have been developed to explain face processing and recognition. One of the most influential was a *serial-stage model* by Bruce and Young (1986)[16]. According to this model, there is a wide range of information that can be detected from faces, and there are major differences in the processing of familiar and unfamiliar faces. Moreover, there are two separate, not completely independent, processing routes dedicated to elaborate facial identity and facial expression. This separation is important because it helps to recognise a familiar face with an unusual expression, as stated by Young (2018)[17].

Bruce and Young's model has some limitations such as ignoring gaze perception, which is an important element that provides information on what a person is looking at.

Face processing and recognition can be of key importance in the museum environment. For example, when visitors look at portraits (paintings, half-length sculptures, photographs, etc.), how can we improve the memory of these portraits displayed in an exhibition? Since face recognition and object recognition trigger different brain processes, is it better to separate objects based on the subjects depicted (e.g., a section dedicated to portraits) to help the brain function properly?

Visual Imagery and Visual Perception

Up to now we have spoken about perception, but what is *visual imagery* and its function? It is the capacity of the brain to create visual images, and it allows us to predict the visual consequences of performing a specific action. It implies the sense of "having images in the mind", these pictures can be memories of previous visual experiences or syntheses produced by the imagination (e.g., the visualisation of Venus with sunglasses in Botticelli's "The Venus birth"). Moulton and Kosslyn (2009)[18] described it as a process that helps people imagine the consequences of being in a specific situation or performing a specific action by asking themselves the question "what if…".

Visual imagery supports various cognitive functions, such as short-term memory storage and long-term memory retrieval.

An influential theory is the one proposed by Kosslyn (1994)[19]. His *perceptual anticipation theory* states that visual imagery resembles visual perception, and that visual imagery processing occurs primarily in the early visual cortex. Neuroimaging studies provide evidence that similar areas are engaged in visual imagery and visual perception but the latter primarily involves bottom-up processing based on the visual stimuli, while visual imagery engages top-down processing based on knowledge of the object.

Could it be interesting to stimulate museumgoers' visual imagery during their visit? I think, it could. For example, visitors might listen to and visualise scenes from Shakespeare's play in their minds while looking at Blake's painting "Oberon, Titania and Puck with Fairies Dancing" (Tate, 1786; https://www.tate.org.uk/art/artworks/blake-oberon-titania-and-puck-with-fairies-dancing-n02686). Or, while visiting a submarine or warship, visitors could listen to letters sent by the crew to their families and imagine their lives, and so forth.

Children's educational activities could also take advantage of visual imagery. Children are very good at this activity, which could be exploited in numerous ways.

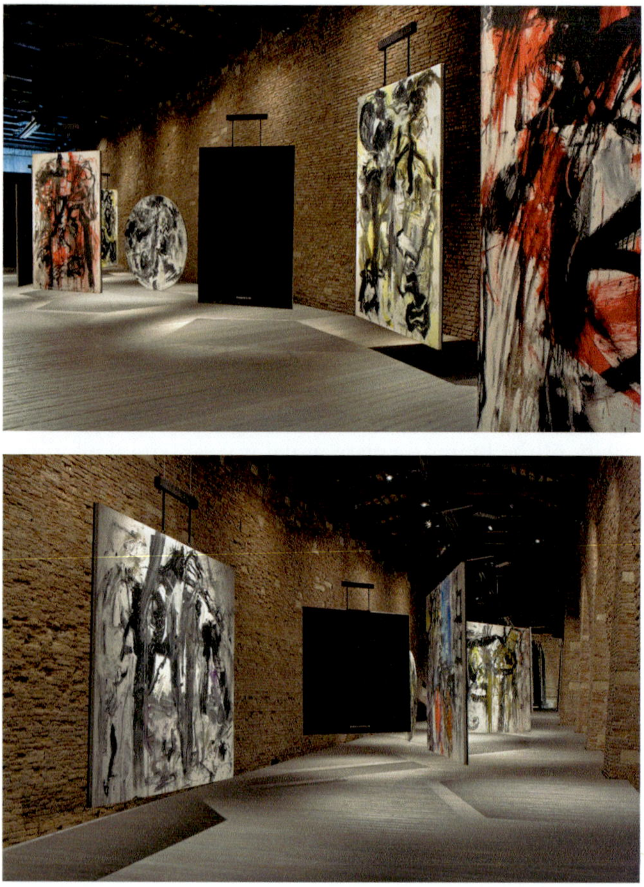

Figure 3.5 Artworks in Motion, "Emilio Vedova/ Renzo Piano" exhibition. Magazzino del Sale, Venice, 2009. Photo: Attilio Maranzano, Berlin © Fondazione Emilio e Annabianca Vedova, Venice. Courtesy of Fondazione Emilio e Annabianca Vedova.

The Complex Issue of Motion

There would be one last very important topic to be tackled in this chapter which is the perception of motion. It addresses the issue of how we interact (process and respond) with an ever-changing visual world.

As stated by Reitstätter et al. (2020), the combined activity of seeing and moving was already assessed in the early visitor studies (e.g., Robinson, 1928; Melton, 1935; Porter, 1938) and continues to be explored over time up to the present day (e.g., Yalowitz & Bronnenkant, 2009). The movement of visitors in

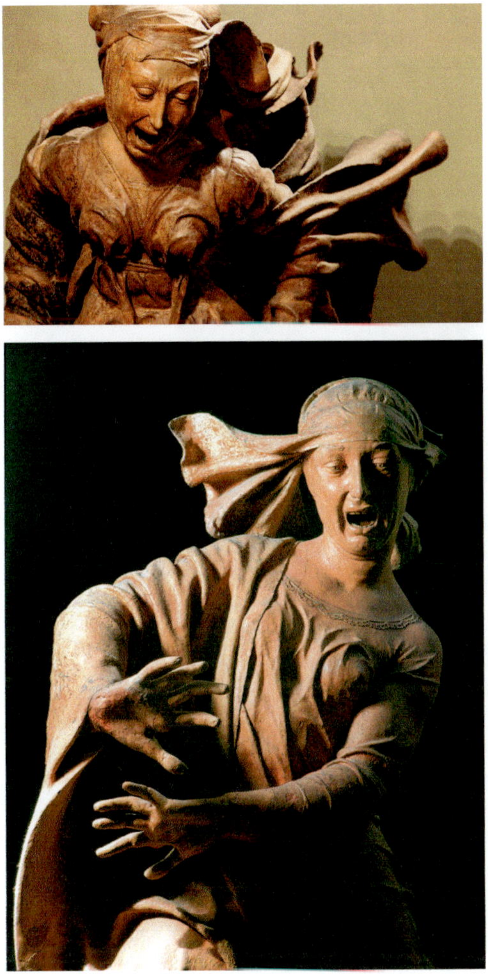

Figure 3.6 Mary Magdalene and Mary of Clopas Belonging to the Sculptural Group of "Compianto sul Cristo morto" by Niccolò dell'Arca. Church of Santa Maria della Vita. Photo: Andrea Samaritani. Courtesy of Genus Bononiae. Museums in the City.

museum spaces or around large objects is one of the important topics when it comes to motion. However, there are other issues that need our attention. For example, how do we perceive objects in motion (3D) such as Calder's "Mobile" (Tate, 1932; https://www.tate.org.uk/art/artworks/calder-mobile-l01686) or Vedova's paintings in motion (2D) displayed at Magazzino del Sale in Venice (Figure 3.5)?

Or, how do we perceive movement in static objects such as Niccolò dell'Arca's statues "Lamentation over the dead Christ" (1462–63; Figure 3.6) or Boccioni's painting "Riot in the gallery" (1910; Figure 3.7)?

Issues related to motion in the museum environment will be addressed in further publications given the complexity of this topic and the fact that in the majority of museums around the world visitors generally *stop* to observe a *static* object.

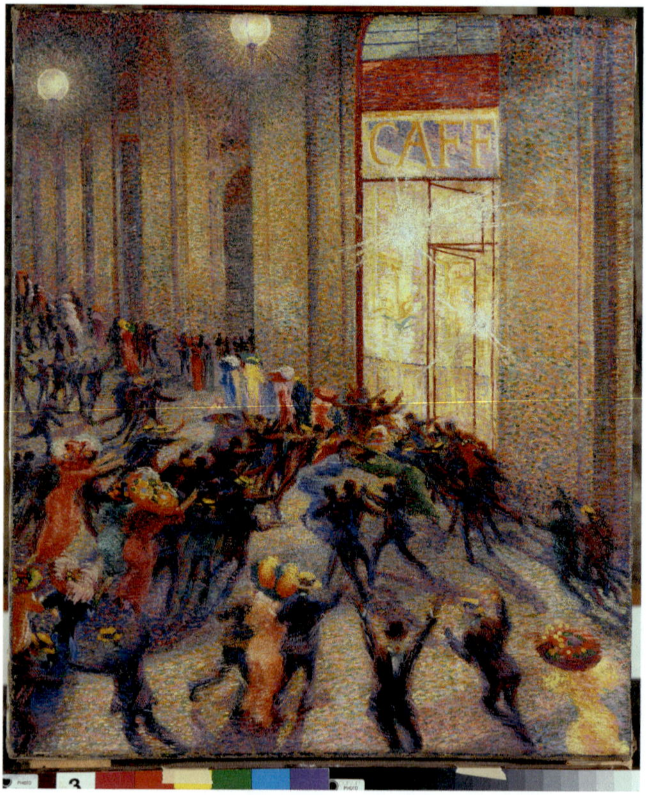

Figure 3.7 Umberto Boccioni, *Riot in the Gallery*, 1910, Oil on Canvas © Pinacoteca di Brera, Milan. Courtesy of the Pinacoteca di Brera.

Notes

1 The first Museum of Illusions (https://www.museumofillusions.com/) was founded in Croatia (2015) by Roko Zivkovic. Illusions deceive visitors' confidence in their senses by introducing them to complex topics such as perception and the human brain.
2 https://www.pem.org/neuroscience-initiative/from-neuroscience-to-museum-practice, accessed 9 February 2021.
3 https://dictionary.apa.org/visual-area, accessed 14 June 2021.
4 See reference in Eysenck and Keane (2020, p. 48).
5 See reference in Eysenck and Keane (2020, p. 55).
6 See reference in Eysenck and Keane (2020, p. 63).
7 See reference in Eysenck and Keane (2020, p. 75).
8 See reference in Eysenck and Keane (2020, p. 95).
9 https://dictionary.apa.org/gestalt-psychology, accessed 18 June 2021.
10 See reference in Eysenck and Keane (2020, p. 101).
11 See reference in Eysenck and Keane (2020, p. 105).
12 See reference in Eysenck and Keane (2020, p. 111).
13 Example of reversible images and prime stimuli: https://www.researchgate.net/figure/Samples-of-the-stimulus-items-the-Eskimo-indian-and-liar-face-ambiguous-figures-are_fig1_49827588, accessed 14 March 2021. The upper images are ambiguous pictures, such as Eskimo/Indian and Liar/face, and the lower images are the *primes,* which individually precede the reversible images and influence their interpretation.
14 See reference in Eysenck and Keane (2020, p. 116).
15 See reference in Eysenck and Keane (2020, p. 122).
16 See reference in Eysenck and Keane (2020, p. 125).
17 See reference in Eysenck and Keane (2020, p. 126).
18 See reference in Eysenck and Keane (2020, p. 131).
19 See reference in Eysenck and Keane (2020, p. 131).

References

Bruce, V., & Young, A.W. (1986). Understanding face recognition. *British Journal of Psychology*, 77, 305–327.

Bruno, N., & Cutting, J.E. (1988). Mini-modularity and the perception of layout. *Journal of Experimental Psychology*, 117, 161–170.

Cerasa, A., & Tomaiuolo, F. (2019). *La Scatola Magica. All'origine delle neuroscienze*. Milano: Hoepli.

Ernst, M.O., & Bülthoff, H.H. (2004). Merging the senses into a robust percept. *Trends in Cognitive Sciences*, 8, 162–169.

Eysenck, M.W., & Keane, M.T. (2020). *Cognitive Psychology. A Student's Handbook*. Oxon-New York:Routledge.

Goolkasian, P., & Woodberry, C. (2010). Priming effects with ambiguous figures. *Attention, Perception, & Psychophysics*, 72, 168–178.

Haak, K.V., & Beckmann, C.F. (2018). Objective analysis of the topological organisation of the human cortical visual connectome suggests three visual pathways. *Cortex*, 98, 73–83.

Jain, A.K., & Duin, R.P.W. (2004). Pattern recognition. In R.L. Gregory (Ed.), *The Oxford Companion to the Mind* (pp. 698–703). Oxon: Oxford University Press.

Kosslyn, S.M. (1994). *Image and Brain: The Resolution of the Imagery Debate*. Cambridge, MA: MIT Press.

Marr, D. (1982). *Vision: A Computational Investigation into the Human Representation and Processing of Visual Information*. San Francisco: W.H. Freeman.

Melton, A.W. (1935). *Problems of Installation in Museums of Art* (New Series). American Association of Museums.

Milner, A.D., & Goodale, M.A. (1995). *The Visual Brain in Action*. Oxon: Oxford University Press.

Milner, A.D., & Goodale, M.A. (2008). Two visual systems re-viewed. *Neuropsychologia*, 46, 774–785.

Moulton, S.T., & Kosslyn, S.M. (2009). Imaging predictions: Mental imagery as mental emulation. *Philosophical Transactions of The Royal Society B Biological Sciences*, 364, 1273–1280.

Palmer, S.E., & Rock, I. (1994). Rethinking perceptual organization: The role of uniform connectedness. *Psychonomic Bulletin & Review*, 1, 29–55.

Porter, M. (1938). *Behavior of the Average Visitor in the Peabody Museum of Natural History Yale University* (New Series). American Association of Museums.

Reitstätter, L., Brinkmann, H., Santini T., Specker, E., Dare, Z., Bakondi, F., Miscená, A., Kasneci, E., Leder, H., & Rosenberg, R. (2020). The display makes a difference: A mobile eye tracking study on the perception of art before and after a museum's re-arrangement. *Journal of Eye Movement Research*, 13, 6.

Robinson, E.S. (1928). *The Behaviour of the Museums Visitor* (New Series). American Association of Museums.

Tizi, L., Toffalini, E., Pavan, E., & Pazzaglia, F. (2019). Atmosfera percepita di due allestimenti museali in relazione a fattori ambientali e variabili cognitive, affettive e rigenerative. Analisi delle caratteristiche psicometriche dell'adattamento italiano del Perceived Atmosphere Instrument. *Giornale italiano di psicologia*, 4, 959–983.

Tymkiw, M., & Foulsham, T. (2020). Eye tracking, spatial biases and normative spectatorship in museums. *Leonardo*, 53, 542–546.

Wang, P., Gauthier, I., & Cottrell, G. (2016). Are face and object recognition independent? A neurocomputational modeling exploration. *Journal of Cognitive Neuroscience*, 28, 558–574.

Watson, T.L., & Robbins, R.A. (2014). The nature of holistic processing in face and object recognition: Current opinions. *Frontiers in Psychology*, 5 (Article 3).

Yalowitz, S.S., & Bronnenkant, K. (2009). Timing and tracking: Unlocking visitor behavior. *Visitor Studies*, 12, 47–64.

Young, A.W. (2018). Face, people and the brain: The 45th Sir Frederic Bartlett lecture. *Quarterly Journal of Experimental Psychology*, 71, 569–594.

Zeki, S. (1993). *A Vision of the Brain*. Oxon: Blackwell.

Zeki, S. (2001). Localisation and globalization in conscious vision. *Annual Reviews of Neuroscience*, 24, 57–86.

4 Attention, Memory, and Learning in Museums

Annalisa Banzi

When visitors enter a museum, some of them assume that they have to visit it entirely. At some point of the tour, when they start to feel tired, they give up and look for the exit. Our brain is not made to absorb an overwhelmingly large number of stimuli. It takes time to analyse, re-elaborate, and remember these stimuli, especially if a person is not familiar with them. It is very important to help everyone understand that the brain has these needs.

In 2001, Smith and Smith carried out a study at the Metropolitan Museum of Art to evaluate the average amount of time visitors spend looking at artworks (mean amount of time: 27.2s, median: 17.0s, and mode: 10.0s). In 2017, Smith et al. repeated that study at The Art Institute of Chicago. They expanded it to include a larger sample size, more artworks, and separate observations for the time spent looking at exhibits and reading captions. As with the original study, the researchers also analysed the effects of gender, age, and group size on the time spent observing. The findings were very similar to those collected in 2001 (mean amount of time: 28.63s, median: 21.00s, and mode: 10.00s.). Note that in the latest study (2017), the researchers detected that a large number of visitors take *arties* (i.e., selfies taken with the artworks) regardless of the visitors' gender, apparent age, or group size. These findings (sadly) show that the time people spend viewing artworks has not changed much. However, what has changed is how museumgoers spend that time (e.g., arties).

Focused Auditory Attention, Focused Visual Attention, and Divided Attention

Attention is of key importance in museums; therefore, the first part of this chapter addresses this topic and refers to focused auditory attention, focused visual attention, and divided attention when performing two tasks. Note that at the end of this chapter, there is an example of the concrete application of psychology and neuroscience in the museum environment (section: "Practical application of psychology and neuroscience in the museum environment").

Attention is a state in which cognitive resources are focused on specific aspects of the environment rather than others and the central nervous system is ready to respond to stimuli[1].

DOI: 10.4324/9781003304531-4

There are three main preliminary distinctions concerning attention:

- *active attention* (when driven by the individual's expectations or goals: top-down processes) and *passive attention* (when driven by environmental stimuli: bottom-up processes)
- *focused or selective attention* (when an individual tries to respond only to one stimulus presented together with others) and *divided attention*, also known as *multi tasking* (when an individual performs two tasks at the same time)
- *external attention* (which is the selection and modulation of sensory information) and *internal attention* (which is the selection, modulation, and maintenance of internally generated information, as stated by Chun et al., 2011)[2]

Imagine we are in a crowded and noisy museum room, how can we follow the museum guide explaining an object while many people are talking? This is the *cocktail party problem*, as it is called by psychologists.

McDermott (2009)[3] points out that listeners have to deal with two problems when focusing on one voice among many, which is the phenomenon called *focused auditory attention*. In the case of museumgoers, they have first to isolate which sounds belong together (i.e., sound segregation) and secondly they have to concentrate on listening to the museum guide (i.e., sound source of interest) while ignoring other auditory inputs. According to McDermott, auditory segregation is more difficult than visual segregation due to signals overlapping from different sound sources in the cochlea located inside the ear (visual objects usually involve several areas of the retina).

There is evidence that top-down processes, based on the expectations and/or knowledge of individuals, are involved in achieving the complex task of selecting the auditory input of interest (e.g., the voice of the museum guide) and ignoring the others.

Auditory attention has been less investigated than visual attention because vision is our major sense modality involving the cortex more than any other sense.

Depending on the specific situation and the individuals' goal, focused or selective visual attention can resemble:

- a spotlight (Posner, 1980)[4] when focused on a quite small area
- a zoom lens (e.g., Eriksen & St. James, 1986)[5] when increasing or decreasing the area of focal attention
- multiple spotlights (Awh & Pashler, 2000)[6] when attention is directed to two or more not-adjacent areas in the space (this phenomenon is called *split attention*)

The metaphors adopted in these theories, such as attention resembling a spotlight, describe the experimental findings collected on visual attention but do not explain the underlying brain mechanisms, as stated by Di Lollo (2018)[7].

Focused or selective visual attention can select a specific area of space (*space-based attention*), a given object (*object-based attention*), or a particular feature such as colour or shape (*feature-based attention*). These three types of attention often interact with each other to improve object processing, as stated by Kravitz and Behrmann (2011)[8].

There are phenomena that could be interesting to investigate in the museum environment. The first is called *inhibition of return*, which is the reduced likelihood of visual attention returning to a recently attended place or object. The second is called *covert attention*, which is the attention given to an object without the eye movement towards it. As claimed by Chen and Zelinsky (2019)[9], most of the research studies on the allocation of attention have been carried out in non-naturalistic conditions. What if we study these attentional processes in museums for the benefit of visitors? For example, what would be the consequences of inhibition of return and covert attention in the process of looking at museum objects?

Bitgood (2009) provided a list of phenomena that seem to have an impact on decreasing attention over successive object viewing: fatigue (mental and/or physical exhaustion), satiation (lack of variety), competition (increasing number of alternatives available at any moment), information overload (there are too many inputs at once or too many are presented too quickly), distraction, choice, interactions (when the aforementioned phenomena interact), and poor design.

According to PEM, visitors do not necessarily pay attention to the important elements in an exhibition just because these are present. Exhibition designers have to create displays and environments to activate focused attention while being aware that this type of attention processing cannot be sustained for the duration of an entire exhibition[10]. It is a wise advice that proposes to consider how to trigger the best attention performance, which is limited in time and needs to be recharged. To this end, I would like to mention the Fundació Joan Miró in Barcelona (Spain). Daniel (private communication, 2020), director of this museum, explained to me how Miró was sensitive to adequately involve visitors while also thinking about their cognitive needs (including attention). Miró himself wanted to build the foundation (opened in 1975). He chose to place it on the Montjuïc hill, overlooking Barcelona, because he desired to combine his passions: art, nature, and landscape. When he asked his friend, architect Josep Lluís Sert, to build the museum, he had very clear in mind what kind of visit to offer to the public. Miró marked on the architect's drawings and maps the points in which to insert open spaces overlooking the city or the verdant landscape of Montjuïc. These are intervals that allow people to sit back, relax, and entertain themselves with the panorama, and to have the time to process the information acquired by visiting the first rooms of the foundation. Without leaving the museum, these stops create a temporary separation from the aesthetic solicitations of paintings and sculptures. Miró thought about the rhythm of the museum visit, modulating its intensity and the pauses devoted to relaxing the mind or to activities other than the contemplation of art.

Nature is a different stimulus from that proposed by artistic language, as well as representing in itself a moment of regeneration. Miró, in addition to the priceless gift of his art, has created a museum that wants to easily communicate with our brain. It would be very useful to verify and collect evidence on the idea of Miró by measuring the cognitive reactions of visitors through neuroscience tools and psychological theories, as suggested by the BFM approach. In this regard, there are studies that demonstrate a restorative and beneficial effect of nature on individuals in terms of psychological recovery from attention fatigue and the restoration of mental resources previously used in activities that required attention (Amicone et al., 2018). Mason et al. (2021) examined 14 studies reporting investigations which involved students of different levels of education (elementary and secondary schools, and university), in a brief exposure to nature lasting from 10 to 90 minutes during a school day. The review shows that 12 out of 14 studies report cognitive benefits in terms of direct restoration of attention from mental fatigue due to contact with greenery. Nature also has a positive impact on affects as it reduces psychophysiological stress, anxiety, rumination, and negative emotions. Positive affect favours cognitive functioning and academic achievement (Mason et al., 2021).

Attention has been extensively studied by researchers. They suggested several theories based on two major networks: one goals-directed or endogenous and the other stimulus-driven or exogenous. For example, Corbetta and Shulman's (2002)[11] influential approach proposed two attention systems that can interact effectively with each other:

- the goal-directed or top-down system (*dorsal attention network*) is triggered when a cue predicts the feature of an imminent visual stimulus and is influenced by the expectations, knowledge, and objectives of individuals
- the stimulus-driven or bottom-up system (*ventral attention network*) is activated when an unexpected and important stimulus shows up

This theoretical approach has some limitations. For example, additional attention-related brain networks have been identified in recent years, such as the *default mode network,* which is engaged in internal processes (e.g., mind wandering).

Of course, attention impacts our everyday life. For example, *visual search* is the activity that involves the fastest possible detection of a specific stimulus (target). This process is also vital in the museum environment, when we are looking for a museum object that we would like to see or when we are searching for a guide in the bookshop, etc.

There are several theories that try to explain visual search. According to Treisman and Gelade's *feature integration theory* (1980),[12] there are two phases of elaboration: a first-processing stage in which the basic visual object's features are processed quickly and in parallel, and a second-processing stage in which the focused attention combines these features to form the object by means of a slower serial process. Most recent theories underline the important role played by perception in visual search.

Note that the research studies introduced so far are focused on only one modality (visual or auditory); but, in real life, like in a museum, people usually coordinate attention through two or more modalities at the same time (e.g., visitors listen to the museum guide while they look at the exhibits). This phenomenon is called *cross-modal attention*. Its effects have been studied by collecting empirical findings but it still lacks a theoretical understanding. Moreover, these results were not collected in natural scenes and individual differences were generally ignored.

As mentioned at the beginning of this chapter, attention can be focused (selective) or divided (multi tasking). Focused attention has already been discussed. Let's now turn to divided attention, which is a dual-task performance[13]. The execution of these two tasks is influenced by:

- similarity, that is the situation in which stimuli or responses are in the same modality (visual or auditory); in this case, the performance is worse than when they are in different modalities
- practice, which determines how well the two tasks can be accomplished together

Individuals perform the two tasks by taking advantage of parallel processing or serial processing. Parallel processing involves processing the two tasks simultaneously. Serial processing involves shifting attention back and forth between the two tasks with only one task being processed at any given moment.

What happens in a dual-task performance when the second stimulus is presented shortly after the first one? Typically, the response to the second stimulus is significantly slowed. This phenomenon is called *psychological refractory period* (PRP) effect[14]. It can be influenced by *crosstalk* (i.e., the direct interference between two tasks that generally occurs when the stimuli and/or the responses of the two tasks are similar) and by practice (which could reduce the PRP effect). In general, divided attention research studies report that practice often greatly enhances performance. It has been supposed that this improvement occurs because some processes become automatic due to long practice.

According to PEM, when designing an exhibition we have to consider:

- how the visually salient elements of artworks will influence attention
- how top-down factors will affect the attention of visitors
- how we can take advantage of the various contextual elements to grab attention[15]

I think we can adapt these suggestions to different types of museums.

In my opinion, silence is another element that should be taken into account in a museum. It can improve attention. What if we introduced the *hour of silence* in the museum, once a week, to allow people sensitive to noise to focus on museum objects? This initiative can be appreciated by specific audiences, such as autistics, but not only by them because everyone can benefit from this moment of silence away from the commotion of everyday life.

One last thought to conclude this part. I am aware that what I am about to say now may seem a utopia but perhaps it may be a provocation that can generate applicable ideas. In some ways, as anticipated in the introduction, this book is a kind of brainstorming. Compatibly with conservation issues, museum size storage, security requirements, etc., maybe there is the option for some museums to organise their collections in terms of "alternating collections". Rotating museum objects would involve designing mini tours based on specific topics and thematic units relevant for the museum itself. The rotation system might have some advantages. First, it could favour focused visual attention as visitors would not be distracted by too many stimuli. Museumgoers could focus on a limited number of exhibits, helping the brain to adequately absorb the proposed stimuli. Second, it could help museums to generate more interest from their visitors because it is like re-discovering the museum every time. The *surprise* and *excitement* generated by seeing again an object, which is not always available, is an effective basic human mechanism. Third, it could give some "rest" to museum objects, as many of them are very delicate and sensitive to factors such as light.

Short-term Memory, long-term Memory, and Learning

The second part of this chapter introduces short-term memory (STM) and long-term memory (LTM), explicit and implicit learning, and the reasons responsible for forgetting in long-term memory. All these aspects are relevant to consider when designing exhibitions and their related activities.

According to many theorists, *short-term memory* is a type of memory in which information is hosted for a brief period of time and differs from *long-term memory* not only in terms of durations (a few seconds vs. several decades) but also in terms of capacity, because it can store only a few items compared to long-term memory, which has essentially unlimited capacity[16].

Several hypotheses have been proposed to explain the loss of information from short-term memory. One explanation could be that short-term memory capacity is limited; therefore, new information often displaces the ones already present in it. Another hypothesis suggests that in the absence of practice (rehearsal), information stored in short-term memory decays over time. Interference from information presented during the retention interval can be another factor that causes forgetting.

According to Baddeley and Hitch (1974)[17], short-term memory is of key importance in performing various tasks in daily life that are not explicitly memory tasks. They put forward the influential *working memory model*,

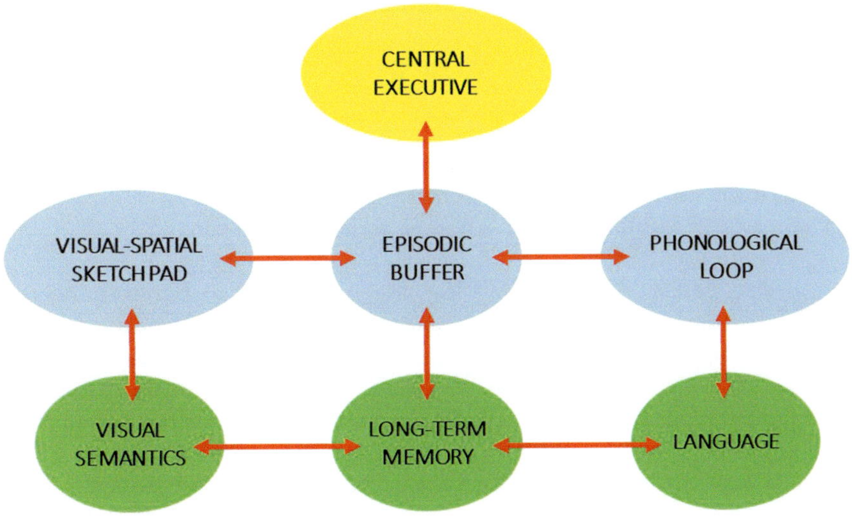

Figure 4.1 The Working Memory Model Consists of Four Components. The Schema Is Inspired by the One Proposed in the Book by Eysenck and Keane (2020, p. 246).

replacing the concept of short-term memory with that of *working memory*, which is a system composed of (Figure 4.1):

- a *central executive*, which resembles an attentional system
- a *phonological loop*, which processes and temporarily stores speech-based information
- a *visuo-spatial sketchpad*, which processes and temporarily stores visual and spatial information
- an *episodic buffer*, which is a temporary storage for integrated information (phonological loop + visuo-spatial sketchpad). It links to perception and long-term memory

This model remains influential over time also because there is compelling empirical evidence for all of its components listed earlier. However, it has some limitations, for example, it needs more information on the interaction between these four components. It also needs further investigation because it does not take into account some types of information such as those relating to smell, taste, etc.

Recently, there have been many contributions to improve working memory knowledge by developing two main theoretical approaches. Some theorists have analysed the working memory capacity, which is the ability to evaluate the amount of information that can be processed and stored at the same time. This capacity is positively related to intelligence and attentional control, meaning that individuals with high working memory capacity have higher *fluid intelligence* (i.e., a form of intelligence based on rapid understanding of novel relationships), and greater *attentional control* (i.e., a better control of external and internal distracting information) than those with low capacity. Other theorists have developed the second theoretical approach based on replacing the unitary central executive with several more specific executive functions, which are the processes used to organise and coordinate the functioning of the cognitive system to achieve goals.

Memory and learning require different stages of processing:

- *encoding* (which occurs during learning) is devoted to transforming the information contained in external stimuli into a representation
- *storage*, in this stage the representation is stored in the memory system
- *retrieval*, which is the process needed to recover information from the memory system (forgetting occurs if retrieval attempts fail)

We turn now to the learning processes that determine the storage of information in long-term memory. According to Kandel et al. (2000), learning is the process by which we acquire knowledge about the world. It can be divided into two categories:

- *explicit learning*: when we are aware of what has been learned
- *implicit learning*: when we are not aware of what has been learned

This distinction has been demonstrated by evidence from behavioural and neuroimaging studies. It is not easy to define which brain areas are associated with these two types of learning because learners often use both (individual differences and the stage of learning influence the extent to which learners are aware of what they are learning). The medial temporal lobe, including the *hippocampus*, is typically associated with explicit learning while the *basal ganglia*, including the *striatum*, are generally associated with implicit learning.

Regarding implicit learning, it is often assumed that it is less dependent on attention and working memory than explicit learning. There is a distinction between implicit learning and implicit memory and between explicit learning and explicit memory. *Implicit memory* (or *non-declarative memory*) is a form of long-term memory that does not involve conscious recollection. *Explicit memory* (or *declarative memory*) is a form of long-term memory that involves conscious recollection.

Typically, implicit learning is followed by implicit memory, whereas explicit learning is followed by explicit memory.

A concrete example of explicit learning is *learning through retrieval*[18] (i.e., performing tests on previously studied material which leads to better retention than re-studying that material for an equivalent time).

The discovery that long-term memory is improved thanks to this retrieval process is called the *test effect*. As stated by APA, although testing is an assessment tool, this finding suggests that testing (or retrieval practice) can also be considered a learning tool. Exams or tests appear to activate retrieval processes that facilitate learning and ensure that knowledge is stored more effectively in long-term memory[19].

Some theorists, on the basis of results collected, stressed the importance of retrieval effort: the testing effect is greater when the retrieval effort during the learning period is high rather than low.

Regarding museums, Simon (2010) argued that much of contemporary learning theory is based on the idea of "instructional scaffolding", whereby educators (or didactic material) provide a supporting guide on which visitors can build their confidence and talents. Falk and Dierking (2000) contended that people are highly motivated to learn when:

- they are in supportive environments
- they are involved in meaningful activities
- they are freed from anxiety, fear, and other negative mental states
- they have choices and control over their learning
- the challenges of the task meet their skills

Additionally, Hein (1998) pointed out that explicitly informing visitors, prior to the museum tour, of what they will be able to see or what the purpose of the exhibition is, leads them to relax and be more open to engage in acquiring new knowledge. It is important to give the possibility to choose and control one's own learning, and to tackle tasks that are proportionate to one's abilities.

Museumgoers' comfort is another important requisite for visitors' learning in museums: it is a necessary, albeit not sufficient, element for learning. Comfort covers a wide range of factors from physical environment to psychological conditions. Gilman (1916), for example, observed the museum fatigue that is due to the muscular effort of looking carefully at objects.

As mentioned earlier, retrieval practice is of key importance to improve the long-term memory. I thought of offering you the *time-dilated museum experience*, which is a flexible method that can be tailored to one's needs. As mentioned in the introduction, this is one of the proposals that needs to be verified in the museum setting. It is based on a multiple-guided tour (at a special price) of the same group of exhibits. The first session is of a standard type: the museum staff introduces the initiative (practical details) and then explains the specific topic relating to a limited number of previously selected objects. The duration of this session depends on how you want to personalise it. However, it cannot last more than 30 minutes to avoid mental or physical fatigue. The second and the third time the museum staff asks questions (like a quiz or a game) to visitors about the content provided in the previous meeting (*retrieval process*) in about 5/10 minutes. This step can help museumgoers better remember what they want to learn. Then, the museum staff add new concepts on the selected group of exhibits. At the end of each approximately 30-minute session, the museum staff can share references or mention similar objects displayed elsewhere to give interested participants the opportunity to explore the concept(s) addressed in that session. This step should encourage visitors to realise that museum learning does not occur only within the limited time and physical space of the museum. An extra session (or the last one) could be dedicated to a complementary activity, such as mindfulness session or a drawing session, focused on one of the museum objects described and analysed in the previous meetings. What could be the benefits? First, visitors could remember information more effectively through retrieval process discussed earlier. Second, this activity could be a potential socialising opportunity because museumgoers have the chance to meet the same people three times (or even four, if you consider the extra activity). Third, visitors become familiar with the museum: it should begin to be perceived as a safe and happy place to go and enrich their lives.

Let's now turn to the problem of long-term memory forgetting. Most of the studies conducted in this field have focused on explicit memory (forgetting is often faster in explicit memory than implicit memory). According to Nørby (2015)[20], forgetting has three main functions:

- reduces access to painful memories to increase psychological wellbeing
- deletes outdated information to avoid interference with current (and useful) information
- cancels the details that are not useful for remembering what we have read or heard because this process is typically more efficient when focusing on the overall gist rather than details

Several hypotheses have been formulated to identify the factors responsible for forgetting, such as decay, which occurs within memory traces, and interference. Lacking the appropriate retrieval cues (*cue-dependent forgetting*) may be another explanation for forgetting (e.g., suppose you have forgotten the name of the artist who painted "Guernica", if you are presented with a list of four names, however, you should recognise the correct one). According to Sadeh et al. (2016)[21], decay should be the cause of forgetting detailed memories (which contain contextual information), while interference should be the cause of forgetting weak memories (which lack contextual information).

Long-term Memory Systems

The third part of this chapter is devoted to long-term memory, which is the storage of an incredible variety of information[22]. It also introduces the traditional theoretical approach based on the distinction between explicit/declarative memory and implicit/non-declarative memory, and the more recent theories that overcome this clear-cut distinction.

The traditional theoretical account, based on different long-term memory systems (Figure 4.2), provides a division into two main groups:

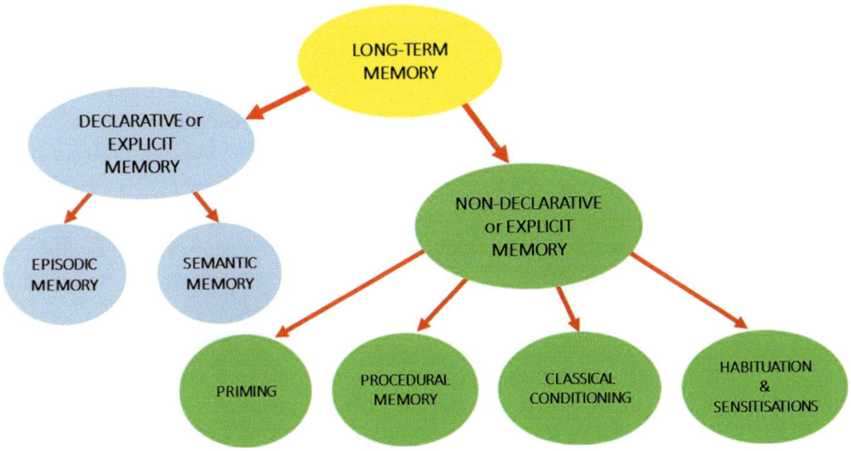

Figure 4.2 The Long-Term Memory Systems as Proposed by the Traditional Theoretical Approach.

- **declarative memory (or explicit memory)**, which involves conscious recollection of facts and events and is divided into:
  - *episodic memory*, which refers to personal experiences of events that happened in a given place, at a specific time. It is also used to imagine or to plan the future, and to influence *divergent creative thinking* (which explores unusual uses of common objects)

    There are two main types of tests to assess episodic memory after learning:

    - *recognition-memory test*: participants are presented with various items and have to decide if each of them has been previously presented. This test can involve *recollection* (where recognition relies on conscious retrieval of contextual information) or *familiarity* (where recognition lacks of conscious retrieval of contextual information). Note that *recognition memory* is a form of episodic memory
    - *recall* tests:
      - *free recall*: items to remember are recalled in any order
      - *serial recall*: items to remember have to be recalled in the order of presentation
      - *cued recall:* items to remember are recalled in response to specific cues (e.g., the learning items can be *Palladio-Villa Almerico-Capra* and the cue during the test can be *Palladio-???*)

- *semantic memory*, which refers to the general knowledge about the world and consists of:
    - *concepts*, which are mental representations of categories of items, such as words, objects, or facts, which include information from different sense modalities (multimodal representations)
    - *schemas*, which are larger information structures organised into information packets
    - *scripts*, which are schemas that include information about sequences of events (e.g., your museum visit script probably is made up of buying a ticket, checking the museum map, and visiting the museum and the bookshop)

    Episodic memory and semantic memory are often interdependent. For example, *personal semantics* are aspects of one's autobiographical memory that combine elements of both memories. There is also another phenomenon to consider as evidence of the connection between these two types of memories. It is called *semanticisation*, which is the transformation of episodic memories into semantic memories over time (Robin & Moscovitch, 2017)[23]. For example, the first time you visited a museum as a child, you created an episodic memory of this experience. Later, as an adult, you still remember that visit but you have probably forgotten some personal and contextual information related to those childhood memories.

- **non-declarative memory (or implicit memory)**, which does not involve conscious recollection and can be detected by observing changes in behaviour (e.g., consider someone learning to paint, their ability will improve over time but they will not consciously recollect what they have learned). It is divided into:
    - *procedural memory* (or *skill learning*), which is the memory of skills
    - *priming*, which facilitates the processing of a recently presented stimulus (priming will be detailed in the section "Practical application of psychology and neuroscience in the museum environment" as it is the psychological phenomenon selected to implement experiments in the museum environment to improve the memory and learning of visitors)
    - simple *classical conditioning* (also called Pavlovian conditioning)
    - *habituation* and *sensitisation*

There are two main differences between priming and procedural memory (which are the two major types of non-declarative memory): the former is often fast and is quite closely related to specific stimuli, whereas the latter is generally slow and can be related to numerous stimuli. There is evidence that these two types of non-declarative memory involve processes and brain areas other than those involved in declarative memory.

The theoretical traditional approach emphasises that the difference between these two memory systems (declarative/explicit memory vs. non-declarative/implicit memory) relies on the role of consciousness in accessing stored information. It also proposes that the medial temporal lobe, particularly the hippocampus, is generally related only to explicit memory. According to this approach, each memory system is associated with a few brain areas and operates independently. Recently, several theorists believe these assumptions are oversimplified. For example, Henke's (2010)[24] *processing-based model* focuses on memory processes rather than memory systems, and the *component-process model* (Cabeza et al., 2018)[25] states that memory is based on a flexible combination of numerous brain areas and processes.

Moreover, neuroimaging techniques provide evidence that one or more networks, which are made up of several brain areas, are associated with each type of memory. For example, semantic memory involves a left-hemisphere network of seven brain regions (Binder et al., 2009)[26] rather than just the medial temporal lobes proposed by traditional approach.

Let's now turn to two types of memory, autobiographical and prospective, which are strongly influenced by our everyday goals. The *autobiographical memory* is a long-term memory, which stores the events of a person's life. There is a relationship between this type of memory and episodic memory because they are both related to personal past experiences. However, in the episodic memory much information is superficial and, thus, is not stored for a long time, whereas, in autobiographical memory, the information is concerned with personal significant events or experiences and therefore is stored for a long time.

Neuroimaging research provides evidence that autobiographical memory[27] is more complex and activates more brain areas than episodic memory.

According to Bluck and Alea (2009)[28], autobiographical memory has:

- a social function: it helps us to get emotionally closer to others
- a directive function: it allows us to use the past as a guide to the future
- a self-function: it gives us the opportunity to create a sense of self-continuity over time
- a self-enhancement function: individuals are generally closer to their positive memories than to their negative memories; this function has been added by Demiray and Janssen (2015)[29]

Flashbulb memories, as claimed by Brown and Kulik (1977)[30], are vivid and detailed autobiographical memories of dramatic public events, such as the burning of Notre-Dame de Paris cathedral in 2019.

Another example of autobiographical memory is the *reminiscence bump*, which is the tendency of the elderly to recall many personal memories especially of the time period between 10 and 30 years. In contrast, autobiographical memories related to the first three years of life lack in all adults (this phenomenon is called *childhood amnesia* or *infantile amnesia*).

The other type of memory, the *prospective memory*[31], consists in remembering to perform the planned actions without the aid of an explicit reminder to do so. It differs from *retrospective memory* because the latter is focused on remembering the past (e.g., events, people, etc.). It typically requires several separate processes (i.e., intention formation, retention interval, cue detection, intention recall, and intention execution) as stated by Zogg et al. (2012)[32], and is divided into:

- *time-based prospective memory*, which is the execution of a given action at a specific time
- *event-based prospective memory*, which is the execution of a given action in the appropriate circumstances

Practical Application of Psychology and Neuroscience in the Museum Environment

In the last part of this chapter, I focus on the definition and features of priming (a type of non-declarative or implicit memory) and introduce the experiments[33] carried out in the Pinacoteca Ambrosiana (an art gallery located in Milan, Italy) to enhance the visitors memory and learning. These pilot studies represent an example of concrete application of psychology and neuroscience to the museum environment.

Priming, as defined by McNamara (2005), is an improvement in performance (i.e., in speed or accuracy to respond to a stimulus), in a perceptual or cognitive task, relative to an appropriate baseline, produced by the context or prior experience. Summing up, priming is a phenomenon that is based on the influence of one stimulus (*prime*) on another (*target*), generating an improvement in subsequent performance in terms of speed and accuracy of the response.

Consider this example: a person reads a list of words including *diorama*. The person is then asked to complete a word starting with *di*. The probability that the answer will be *diorama* is increased by the fact that this word was previously "primed". Therefore, if a stimulus is primed, later experiences of this stimulus will be processed more quickly and precisely by the brain.

Researchers have made a distinction between *conceptual priming,* in which the repetition of a stimulus facilitates the processing of its meaning, and *perceptual priming*, in which the repetition of a stimulus facilitates the processing of its perceptual features. There are different kinds of priming, such as *masked priming*, *affective priming*, and *structural priming*. In the case of the experiments in the Pinacoteca Ambrosiana, the following were used:

- *repetition priming*, which facilitates performance based on prior encounter with the same stimulus (*prime* = *target*). Stimulus repetition, as it occurs in repetition priming, is generally associated with *repetition suppression* (i.e., the brain activity decreases with the repetition of the stimulus) but can sometimes be associated with *repetition enhancement* (i.e., the brain activity increases with the repetition of the stimulus). According to Ferrari et al. (2017)[34], repetition suppression occurs when the stimuli are repeated many times in rapid succession, whereas repetition enhancement occurs when stimuli are spaced out over time

- *perceptual priming*, which is defined by enhanced processing of previously seen visual material with respect to novel visual material. This type of priming is not influenced by small changes in orientation: rotations in depth up to 67°. However, it is eliminated by large changes in orientation: rotations in depth ≥ 80°. Priming is also weakened by changes in the exemplar of an object (i.e., the same-named object in a different picture) and changes in the typography of a word from the study phase to the test phase (Wiggs & Martin, 1998)
- *semantic priming*, which refers to improving the speed or accuracy of responding to a stimulus when it is preceded by a semantically related or associated stimulus versus when it is preceded by a semantically unrelated or unassociated stimulus. For example, cat-dog versus table-dog. Semantic priming is a generic expression that comprises priming caused by many different types of relations that include both associative relations and true relations of meaning, as stated by Healy & Proctor (2003)

Priming has interesting features, such as long-lasting effects, stability despite age, and imperviousness to attention degree, that can be exploited in museum environment. This strong persistent type of memory could encourage visitors to learn more and better.

In 2011, I implemented two pilot studies in the Pinacoteca Ambrosiana, designed to concretely assess perceptual repetition priming effects and semantic repetition priming effects in the museum setting.

The experiments took into account semantic and perceptual repetition priming avoiding other more sophisticated types of priming. As mentioned earlier, prime and target are the same stimulus in repetition priming, this is the easiest way to trigger memory in the general public, which may not have preliminary or adequate knowledge of the museum objects. This means that the concepts or perceptual features were introduced prior to the visit to the museum collections (in a room next to the lobby of the art gallery) and were proposed again during the visit.

Overall, the pilot studies required three groups (a prime group, a neutral group, and a control group) to evaluate whether priming had occurred and whether it was effective in remembering museum objects and their features.

The first experimental setup took advantage of perceptual repetition priming (prime and target are the same). Here is a brief presentation of the procedure:

- prime group: each participant looked at a PowerPoint consisting of five prime stimuli (colours: red, green, blue, brown, and white) related to the colours of five paintings, alternated with neutral stimuli (objects in black and white not depicted in paintings: luggage, phone, baby bottle, vacuum cleaner, and headband) for a short period of time (about one minute). Each participant then freely visited the museum
- neutral group (this group was included to demonstrate that only specific stimuli trigger perceptual repetition priming): each participant looked at a PowerPoint consisting of 10 stimuli unrelated to the paintings (objects in black and white not depicted in the paintings, such as sunglasses) for a short period of time (about one minute). Each participant then freely visited the museum
- control group: each participant visited the museum freely without being engaged in any perceptual stimulus; the collected data related to this group provide the baseline to assess whether there has actually been a better performance by those who have been subjected to the visual-perceptual stimuli (prime group; Table 4.1).

At the end of their tour, all participants were asked to answer some questions about the paintings chosen for this experiment in order to verify if the prime stimuli (colours) helped them to remember the colours of the artworks (target).

In addition, Folgieri (Banzi & Folgieri, 2012) recorded subjects' EEG signals using a Neurosky MindWaveTM BCI device, a wireless brainwave sensing headset (the brain signals are transmitted via Bluetooth to a host computer).

The experiments were set up to improve the design of mini tours focusing on specific topics. For example, the second experimental setup exploited the semantic repetition priming (prime and target coincide) and was designed to develop a hypothetical mini tour related to the iconographic theme of the *Adoration of the Magi/Adoration of the Christ Child.*

Here is a brief presentation of the procedure:

- prime group: each participant watched a video (about five minutes) explaining the selected iconographic theme. Some keywords (prime stimuli) appeared on the screen as soon as the speaker pronounced

Table 4.1 List of prime stimuli (colours) related to a selected group of paintings

Portions of the artworks colours	*Selected artworks exhibited in the Pinacoteca Ambrosiana*
Green	Bonifacio de' Pitati, The Holy Family, St. John, Tobias, and the Archangel Raphael
Red	Giovanni Ambrogio Figino, Portrait of St. Charles Borromeo
Blue	Martino Piazza, Adoration of the Christ Child
White	Workshop of Tiziano Vecellio (Titian), The Madonna with Child, St. John the Baptist, and St. Cecilia
Brown	Iacopo Bassano, The rest on the flight into Egypt

them, while telling the story of the *Adoration of the Magi/Adoration of the Christ Child*. Each participant then freely visited the museum. Note that the keywords have been written in a second caption added next to each artwork

- neutral group (this group was included to demonstrate that only specific stimuli trigger semantic repetition priming): each participant watched a video, without keywords, that told the story of Cardinal Federico Borromeo, the founder of this museum (this story is not linked to the iconographic theme of the *Adoration of the Magi/Adoration of the Christ Child*). Each participant then freely visited the museum
- control group: each participant visited the museum freely without being engaged in any semantic stimulus; the collected data related to this group provide the baseline to assess whether there has actually been a better performance by those who have been subjected to the semantic stimuli (prime group; Table 4.2).

As for the previous experiment, at the end of their tours, all participants were asked to answer some questions about the paintings chosen for this experiment in order to verify if the prime stimuli (keywords) helped them to remember the details related to the theme and the paintings of the *Adoration of the Magi/ Adoration of the Christ Child* (target). Each participant's EEG signals were also collected via MindWave.

I have not reported and commented on the results of the two pilot studies in this book as my aim now is to give a practical example of the procedure of applying a cognitive process (psychology) and an EEG device (neuroscience tool) in the museum setting. In these experiments, the technology was used to evaluate the cognitive processes of the brain.

Priming is assessed with various tasks, such as *word-fragment completion* (e.g., s_l_ _n_) and *word-stem completion* (e.g., sal______), which can also be used as a game for children and teenagers after the museum tour. For example, a word-fragment completion task could be proposed to participants. Let's make a

Table 4.2 List of prime stimuli (keywords) related to a selected group of paintings

Keywords	*Selected artworks exhibited in the Pinacoteca Ambrosiana*
Gospel of St. Matthew	Morazzone, Adoration of the Magi
Three ages of life	Andrea Schiavone, Adoration of the Magi
Melchior, Gaspar, and Baldassarre	Tiziano Vecellio (Titian), Adoration of the Magi
Gold, incense, and myrrh	Maestro del Santo Sangue, Adoration of the Magi
Virgin Mary and the Child	Bramantino, Adoration of the Christ Child
Red and blue	Workshop of Ghirlandaio, Adoration of the Christ Child
Joseph	Giampietrino, Adoration of the Christ Child with St. Roch
Shepherds	Martino Piazza, Adoration of the Christ Child

concrete example. Suppose there is an exhibition focusing on pollution and climate change in a natural history museum. You can ask the children to read a list of words related to this exhibition (e.g., nature, planet, plastic, pollution, etc.) before entering the exhibition. At the end of the visit, you can ask them to fill in the word-fragment completion task (e.g., n_ t _ _ e, p_ _ _ u_ i_ _) as quickly as possible. The first one who completes the list correctly wins the competition. In the meanwhile, you have collected data that could help you to understand if the young participants remember what they saw.

The priming-based model, once fully developed, can be easily adapted to the entire cultural heritage. It could also become a means of breaking down cultural barriers, welcoming audiences with different backgrounds, as it takes advantages of mechanisms common to all human beings.

Notes

1 https://dictionary.apa.org/attention, accessed 22 February 2021.
2 See reference in Eysenck and Keane (2020, p. 179).
3 See reference in Eysenck and Keane (2020, p. 179).
4 See reference in Eysenck and Keane (2020, p. 184).
5 See reference in Eysenck and Keane (2020, p. 184).
6 See reference in Eysenck and Keane (2020, p. 184).
7 See reference in Eysenck and Keane (2020, p. 186).
8 See reference in Eysenck and Keane (2020, p. 189).
9 See reference in Eysenck and Keane (2020, p. 189).
10 https://www.pem.org/neuroscience-initiative/from-neuroscience-to-museum-practice, accessed 26 February 2021.
11 See reference in Eysenck and Keane (2020, p. 192).
12 See reference in Eysenck and Keane (2020, p. 202).
13 Theories such as *multiple resource theory* or *threaded cognition model* try to explain dual-task performance claiming it depends on several processing resources with limited capacity.
14 The most influential explanation of the PRP effect is the *bottleneck model*. It is often argued among psychologists that task performance requires three successive stages: 1st perceptual, 2nd central response selection, and 3rd response execution. In the bottleneck model, the PRP effect is a consequence of the waiting time of the second task. This delay is due to the bottleneck in the response selection phase of the first task (Mittelstädt and Miller, 2017—see reference in Eysenck and Keane (2020, p. 223).
15 https://www.pem.org/neuroscience-initiative/from-neuroscience-to-museum-practice, accessed 26 February 2021.
16 The distinction between these two types of memory underlies *multi-store models*, such as that of Atkinson and Shiffrin (1968—see reference in Eysenck and Keane (2020, p. 240) based on three separate kinds of memory stores (i.e., sensory stores associate with each of our senses, short-term store, and long-term store). More recently, *unitary-store models* have proposed a less clear-cut distinction between short-term and long-term memory.
17 See reference in Eysenck and Keane (2020, p. 246).
18 There is evidence that learning through retrieval is very effective with many different types of learning materials.
19 https://dictionary.apa.org/testing-effect, accessed 19 March 2021.
20 See reference in Eysenck and Keane (2020, p. 278).
21 See reference in Eysenck and Keane (2020, p. 280).

22 Thus, is not well represented by Atkinson and Shiffrin's (1968) notion of a single long-term memory store (footnote n. 16).
23 See reference in Eysenck and Keane (2020, p. 304).
24 See reference in Eysenck and Keane (2020, p. 333).
25 See reference in Eysenck and Keane (2020, p. 338).
26 See reference in Eysenck and Keane (2020, p. 337).
27 All these findings are of interest to researchers who have developed many theories of autobiographical memory over time, such as the *self-memory system model* by Conway and Pleydell-Pearce (2000—see reference in Eysenck & Keane, 2020, p. 355).
28 See reference in Eysenck and Keane (2020, p. 347).
29 See reference in Eysenck and Keane (2020, p. 347).
30 See reference in Eysenck and Keane (2020, p. 349).
31 The *multiprocess framework* (Einstein & McDaniel, 2005—see reference in Eysenck & Keane, 2020, p. 382) and the *dynamic multiprocess framework* (Shelton & Scullin, 2017—see reference in Eysenck & Keane, 2020, p. 382) are examples of theories that attempt to explain prospective memory.
32 See reference in Eysenck and Keane (2020, p. 377).
33 They are pilot studies, which are small preliminary experiments, aimed at evaluating procedures and measurements in view of a subsequent and more in-depth research project. Even if they are carried out to collect information about the feasibility of a project and to make necessary changes, pilot studies can also supply useful initial data on the subject of study and suggest ideas for future research (https://dictionary.apa.org/pilot-study, accessed 07 April 2021).
34 See reference in Eysenck and Keane (2020, p. 327).

References

Amicone, G., Petruccelli, I., De Dominicis, S., Gherardini, A., Costantino, V., Perucchini, P., & Bonaiuto, M. (2018). Green breaks: The restorative effect of the school environment's green areas on children's cognitive performance. *Frontiers in Psychology*, 9, 1579.

Atkinson, R.C. & Shiffrin, R.M. (1968). Human memory: A proposed system and its control processes. In K.W. Spence & J.T. Spence (Eds.), *The Psychology of Learning and Motivation* (Vol. 2; pp. 89–195). London: Academic Press.

Awh, E., & Pashler, H. (2000). Evidence for split attentional foci. *Journal of Experimental Psychology Human Perception & Performance*, 26, 834–846.

Baddeley, A., & Hitch, G.J. (1974). Working memory. In G.A. Bower (Ed.), *Recent Advances in Learning and Motivation* (Vol. 8; pp. 47–89). New York: Academic Press.

Banzi, A. (2012). The case for implicit memory process as a tool to improve visitors' learning in museums of fine arts. *The International Journal of the Inclusive Museum*, 4, 27–36.

Banzi, A., & Folgieri, R. (2012). EEG-based BCI data analysis on visual-priming in the context of a museum of fine arts. DMS 2012, 18th International Conference on Distributed Multimedia Systems.

Binder, J.R., Desai, R.H., Graves, W.W., & Conant, L.L. (2009). Where is the semantic system? A critical review and meta-analysis of 120 functional neuroimaging studies. *Cerebral Cortex*, 19, 2767–2796.

Bitgood, S. (2009). When is "museum fatigue" not fatigue? *Curator*, 52, 193–202.

Bluck, S., & Alea, N. (2009). Thinking and talking about the past: Why remember? *Applied Cognitive Psychology*, 23(8), 1089–1104.

Brown, R., & Kulik, J. (1977). Flashbulb memories. *Cognition*, 5, 73–99.

Cabeza, R., Stanley, M.L., & Moscovitch, M. (2018). Process-specific alliances (PSAs) in cognitive neuroscience. *Trends in Cognitive Sciences*, 22, 996–1010.

Chen, Y., & Zelinsky, G.J. (2019). Is there a shape to the attention spotlight? Computing saliency over proto-objects predicts fixations during scene viewing. *Journal of Experimental Psychology: Human Perception and Performance*, 45, 139–154.

Chun, M.M., Golomb, J.D., & Turk-Browne, N.B. (2011). A taxonomy of external and internal attention. *Annual Review of Psychology*, 62, 73–101.

Conway, M.A., & Pleydell-Pearce, C.W. (2000). The construction of autobiographical memories in the self-memory system. *Psychological Review*, 107, 261–288.

Corbetta, M., & Shulman, G.L. (2002). Control of goal-directed and stimulus-driven attention in the brain. *Nature Reviews Neuroscience*, 3, 201–215.

Demiray, B., & Janssen, S.M. (2015). The self-enhancement function of autobiographical memory. *Applied Cognitive Psychology*, 29, 49–60.

Di Lollo, V. (2018). Attention is a sterile concept; iterative reentry is a fertile substitute. *Consciousness and Cognition*, 64, 45–49.

Einstein, G.O., & McDaniel, M.A. (2005). Prospective memory: Multiple retrieval processes. *Current Directions in Psychological Science*, 14, 286–290.

Eriksen, C.W., & St. James, J.D. (1986). Visual attention within and around the field of focal attention: A zoom lens model. *Perception & Psychophysics*, 40, 225–240.

Falk J.H., & Dierking L.D. (2000). Learning from museums. *Visitors Experiences and the Making of Meaning*. Walnut Creek: Altamira Press.

Ferrari, V., Codispoti, M., & Bradley, M.M. (2017). Repetition and ERPs during emotional scene processing: A selective review. *International Journal of Psychophysiology*, 111, 170–177.

Gilman, B.I. (1916). Museum fatigue. *Scientific Monthly*, 2, 62–74.

Healy, A.F., & Proctor, R.W. (2003). *Handbook of Psychology. Experimental Psychology*. Vol. IV. New Jersey: Publishing House Wiley.

Hein, G.E. (1998). *Learning in the Museum*. London: Routledge.

Henke, K. (2010). A model for memory systems based on processing modes rather than consciousness. *Nature Reviews Neuroscience*, 11, 523–532.

Kandel, E.R., Schwartz, J.H., & Jessell, T.M. (2000). *Principles of Neural Science*. New York: McGraw-Hill.

Kravitz, D.J., & Behrmann, M. (2011). Space-, object-, and feature-based attention interact to organize visual scenes. *Attention, Perception & Psychophysics*, 73, 2434–2447.

Mason, L., Ronconi, A., Scrimin, S., & Pazzaglia, F. (2021). Short-term exposure to nature and benefits for students' cognitive performance: A review. *Educational Psychology Review*, 34, 609–647.

McDermott, J.H. (2009). The cocktail party problem. *Current Biology*, 19, 1024–1027.

McNamara, T.P. (2005). *Semantic priming: Perspectives from memory and word recognition*. New York: Psychology Press.

Mittelstädt, V., & Miller, J. (2017). Separating limits on preparation versus online processing in multitasking paradigms: Evidence for resource models. *Journal of Experimental Psychology: Human Perception and Performance*, 43, 89–102.

Nørby, S. (2015). Why forget? On the adaptive value of memory loss. *Perspectives on Psychological Science*, 10, 551–578.

Posner, M.I. (1980). Orienting of attention. *The Quarterly Journal of Experimental Psychology*, 32, 3–25.

Robin, J., & Moscovitch, M. (2017). Details, gist and schema: Hippocampal–neocortical interactions underlying recent and remote episodic and spatial memory. *Current Opinion in Behavioral Sciences*, 17, 114–123.

Sadeh, T., Ozubko, J.D., Winocur, G., & Moscovitch, M. (2016). Forgetting patterns differentiate between two forms of memory representation. *Psychology Science*, 27, 810–820.

Shelton, J.T., & Scullin, M.K. (2017). The dynamic interplay between bottom-up and top-down processes supporting prospective remembering. *Current Directions in Psychological Science*, 26(4), 352–358.

Simon, N. (2010). The participatory museum. https://www.participatorymuseum.org/.

Smith, L.F. & Smith, J.K. (2001). Spending time on art. *Empirical Studies of the Arts*, 19(2), 229–236.

Smith, L.F., Smith, J.K., & Tinio, P.P.L. (2017). Time spent viewing art and reading labels. *Psychology of Aesthetics, Creativity, and the Arts*, 11, 77–85.

Treisman, A.M., & Gelade, G. (1980). A feature-integration theory of attention. *Cognitive Psychology*, 12, 97–136.

Wiggs C.L., & Martin, A. (1998). Properties and mechanisms of perceptual priming. *Current Opinion in Neurobiology*, 8, 227–233.

Zogg, J.B., Woods, S.P., Sauceda, J.A., Wiebe, J.S., & Simoni J.M. (2012). The role of prospective memory in medication adherence: A review of an emerging literature. *Journal of Behavioral Medicine*, 35, 47–62.

5 What is the Right Language and Type of Communication to Engage Different Kinds of Museum Audiences?

Annalisa Banzi

This is a complex question to answer. Hastings (Hastings & Meyer, 2020), Netflix co-founder, shared a personal experience that made me think a lot. In 1983, he moved to Swaziland (Africa) and worked as a Peace Corps volunteer teaching mathematics to teenage students. A few weeks after his arrival, he presented them with a mathematical problem that he expected would be easily solved by his pupils: consider a room measuring 2 metres by 3. How many 50-centimetres-long tiles are needed to cover the floor? Nobody answered. The next day he wrote this problem on the blackboard and asked them again to solve it. At some point, a guy called Thabo raised his hand and asked what a tile was. Hastings' students lived in rounded huts and the floor was made of mud or cement. They couldn't solve the problem not because they were stupid but because they didn't know the meaning of the word "tile".

... How can we improve museum communication aimed at different types of visitors, especially those with cultural backgrounds different from ours?

I report a personal experience of Cialdini (2017) that enlightened me. Cialdini wanted to teach his son Chris to swim. Even though Chris loved the water, he didn't want to leave his swimming ring. Cialdini made several unsuccessful attempts. Eventually, he decided to ask a swimming teacher for help. No results, the teacher gave up. One day, Cialdini went to pick up his son from the summer camp he was attending. He saw Chris dive off the diving board into the deepest part of the pool. At the beginning, Cialdini panicked and his first reaction was to save his son but he stopped when he saw Chris emerge from the water and safely reach the edge of the pool. He enthusiastically told Chris that he could swim then and his son replied that he had learned that very day. Cialdini then asked his son why he hadn't worn the swimming ring that day and Chris replied that he was three, and his friend Tommy was three too. If Tommy could swim without a swimming ring, so could he. Chris relied on Tommy, not the swimming teacher, as a valuable and trusted source of information on how to behave.

The take-home message is that when we are not sure of what to do, we are willing to be guided by someone similar to us rather than one who is different

DOI: 10.4324/9781003304531-5

from us. Cialdini in his book reported several research studies explaining how this principle works for both children and adults.

Hastings and Meyer (2020), while talking about the diversity of giving honest and sincere feedback according to people's nationality, introduced an example that, in my opinion, reconfirmed the aforementioned principle from a cultural standpoint. This example was about the Japanese culture, in which Japanese people experience difficulties in providing straightforward feedback (as required by Netflix's philosophy). Hastings and Meyer reported the memory of Yuka, one of the Japanese managers involved in a meeting with US managers whose purpose was to help them with this issue. The four Americans led the session explaining how to provide and receive feedback. At the end of the meeting, the Japanese applauded but did not find it helpful. An American giving feedback to another American in English is not a challenge, they had seen it many times before. What they really needed was to see a Japanese giving feedback to another Japanese, possibly in Japanese, in a way that the *Japanese consider* appropriate, respectful and that does not threaten the relationship.

I think we can adapt this principle to enhance the museum communication. The goal is to get close to potential visitors who are unsure of what to do and are looking for hints and evidence that can help them make a decision.

People who are already oriented and are familiar with a topic or a museum do not need support. Those who are definitely not interested in museums have the right to be left alone. Hence, our target is "uncertain people": how can we communicate with them based on Cialdini's and Hastings' experiences? For instance, we can ask some of the most enthusiastic visitors of different ages (a child, a teenager, a young adult, and an elderly person) to present their experiences to their peers, in a video. They can share *their* emotions and thoughts about *their* favourite museum object, why they think this visit was great, and what they learned. It is very important to cover all age groups. This strategy can also be useful for approaching autistic, blind, deaf, and other audiences with specific needs.

Another example: If we want to reach Japanese visitors, we can ask a Japanese who is happy with the museum visit to present *their* museum experience in a video, in *their* native language, to the Japanese public.

This approach can also be used for practical information (e.g., what there is to see or do). This has to be presented clearly in a way that is easily accessible and understandable. For instance, a family who is familiar with the museum can explain to other families where the cafeteria, the restroom, and the cloakroom are located; they can also present the educational activities *their* children participated in.

We can make the videos available on the museum's official website and on social media to anyone who wants to get an idea of the museum.

There is an interesting study carried out by Li et al. (2009)[1] that should be taken into account when thinking and writing the contents explaining the museum objects. English, Japanese, and Mandarin speakers were involved in this experiment. Participants saw objects, such as a metal whisk, labelled by a novel noun in neutral syntax. The findings revealed that English speakers are more likely to assume the noun refers to the object itself, while Mandarin and Japanese speakers are more likely to assume the noun refers to the substance. Let's stop and consider only this part of the experiment: what could be the impact of these differences (English speakers vs. Mandarin and Japanese speakers) in the communication style of a museum?

Considering the culture and mindset of our visitors can help us communicate successfully with them. Thus it is not just about translating explanatory texts. It is about proposing the contents in a way that can be understood by people with a different cultural background, paying particular attention to concepts that are unfamiliar to the group of visitors with whom we are intended to communicate (e.g., the word "tile" for the Hastings' students). I am aware that there are museums which are already working hard in this direction but perhaps there are others that feel the need to improve their way of approaching their public and involving new local and international visitors.

A Brief Introduction on Language in Cognitive Psychology

"The Hastings' tile" is one of several examples that remind us of the importance of language. Let's focus now on cognitive psychology to understand a little better what language is and how it works. Language theories and notions will be discussed in depth in further publications since most research so far has been limited to the study of the English language (e.g., that relating to reading and parsing) while the BFM approach is aimed at museums around the world. This means that every language is as important as other factors in museums and deserves to be considered thoroughly.

Language is a system for expressing thoughts and feelings through speech sounds or written symbols (such as words)[2]. Research on this topic began in the late 1950s. According to behaviourists, such as Skinner (1957)[3], there is nothing special about language and it can be developed by other species. Chomsky (1957, 1959)[4] considered the behavioural approach to language to be poor. He claimed that language has several unique characteristics and is a communication system uniquely acquired and used by human beings. After the pivotal work by Chomsky, language research increased and became of central importance in cognitive psychology.

Two important issues were debated from the beginning: whether language is innate and whether it is special (i.e., it is different from other cognitive functions). Chomsky believed that there was a universal grammar consisting of linguistic universals, which are features common to the vast majority of the world's languages. Examples of linguistic universals are word order (e.g., subject-verb-object) and lexical categories (e.g., nouns and adjectives). In contrast, there are theorists, such as Christiansen and Chater (2008)[5], who claimed that languages differ enormously. There is evidence that human beings are naturally inclined and motivated to learn language and communicate with each other. The findings collected in various studies, however, do not support the theory of universal grammar. Neuroimaging research revealed that language is less special than Chomsky claimed. For example, language comprehension and production depend on general cognitive processes (e.g., attention).

There is a theoretical assumption, called the *Whorfian hypothesis*, according to which language can influence thinking and performance in several ways, and is based on the linguistic relativity (i.e., individuals who speak different languages think differently). However, it is still a crucial issue to detect the conditions under which language influences our thoughts or not.

According to theorists, there are four main language skills:

- listening to speech (speech perception)
- reading
- speaking
- writing

Some of the Main Features of Speech Perception and Reading

Speech perception and reading on the one hand are similar because, for example, they are both fast and incremental, which means that a lot of processing occurs while paying attention to a word (Rayner & Clifton, 2009)[6]. On the other hand, they are different because, for example, most of the written words can be perceived as a whole and remain in vision (in reading), while the spoken words are distributed over time and are transitory (in listening to speech). In addition, they involve slightly different brain areas and cognitive processes.

Speech perception consists of several stages, including the identification and isolation of the speech sounds from the acoustic background, word recognition and statement recognition. It is a very important type of auditory perception. Music is another form of auditory perception and shares some similarities with speech perception. However, they trigger different brain areas and cognitive processes.

Reading involves various cognitive processes (e.g., perceptual processes) and requires a good knowledge of language and grammar (i.e., the set of rules determining the structure of a language). It needs various types of stored information, such as word meaning and linguistic knowledge. This stored information is used to achieve word identification and text comprehension. The latter requires elaborating the grammatical structure of each sentence, drawing inferences, and producing an integrated mental representation. Reading processes occur in a flexible order.

Eye-movement research improves our knowledge about word reading within sentences. The rapid eye movements, as previously mentioned, are called *saccades* (lasting 20/30 ms). They cover a length of 8 letters/spaces and cannot change their direction once started. 10% of saccades are related to moving the eye backwards in the text (regression). Saccades are interspaced with *fixations* (lasting 200/250 ms), whose role is important because information is extracted from the text only when fixations occur.

Let's turn now to sentence comprehension which is based on the analysis of the grammatical structure of each sentence and the examination of the literal or intended meaning of the sentence. Pragmatics studies the intended meaning, which can be influenced by the context in which a sentence is spoken.

When we read a text, which is made up of larger units of language, we need to integrate the information within it. This integration process requires several stages, such as drawing inferences and identifying the main topics introduced in the text. Theorists have found various types of inferences:

- *logical inference*, which is based only on the meanings of words
- *bridging inference* (or *backward inference*), which provides consistency between the current part of the text and the previous one
- *elaborate inference*, which contributes to expanding textual information by means of knowledge of the world. An important type of elaborate inference is *predictive inference* (or *forward inference*, which is the prediction of what will happen next in a text or in a speech)

Regarding museums, we have to keep in mind that continuously switching from reading long museum text panels, leaflets, etc. to looking at objects is a very demanding task for the brain, as clearly explained by Antinucci (2006). The interference between reading and looking at decreases if:

- the text is very short (as in the case of captions)
- the verbal stimuli are very simple
- you listen to the information while looking at the exhibit (i.e., listening to the explanations of an expert)

When I visited the exhibition "Il sarcofago di Spitzmaus e altri tesori" (Spitzmaus Mummy in a Coffin and Other Treasures)[7] at Fondazione Prada (Milan, Italy), the captions were (only) shown on a flyer available at the entrance to the exhibition. On the leaflet, each group of objects displayed together was reproduced as a group of silhouettes and accompanied by captions (i.e., a drawing combined with a short text). This solution could be an application of the concept introduced by Antinucci to mitigate brain fatigue. Especially if the museum is crowded, it could also avoid visitors getting stuck next to the exhibit captions when trying to read them (such as when these hang on the wall). Additionally, it could be a memento of the exhibition, and a starting point for deepening the knowledge of the objects on display (Figure 5.1).

Note that to avoid visual fatigue, we have to consider that perhaps the font should be simple and clearly written in a large size to meet the needs of different target audiences (e.g., dyslexic people and presbyopes).

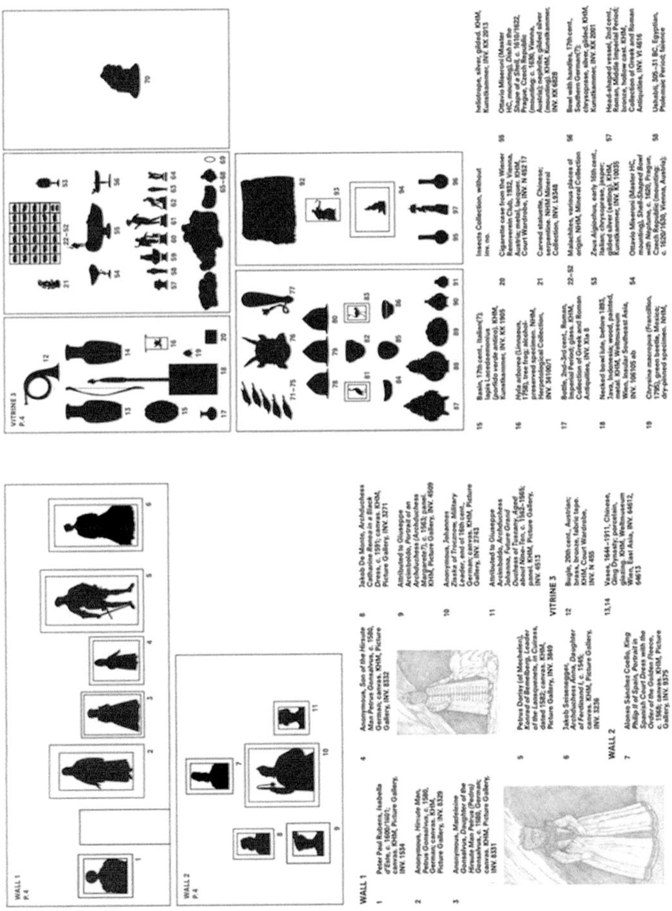

Figure 5.1 Leaflet of the exhibition "Il sarcofago di Spitzmaus e altri tesori" at Fondazione Prada, Milan (20 Sep 2019 to 13 Jan 2020). Organised by Fondazione Prada in collaboration with the Kunsthistorisches Museum in Vienna. Courtesy of Fondazione Prada.

These assumptions have to be verified through experiments to be generalised and systematically adopted in museums.

A Few Notes on Speaking and Writing

So far, researchers have focused more on language comprehension than on language production because it is more difficult to control an individual's language production. Moreover, in the study of the latter, motivational and social factors have to be taken into account together with linguistic factors. Speech production, in turn, is better known than writing. People spend more time talking than writing.

According to Boiteau et al. (2014)[8], language production is often more cognitively demanding than language comprehension, especially in terms of attention. There are some strategies used by speakers to reduce these cognitive demands when producing a speech:

- reuse aspects of a speech that an individual has just heard (e.g., *syntactic priming*, in which speakers reproduce a syntactic structure)
- *preformulation*, which occurs when an individual repeats previously frequently used phrases
- *underspecification*, which occurs when an individual uses simplified expressions avoiding specifying the full meaning

Language production requires four stages: *semantic level*, *syntactic level*, *morphological level*, and *phonological level*.

What speakers say when they talk to other people is increasingly being investigated by language theorists. This research focuses primarily on *audience design*, which refers to how speakers adapt their expressions based on the specific needs and knowledge of their listeners.

Many speakers are inclined to include gestures as they talk because it makes their communication more efficient and easier to process. Gerwing and Allison (2011)[9] conducted an experiment asking people to describe an ornamented dress to present or not present listeners. Surprisingly, the number of gestures was comparable in both conditions, although in the face-to-face condition people's gestures were much more informative. Holler and Wilkin (2011)[10] analysed and compared speakers' gestures before and after receiving feedback from their audience. First, they found that when listeners confirmed they understood what speakers were saying, the number of gestures decreased. Second, they found that when listeners asked for clarification or correction, speakers produced more precise, wider, or more visible gestures.

Regarding the efficiency of communication by gesturing, I would like to share a personal experience which is not necessarily a generalisable principle. I remember once I visited the British Museum in London, I attended a tour led by a staff member: I was struck by his effective explanation, accompanied by gestures, of the sculptures on display. I still have a clear and vivid memory of that episode, not only because his speech was very clear and interesting but also for those gestures. He used his body to reproduce the positions and movements of the sculptures to make his description more incisive and explanatory. I liked this style of explanation so much that I copied it when I was working as a museum guide while attending university.

Speakers can improve listeners' understanding by also using prosodic cues (e.g., rhythm, stress, and intonation) and discourse markers (e.g., *well*, *I mean*, or *you know*), which are spoken words or phrases that do not directly contribute to the content of the conversation.

Writing extended texts requires various processes which are demanding and effortful. Chenoweth and Hayes (2003)[11] identified four processes of writing:

- *proposer*, which provides ideas in high-level planning processes
- *translator*, which converts the proposer's message into word strings
- *transcriber*, which translates word strings into written text
- *evaluator/reviser*, which assesses what has been written and proceeds to review any errors

These stages can be used flexibly by writers, who can quickly switch between them. Practice and high working memory capacity are some of the factors that can positively influence writing. Additionally, an experienced writer spends more time revising and detects far more problems in a text than a non-expert.

Writing content for the museum's social media can be challenging. The Art Newspaper[12] has carried out a survey on the most followed museums in the last two years (2020 and 2021): the MoMA (USA) is the most appreciated on social media. The newspaper interviewed Rob Baker, MoMA's director of marketing and creative strategy, who answered the question as to why MoMA is so popular online. He thinks one of the reasons for this success is the effort to keep offering content that adds value, which means sharing good content that people want to interact with and being attuned with what is happening in the world. For example, on the US Election Day in 2020, MoMA posted a short video of Monet's *Water Lilies* (1914–26) to help people relax in that very tense time.

Last but not least, it should be remembered that museums are places that by their nature cannot help to fully communicate museum objects. As Antinucci (2006) stated, museums are the greater "decontextualisers" of exhibits. For instance, when an African mask is displayed in a museum it is deprived of the costume it was matched with, the body of the person wearing it, and the performance. As institutions that collect objects not originally created for them, museums do not automatically provide information about the objects' original contexts (which is an essential piece of information for the understanding of these exhibits). This delicate task is left to museum experts who always have to strive to recall these contexts.

As we all know, one of the best ways to communicate and grab the attention of visitors is the well-known storytelling. Narration is one of the most effective ways to communicate with children, young people, and adults. A story can tell the original context of an object. It can also introduce any other information that helps museumgoers to interpret and understand the message of this exhibit. In general, these objects are ancient and were made for an audience who could easily decode this message and their function because it was part of their culture. Comparing the museum objects to daily-life objects or historical characters to contemporary ones (when possible) connects the past to the present. Comparing, as stated by Antinucci (2006), also means emphasising the differences between ancient and contemporary objects/people in order not to propose false equivalences. Comparison makes the past more comprehensible and easier to remember. It can be particularly effective with targets such as school groups and families. As stated by Hooper-Greenhill (1994), research indicates that museums can present ideal opportunities for families to exchange ideas, explore together, and learn by comparing what they already know with the new. From apparently trivial exchanges, productive family opportunities arise. Parents and children together relate the museum experience to their familiar world of experiences. This process helps them strengthen their relationship and extend their awareness and knowledge of unfamiliar objects/topics.

Notes

1 See reference in Eysenck and Keane (2020, p. 399).
2 https://dictionary.apa.org/language accessed 4 May 2021.
3 See reference in Eysenck and Keane (2020, p. 393).
4 See reference in Eysenck and Keane (2020, p. 393).
5 See reference in Eysenck and Keane (2020, p. 395).
6 See reference in Eysenck and Keane (2020, p. 403).
7 The exhibition was curated by Wes Anderson and Juman Malouf. It was organised by the Fondazione Prada in collaboration with the Kunsthistorisches Museum in Vienna.
8 See reference in Eysenck and Keane (2020, p. 517).
9 See reference in Eysenck and Keane (2020, p. 548).
10 See reference in Eysenck and Keane (2020, p. 548).
11 See reference in Eysenck and Keane (2020, p. 551).
12 https://www.theartnewspaper.com/blog/how-new-york-s-moma-became-the-world-s-most-followed-museum-on-social-media accessed 5 May 2021.

References

Antinucci, F. (2006). *Comunicare nel museo*. Roma-Bari: Edizioni Laterza.

Boiteau, T.W., Malone, P.S., Peters, S. A., & Almor, A. (2014). Interference between conversation and a concurrent visuomotor task. *Journal of Experimental Psychology: General*, 143, 295–311.

Chenoweth, N.A., & Hayes, J.R. (2003). The inner voice in writing. *Written Communication*, 20, 99–118.

Chomsky, N. (1957). *Knowledge of language: Its nature, origin, and use*. New York: Praeger.

Chomsky, N. (1959). Review of Skinner's "Verbal behaviour". *Language*, 35, 26–58.

Christiansen, M.H. & Chater, N. (2008). Language as shaped by the brain. *Behavioral and Brain Sciences*, 31, 489–558.

Cialdini, R. (2017). *Le armi della persuasione. Come e perché si finisce con il dire di sì.* Firenze: Giunti Editore.
Gerwing, J., & Allison, M. (2011). The flexible semantic integration of gestures and words: Comparing face-to-face and telephone dialogues. *Gesture*, 11, 308–329.
Hastings, R., & Meyer, E. (2020). *No rules rules. Netflix and the culture of reinvention.* Milano: Garzanti S.r.L.
Holler, J., & Wilkin, K. (2011). An experimental investigation of how addressee feedback affects co-speech gestures accompanying speakers' responses. *Journal of Pragmatics*, 43, 3522–3536.
Hooper-Greenhill, E. (1994). *Museums and their visitors.* London: Routledge.
Li, P., Dunham., Y., & Carey, S. (2009). Of substance: The nature of language effects on entity construal. *Cognitive Psychology*, 58, 487–524.
Rayner, K., & Clifton, C. (2009). Language processing in reading and speech perception is fast and incremental: Implications for event-related potential research. *Biological Psychology*, 80, 4–9.
Skinner, B.F. (1957). *Verbal behaviour.* New York: Appleton-Century-Crofts.

6 Problem Solving, Decision-Making, Judgement, Reasoning, and Creativity: The Role of Museums in the Visitors' Cognitive Growth

Annalisa Banzi

Visitor's cognitive growth is a very high-level goal to be achieved and to address this I would like to start with a question. Have you ever thought about the difference between cognitive *skills* and cognitive *habits*? The first time this happened to me was when I read "Creativity. The human brain in the Age of innovation", by the cognitive neuroscientist and neuropsychologist Goldberg (2019). While writing the book, due to his clinical profession, he visited several underprivileged elderly patients from developing countries in Africa and Asia. They had no formal education and even though they lived in the United States they were still tied to their old world. Goldberg administered some neuropsychological tests to understand if these patients had a real cognitive disability. The results were a disaster. He was sure that the tasks were adequate for their cognitive abilities, requiring only a little cognitive effort. After a detailed analysis, he observed that the problem was not due to the fact that the patients did not want to make the cognitive effort necessary to perform a task, but they were not used to making it. They just didn't know how to do it. These considerations led to the distinction between cognitive skills and cognitive habits. Different cultural environments produce different cognitive skills but also different cognitive habits!

Goldberg shared his observations with Bienvenido Nebres, a Filipino scientist and educationalist, who described a similar phenomenon in parts of his country. Goldberg also shared his thoughts with Michael Cole, an American psychologist, who pointed out that the separation of abstract thinking from practical acting is a cultural phenomenon.

Once we become aware of the cultural differences in cognition, I think we cannot underestimate them in the educational approach of museums. They are one of the first fascinating challenges proposed by this chapter. Museums located in culturally diverse areas can be the right places to investigate and compare these cultural differences in cognition for the benefit of their visitors and society.

Museums have long been questioning their role in the cognitive growth of visitors. Critical thinking, problem solving, and creativity are some of the 21st-century skills they can foster, along with libraries (Institute of Museum and

DOI: 10.4324/9781003304531-6

Library Services, 2009[1]). Several findings supporting this claim have been collected, especially in art museums. As stated by Sitzia (2018), art museums are learning spaces in which the production of knowledge is not only linked to the acquisition of information but also includes the development of individual cognitive skills (e.g., analytical skills), individual emotional skills (e.g., empathy), psychomotor skills (e.g., moving around artworks), and social skills related to communication.

According to Socrates, true teaching and learning take place through questions (maieutic). Over the past 30 years, many museums have shifted their teaching method towards one based on enquiry, especially when dealing with children and young people. For example, visual thinking strategies (VTS) aim to help people to *think* about art instead of passively absorbing art notions, and rely on open-ended questions, posed by educators to trigger individuals' thoughts based on what they observe in the exhibits. Philip Yenawine, the former director of education at the MoMA, and Abigail Housen, an American cognitive psychologist, developed the VTS in the 1980s to enhance the interaction between viewers and artworks. This strategy underscores the importance of creating viewers' own interpretations of artworks using as little knowledge of the exhibits as possible. Viewers are advised to consider visual information only provided by the artworks, without receiving any information (e.g., the titles of the artworks). Typically, facilitators (i.e., educators) work with small groups inviting participants to look at each artwork for about a minute and then ask them three questions:

- What is going on in this picture?
- What do you see that makes you say that?
- What more can we find?

Facilitators then listen to participants' responses that are shared with the group. At the end of the session, educators give some information about the exhibits.

Housen (2001) reported the educational effects of VTS by analysing participants' comments on exhibits. These data demonstrate how VTS practice enhances language, logical thinking, and critical thinking.

Ishiguro et al. (2021) carried out a study focused on VTS, which is a typical intervention adopted in schools and museums in Japan[2], and observed its educational effect by comparing it to lectures on art history. Undergraduate students, assigned to the VTS condition or the lesson condition, looked at 10 selected artworks, before and after receiving the educational intervention. Students' eye movements and their evaluation of each exhibit were measured and compared. The collected findings show that participants in the VTS condition increased the amount of time they spent viewing artworks compared to students who listened to art history lectures (regardless of the type of paintings involved). Neither educational interventions (VTS vs. art history lesson) influenced participants' preference for artworks.

Another study examined the VTS effects on undergraduate students in museums and in classrooms (Ishiguro et al., 2021). Researchers detected that the VTS programme in the museum was found to be more interesting and better liked than that in the classroom setting. However, in terms of interest, the difference in assessments between the two conditions has been mitigated with the progress of the VTS classes. Plus, students increased art-viewing time throughout the educational programme, regardless of the educational environment (museum vs. classroom).

The VTS method was the result of a joint work of a museum expert and a cognitive psychologist, hence it is also a good example of how psychology enhances a museum experience.

In the next part of this chapter, the different forms of thinking processes based on cognitive psychology are briefly introduced.

Forms of Thinking

Thinking is cognitive behaviour and is based on our capacity to reflect on our lives in complex ways (Eysenck & Keane, 2020). Note that human beings tend to be aware of the *results* of thinking rather than the *processes* involved in it. There are different forms of thinking:

- *problem solving*, which is the activity by which individuals attempt to overcome problems through the use of higher-level cognitive processes: a problem is identified and then solved by means of a series of steps
- *decision-making*, which is the activity of selecting an option from a series of presented possibilities. The selected option (decision) will have personal consequences. It is different from problem solving because in the latter case individuals have to find their own solution rather than choosing from a number of possibilities
- *judgement*, which is the capacity to calculate the probability of various possible events, and is part of the decision-making process
- *deductive reasoning*, which is the ability to draw conclusions that are certainly valid from other premises, that are assumed to be true. Typically deductive reasoning tasks are based on formal logic, but in real life informal (everyday) reasoning is used more than logic to carry out daily tasks
- *informal reasoning*, which is the ability to evaluate the validity of arguments based on one's knowledge and experience. Compared to deductive reasoning, informal reasoning is closer to research on judgement and decision-making because it is based on individual's knowledge and experience
- *inductive reasoning*, which is the capacity to assess whether given statements or hypotheses are true based on available information

Recently, researchers are paying more attention to informal reasoning rather than deductive reasoning because the former is more used by individuals in everyday life.

Problem Solving, Analogical Problem Solving, and Expertise

The second part of this chapter dwells on problem solving, on *analogical problem solving* and *analogical reasoning*, and on *expertise*. Research on expertise typically explores problems that require significant prior knowledge, while research on problem solving focuses primarily on problems that do not require special knowledge. Additionally, expertise research studies the differences between experts and novices in a specific field.

Problem solving is goal-directed, engages controlled processes, and occurs when people do not have the appropriate knowledge to produce an immediate solution. However, this activity is sometimes based on unconscious processes.

Problems can be divided into:

- *well-defined problems*, which are clearly stated in all details
- *ill-defined problems*, which are not clearly laid out (the majority of everyday problems belong to this category)

So far psychologists have mostly investigated well-defined problems because the correct answer is known and usually the best strategy for solving them as well. Thus, researchers can easily detect errors in problem solvers' strategies.

- *knowledge-rich problems* (i.e., special knowledge is required), which can only be solved by individuals who have substantial background knowledge
- *knowledge-lean problems* (i.e., no considerable prior knowledge is required), which provide the information necessary to solve them in the initial problem statement

Compared to knowledge-rich problems, lean-knowledge problems have been more studied because they strongly reduce individual differences in relevant knowledge.

Gestaltists were the first to study problem solving distinguishing between:

- *reproductive thinking*, which is based on the systematic reuse of previous experiences to solve the current problem (it is mainly used with well-defined problems)
- *productive thinking*, which implies a new reorganisation of the problem and is based on insight (it is mostly used with ill-defined problems)

Insight is any sudden understanding, realisation, or solution of a problem that produces a new organisation of the elements of a person's mental representation of stimuli, situations, or events in order to provide an interpretation which is non-obvious or non-dominant (Kounios & Beeman, 2014)[3]. Some theorists (including the Gestaltists) consider insight as very different from other cognitive processes, whereas others argue the opposite (insight and non-insight problems use very similar processes). Insight can be easier if we provide subtle hints.

As stated by Wallas (1926)[4], problem solving can also be facilitated by *incubation*, which is a problem-solving phase in which the problem is put aside for some time: the solution comes to mind after a temporary shift in attention to another topic. It can benefit problem solving because misleading information or unsuccessful strategies are forgotten during this stage. I learned the word "incubation" when I started studying cognitive psychology theories, but I have known this technique empirically for a long time. If you think about your life, perhaps you too have lived it many times. To stop thinking about a problem and take a break or turn our attention to another task can be of great help.

Past experience typically improves our capacity to solve problems. According to Gestaltists, however, it can often prevent us from solving a problem because we tend to adopt a previously successful strategy that is not appropriate for solving the current problem. This phenomenon is called *mental set*, which can be often useful when dealing with successive problems of the same type. One type of mental set is *functional fixedness*, which occurs in problem solving when we inflexibly assume that a given object has only a limited number of familiar uses. Mental set and functional fixedness are examples of how past experience can compromise problem solving.

According to Newell and Simon (1972)[5], the strategies we use to deal with complex problems are influenced by our limited capacity to process and store information. Since our short-term memory is limited, the processing of complex information is usually serial (i.e., one process at a time). Newell and Simon argued that we can solve well-defined problems with our limited processing capacity by means of *heuristics*, which are experience-based strategies (i.e., rules of thumb) that often provide reasonably accurate answers. *Hill climbing* is a simple heuristic, which requires the changing of the current problem state into one closer to the goal. It may work and is often used when problem solvers do not have a clear idea of the problem structure, so they focus on very short-term goals that should help them to reach the final solution. *Means-ends analysis* is the most important heuristic method according to Newell and Simon and is similar to hill climbing. However, in the means-ends analysis problem solvers have a greater awareness of the problem structure which helps them to break the problem down into sub-goals (which reduce the difference between the current state and the final goal state). It is generally assumed that preliminary *planning*[6] occurs when a complex problem is presented. There are important individual differences in the planning of problem-solving tasks.

Let's now turn to analogical problem solving which takes advantage of previous knowledge and experience to solve a problem. An analogy is a comparison that emphasises the similarity between two objects. In this specific case, it stresses the similarities between a current problem and a previous one. It helps to successfully deal with new situations comparing them with similar previous ones. According to Chen (2002)[7], there can be three main types of similarities between two problems:

- superficial similarity (i.e., the details irrelevant to the solution are common to the two problems)
- structural similarity (i.e., the two problems share causal relationships between the principal components)
- procedural similarity (i.e., the two problems share the procedures for transforming the solution principle into concrete operations)

Experts often take advantage of analogies because they help to think about problems in new ways. Specialists use within-domain analogies when discussing issues with their peers, and distant analogies (i.e., connecting different domains) when communicating with non-experts. The different approach is due to the features of within-domain analogies which are more detailed and precise, and thus require specific knowledge (Dunbar 1995, Kretz & Krawczyk, 2014)[8]. How can we encourage people to use analogies in analogical problem solving? According to several researchers, people do not spontaneously think in terms of analogies but can easily adopt them when prompted to do so.

If you work for a museum, is the distant analogies approach already adopted by your institution to explain technical topics? If not, can it be introduced to help visitors better understand the content on offer?

Analogies have also been investigated by means of analogical reasoning[9], which is made up of sequential processing stages. According to Grossnickle et al. (2016)[10], it is composed of four processes:

- *encoding*, which is the processing of the information related to the problem stimuli
- *inferring*, which is the identification of the similarity between two items
- *mapping*, which is the identification of the overall relational pattern that governs the problem
- *applying*, which is the use of the result of the previous process (mapping process) to select the answer that completes the analogy

Let's now turn to expertise, which is a high level of knowledge and performance in a given domain achieved over years of methodical practice. On the one hand, expertise development is similar to problem solving in that experts[11] are very good at solving problems in their area of expertise. On the other hand, problem solving research is focused on knowledge-lean problems (i.e., no considerable prior knowledge is required), whereas expertise research typically involves knowledge-rich problems (i.e., special knowledge is required).

Eye-tracking and the think-aloud technique are among the methods used to investigate expertise. Eye-tracking allows gathering information about visual attention and subconscious processes. Think-aloud helps to understand decision-making. It is based on a transcript of ongoing mental activity, as reported by an individual while performing a task; the goal is to create a record of their cognitive processing for later analysis. What if we used these tools in the museum environment to learn more about museum experts' and visitors' reasoning? It would be interesting to record their eye movements and mental activity while looking at the same object (or more than one) displayed in a museum. The collected data can help us to compare the two thinking approaches (museum experts vs. museumgoers) and could be taken into consideration in the design of exhibitions and more effective educational activities. Additionally, this is a great opportunity to show the thinking method of the museum practitioners to non-experts. The analysis and explanation of the experts' thinking phases can give food for thought to visitors who can freely add these steps to their way of approaching museum objects.

The development of expertise is influenced by various factors such as innate talent, intelligence, and deliberate practice, which is of key importance to becoming an expert in a given area and has four aspects (Ericsson, 2017)[12]:

- the task is appropriate: not too easy, not too difficult
- the learner is provided with feedback on performance
- the learner has adequate possibilities to repeat the task
- the learner has the chance to correct their mistakes

Can we adapt these aspects to museums? I think the answer is *yes, we can.* We can be inspired by them. We can try them out by doing experiments, and we can use them when we design an educational activity in the museum to enhance visitors' expertise. Of course, this is a schematic introduction of the expertise, the features of which need to be examined in depth once a decision is made to conduct the experiments.

Decision-making and Judgement

The third part of this chapter focuses on decision-making, which involves selecting one option from several ones, and judgement, which is an assessment of the probability of a given event when complete information is not available. Judgement[13] requires accuracy and is an essential part of early decision-making process. In everyday life, our assessment of the likelihood of something happening can be modified by new evidence (i.e., this new information can reinforce or weaken the strength of our beliefs).

Individuals, when making a judgement, can exploit the base-rate information which is the frequency related to an event within a specific population (Eysenck & Keane, 2020). Typically, the base-rate information is used when people are highly motivated to use such information (e.g., when they need to demonstrate the validity of what they are arguing) or when they understand the underlying causal factors (i.e., complete causal knowledge is available).

According to Tversky and Kahneman (1974)[14], most individuals, when assigned a judgement task, exploit heuristics[15] (i.e., rules of thumb, which often considerably reduce the effort due to cognitive tasks). Using heuristics can cause people to disregard base-rate information. This happens, for example, when we use the *representativeness heuristics*, which occur when it is decided that an object/individual belongs to a given category because it seems typical of that category. People can also base their judgement upon *availability heuristic*, which is the rule of thumb that evaluates the frequencies of events based on the subjective ease with which these events can be retrieved from long-term memory. Rapid judgements can be influenced by one's emotional response (this phenomenon is called *affect heuristic*). *Anchoring-and-adjustment heuristic* occurs when individuals make an initial assessment, which is the anchor, and then adjust it to produce a final evaluation (the adjustment is usually insufficient). These are some of the numerous heuristics discovered by Kahneman and Tversky; they underlie the judgements in many different contexts.

Life requires us to make a lot of decisions, which are very different from each other in terms of complexity (e.g., making university choices vs. t-shirt colour choices). The influential *prospect theory*, proposed by Kahneman and Tversky (1979, 1984)[16], attempts to explain individuals' behaviours and reactions when making a decision under risk conditions[17]. According to this theory, people are more concerned with potential losses than gains, thus they are open to taking risks to avoid losses. The finding that individuals experience a greater subjective impact of losses than gains of the same magnitude is called *loss aversion*. There are other interesting phenomena to be considered such as *risk aversion* (i.e., the attitude of preferring certain gains rather than potentially larger but uncertain gains), *framing effect* (i.e., a decision can be affected by aspects of the context which are irrelevant to optimal decision-making), and *sunk-cost effect* (i.e., the tendency of individuals to continue investing in something that is not working to justify a previous commitment).

The prospect theory is supported by the results of research on these phenomena, however, it has limitations. For example, it does not provide any unifying principle that can justify the existence of such preferences (Houston et al., 2014)[18].

In everyday life, emotional factors and social factors[19] (e.g., individuals often have to justify their decision to others) are also important in decision-making. Examples of how emotions affect decision-making are:

- *impact bias*, which is the tendency to overestimate the length or the intensity of emotional states related to losses and gains
- *omission bias*, which is the tendency to favour risking harm through inaction over risking harm through action
- *status quo bias*, which is the tendency to maintain the current state of affairs rather than take action to change the decision

Decision-making in the laboratory and in real life differs in terms of consequences that have a greater impact in real life. Additionally, in real life individuals often have to make several decisions to achieve important goals, while in the laboratory a single decision is usually required.

Schwartz et al. (2002)[20], pointed out that there are individual differences in decision-making, and they distinguished between *satisficers* and *maximisers.* Satisficers find less than perfect decisions acceptable, are more optimistic and have fewer regrets than maximisers, who are perfectionists. The latter differ from satisficers in selecting higher goals, and in strategy to achieve these objectives (Cheek & Schwartz, 2016)[21].

There are several theories that attempt to explain the processes involved in complex decision-making such as the *multi-attribute utility theory*, the *two-component model*, and the *elimination by aspects theory*. However, they do not consider factors such as changing the initial preferences and *selective exposure* (i.e., the tendency to favour information that matches one's beliefs rather than information that conflicts with one's beliefs) in the decision-making process. We also need to consider that in the laboratory setting people make decisions from a clear set of options. Conversely, in real life individuals often make decisions in relatively unstructured environments in which they have to produce their own options. Thus, researchers have developed a growing interest in the study of naturalistic environments. For example, Galotti (2002)[22] put forward the *naturalist decision-making theory.* Moreover, Dijksterhuis and Nordgren (2006)[23] pointed out that unconscious thinking can be more effective than conscious thinking when dealing with complex decision-making processes. They proposed the *unconscious thought theory.* Most of the available research does not provide strong evidence for this theory, but sometimes decision-making can be better when conscious thought is followed by unconscious thought.

Forms of Reasoning

Philosophers are used to distinguish between inductive reasoning and deductive reasoning. The former is the capacity to draw inferences and general principles from specific observations and cases. In this case, conclusions are probably, but not necessarily, true. Deductive reasoning[24] is the ability to draw conclusions that are certainly valid from a set of premises considered to be true.

There are forms of deductive reasoning[25]:

- *conditional reasoning*, which implies statements like *If A* (=antecedent) *then C* (=consequent); it is a reasoning based on *if*
- *syllogistic reasoning*, which implies statements like *All A are B, all B are C, therefore all A are C*; it is made up of three elements, one of which is present in both premises

The distinction between inductive and deductive reasoning is not as clear-cut as described above. There is growing evidence that similar processes are involved in both types of reasoning.

Since deductive reasoning has little relevance in everyday life[26], there has been an increase in research into informal reasoning, which is a form of inductive reasoning and is based on one's knowledge, education, and experience rather than logic. As Elqayam (2018)[27] stated, we reason with the many degrees of uncertainty and belief and not with the criteria of classical logic.

There are significant differences between deductive and informal reasoning:

- the content of an argument is typically important in informal reasoning but (theoretically) not in deductive reasoning
- contextual factors are relevant in informal reasoning but not in deductive reasoning (e.g., in informal reasoning we give more credit to the explanation of the museum staff than that of a friend who is not expert in this domain)
- informal reasoning deal with probabilities[28] (individuals tend to consider statements, arguments or conclusions as possibly true rather than certainly true or false) whereas traditional research on deductive reasoning is focused on binary logic (Elqayam, 2018)
- usually the motivations of individuals are different: in deductive reasoning, people tend to reason accurately and logically, while in informal reasoning, which generally occurs in social contexts, people are inclined to persuade others

Motivational factors, such as *myside bias*[29], are of key importance in informal reasoning.

Human Thinking and Rationality

The thinking and reasoning performance of most people differs significantly in everyday life and in the laboratory: individuals seem irrational when dealing with laboratory deductive reasoning tasks. Are human beings irrational? Psychologists would answer to this question *yes and no*. By and large, we can assume that everyday thinking is less rational than we can suppose, while thinking in the laboratory is more rational than we can presume. The *Dunning-Kruger effect* (Kruger & Dunning, 1999)[30] is an example of limited human rationality: less-skilled (incompetent) individuals tend to overestimate their abilities more than those who are more skilled.

According to Simon (1957)[31], human beings are characterised by *bounded rationality*, which means that thinking and decision-making are limited (bounded) by environmental and cognitive constraints (e.g., limited short-term memory). Therefore many mistakes of human thinking are related to limited processing ability and environmental limitations rather than irrationality.

Traditionally, an influential approach, supported by famous psychologists such as Piaget, held that rational thought is driven by logic. According to this approach, deductive reasoning should be the means of measuring human rationality. However, as mentioned earlier, logical or deductive reasoning is usually not suitable to solve everyday problems and challenges.

According to Stanovich (2013, 2016)[32] there are two main types of rationality:

- *thin or instrumental rationality*, which is equivalent to behaving in the world in order to obtain exactly what you most want, given the physical and mental resources at your disposal. A little more technically, instrumental rationality can be defined as the optimisation of the achievement of the individual's goal (Stanovich, 2018); it is strictly focused on the current task be to achieved
- *broad rationality*, which takes into account people's personal goals and contextual factors as well as the current task to be achieved. Human beings appear more rational if we consider this type of rationality, which allows us to interpret the reasoning performance in the light of personal objectives and of the social context

Summing up, we can presume that human beings are perceived as rational if we consider Simon's bounded rationality notion and broad rationality (Stanovich). Additionally, heuristic-based[33] apparent *errors* are often not a symptom of *irrationality*. Conversely, human beings appear to be irrational when they act as *cognitive misers* (i.e., when people possess adequate knowledge and skills to reason effectively but fail to do so due to little effort), and when they are not aware of their thinking limitations (Dunning–Kruger effect). Note that poor reasoning is not usually due to insufficient motivation.

Think like Leonardo

I believe that "Think like Leonardo" can be the title of a museum activity to explore and improve creative thinking. Leonardo da Vinci, the famous Italian Renaissance genius, was a prolific inventor. Curiosity, desire to experiment, concentration, and self-awareness are some of Leonardo's unique characteristics.

According to APA, creativity is the ability to produce original work, theories, techniques, and thoughts, while creative thinking are the mental processes that lead to a new invention, solution, or synthesis in any area. A creative person usually shows originality, imagination, and expressiveness. Hollins (2019) stated that we have to consider some aspects when dealing with creativity. First, nothing is completely new; almost everything is a result of adjustments and progresses. Once this concept has been internalised, we can reflect on the importance of improving something that already exists. This is the essence of originality. Second, inspiration does not exist, creativity is a skill that has to be constantly trained with dedication. Third, the excessive degree of involvement in a project can impair the daydreaming and thinking freely which favours creativity. Fourth, consider the positive impact of the "Medici effect", which is the outcome of the continuous exchange of ideas between experts from different fields (a kind of historical think-tank). What is taken for granted in one field can be revolutionary when placed in another context. It is called "Medici effect" because Medici, an important Tuscan Renaissance family, developed the ideal environment for the circulation of ideas. I believe it should be reproduced in museums by inviting local experts from different sectors to participate in monthly informal meetings, without an audience, on topics selected by the museum staff. Another option, for example, is the one proposed by the Denver Center for the Performing Arts which provides the "Mixed Taste" series. It is an evening programme that introduces two speakers at a time who have 20 minutes each to enlighten participants on unrelated topics. After the talks, ideas begin to merge as the audience asks questions and the two speakers discuss the topics together often inventing new and unusual ways of making connections between them. Each event ends with a poem inspired by the themes of the evening[34].

Museums have a unique position in helping the public (children and adults) to grow their creativity by providing the raw material that fuels curiosity, shifting people's brains from subsistence to overdrive, and shaping active engagement with their environment, with other people, with knowledge and ideas. Stimulating creativity could be one of the most valuable public services provided by museums to our society. Some institutions have already developed departments or centres to foster the flourishing of creativity in their audiences (e.g., the Center for Creative Connections at the Dallas Museum of Art). This also applies to children's museums (e.g., the Strong National Museum of Play in New York), which are increasing their commitment to making creative play a cornerstone of the museum experience (Norris & Tisdale, 2014).

«Everybody has a creative potential and from the moment you can express this creative potential you can start changing the world», said Paulo Coelho. Creativity is not a domain for a few; it is a skill that can be developed by everyone through training. A museum activity on creative thinking could explore Leonardo's method of taking notes of every intuition or insight that came to his mind. He collected many of his own drawings, written considerations and thoughts which he could combine to find innovative ideas and solutions. I believe that museums, even the ones that do not possess Leonardo's works, could offer workshops that introduce this method analysing his writings and drawings.

Hollins (2019) reported other techniques used by famous characters such as Salvador Dalí, the surrealist painter, who sought new creative means through the hypnagogic state (i.e., the state of drowsiness that occurs in the transition from wakefulness to sleep). He used to sit down on a chair holding a key in one hand. The key was suspended over a plate and would have fallen if he fell asleep. Why don't we also try Dalí's method in a museum lab? As in the case of Leonardo, the museum does not need to own Dalí's works to test his strategy. Another contemporary famous creator is Walt Disney; his technique might also be suitable for an educational activity. Depending on the type of museum, learning about the strategies of famous inventors can improve visitors' creative thinking. For instance, the methods of Leonardo, Dalí, and Disney can be among the cases of value to be introduced in an art museum activity due to their relationship with visual arts.

Notes

1 Institute of Museum and Library Services (2009). Museums, Libraries, and 21st-Century Skills. https://files.eric.ed.gov/fulltext/ED507729.pdf, accessed 31 May 2021.
2 Amelia Arenas (Yenawine's collaborator at MoMA) introduced VTS to Japan. This strategy was immediately popular and was included in Japanese art education (museums and schools), after being adapted to the Japanese art education environment and is known as *dialogical appreciation* (DA).
3 See reference in Eysenck & Keane, 2020, p. 577.
4 See reference in Eysenck & Keane, 2020, p. 583.
5 See reference in Eysenck & Keane, 2020, p. 588.
6 There is evidence that planning on many problem-solving tasks activates prefrontal areas of our brain.
7 See reference in Eysenck & Keane, 2020, p. 594.
8 See references in Eysenck & Keane, 2020, p. 595.
9 Neuroimaging studies have revealed that the left rostrolateral prefrontal cortex is of key importance in analogical reasoning.
10 See reference in Eysenck & Keane, 2020, p. 596.
11 There are differences in the structure of the brain between experts and non-experts that are often caused by experience or training. These structural changes within the brain are called *brain plasticity*.
12 See reference in Eysenck & Keane, 2020, p. 613.
13 Several theories of judgement have been proposed, among the most influential: the *support theory*, the *fast and frugal heuristics*, and the *dual-process theory*.
14 See reference in Eysenck & Keane, 2020, p. 624.
15 Heuristics are strategies that ignore some information and aim to make decisions faster, more frugally and/or accurately than more complex methods (Gigerenzer & Gaissmaier, 2011 – see reference in Eysenck & Keane, 2020, p. 624).
16 See reference in Eysenck & Keane, 2020, p. 642.
17 The amygdala and the ventromedial prefrontal cortex are involved in risky decision-making.
18 See reference in Eysenck & Keane, 2020, p. 648.
19 The *social functionalist approach* considers social factors of key importance in decision-making.
20 See reference in Eysenck & Keane, 2020, p. 656.
21 See reference in Eysenck & Keane, 2020, p. 656.
22 See reference in Eysenck & Keane, 2020, p. 659.
23 See reference in Eysenck & Keane, 2020, p. 662.
24 *Mental model theory* and *dual-process approach* are two of the most influential theories on deductive reasoning.
25 Neuroimaging studies provide the key brain areas activated during deductive reasoning: Left rostrolateral prefrontal cortex and left parietal cortex.
26 Traditional research on deductive reasoning is considered artificial because it focuses on formal logic and ignores the role of past knowledge.
27 See reference in Eysenck & Keane, 2020, p. 694.

28 The *Bayesian approach* helps to understand the role played by probabilities in informal reasoning.
29 Myside bias is the inclination of individuals to select and interpret information in a way that supports their previous beliefs.
30 See reference in Eysenck & Keane, 2020, p. 705.
31 See reference in Eysenck & Keane, 2020, p. 702.
32 See reference in Eysenck & Keane, 2020, p. 703.
33 It means based on rules of thumbs.
34 https://www.denvercenter.org/tickets-events/mixed-taste/, accessed 11 October 2021.

References

Cheek, N.N., & Schwartz, B. (2016). On the meaning and measurement of maximization. *Judgement and Decision Making*, 11, 126–146.

Chen, Z. (2002). Analogical problem solving: A hierarchical analysis of procedural similarity. *Journal of Experimental Psychology: Learning, Memory, and Cognition*, 28, 81–98.

Dijksterhuis, A., & Nordgren, L.F. (2006). A theory of unconscious thought. *Perspectives on Psychological Science*, 1, 95–109.

Dunbar, K. (1995). How scientists really reason: Scientific reasoning in real-world laboratories. In R.J. Sternberg & J.E. Davidson (Eds.), *The nature of insight* (pp. 365–395). Cambridge, MA: MIT Press.

Elqayam, S. (2018). The new paradigm in psychology of reasoning. In L.J. Ball & V.A. Thompson (Eds.), *The Routledge international handbook of Thinking and Reasoning* (pp. 130–150). Abingdon, Oxon: Routledge.

Eysenck, M.W., & Keane, M.T. (2020). *Cognitive Psychology. A Student's Handbook*. Oxon-New York: Routledge.

Ericsson, K.A. (2017). Expertise and individual differences: The search for the structure and acquisition of experts' superior performance. *WIREs Cognitive Science*, 8, 1–6.

Galotti, K.M. (2002). *Making decisions that matter: How people face important life choices*. Mahwah, NJ: Lawrence Erlbaum Associates.

Goldberg, E. (2019). *Creativity. The human brain in the Age of innovation*. Milano: Adriano Salani Editore.

Grossnickle, E.M., Dumas, D., Alexander, P.A., & Baggetta, P. (2016). Individual differences in the process of relational reasoning. *Learning and Instruction*, 42, 141–159.

Hollins (2019). *Think Like da Vinci: Practical Everyday Creativity for Idea Generation, New Perspectives, and Innovative Thinking*. San Francisco: Pkcs Media, Inc.

Housen, A. (2001). Methods for assessing transfer from an art viewing program. Paper presented at the annual meeting of the American Educational Research Association, Seattle, WA.

Houston, A.I., Fawcett, T.W., Mallpress, J.M., & McNamara, J.M. (2014). Clarifying the relationship between prospect theory and risk-sensitive foraging theory. *Evolution and Human Behavior*, 35, 502–507.

Ishiguro, C., Sato, Y., Takahashi, A., Abe, Y., Kakizaki, H., Okada, H., Kato, E., & Takagishi, H. (2021). Comparing effects of visual thinking strategies in a classroom and a museum. *Psychology of Aesthetics, Creativity, and the Arts*, 15, 735–745.

Ishiguro, C., Takagishi, H., Sato, Y., Seow, A.W., Takahashi, A., Abe, Y., Hayashi, T., Kakizaki, H., Uno, K., Okada, H., & Kato, E. (2021). Effect of dialogical appreciation based on visual thinking strategies on art-viewing strategies. *Psychology of Aesthetics, Creativity, and the Arts*, 15, 51–59.

Kahneman, D., & Tversky, A. (1979). Prospect theory: An analysis of decision under risk. *Econometrica*, 47, 263–291.

Kahneman, D., & Tversky, A. (1984). Choices, values, and frames. *American Psychologist*, 39, 341–350.

Kounios, J., & Beeman, M. (2014). The cognitive neuroscience of insight. *Annual Review of Psychology*, 65, 71–93.

Kretz, D.R., & Krawczyk, D.C. (2014). Expert analogy use in a naturalistic setting. *Frontiers in Psychology*, 5, Article 1333.

Kruger, J., & Dunning, D. (1999). Unskilled and unaware of it: How difficulties in recognizing one's own incompetence lead to inflated self-assessments. *Journal of Personality and Social Psychology*, 77, 1121–1134.

Newell, A., & Simon, H.A. (1972). *Human problem solving*. Englewoodcliffs, NJ: Prentice-Hall.

Norris, L., & Tisdale, R. (2014). *Creativity in Museum Practice*. Oxon-New York: Routledge.

Schwartz, B., Ward, A., Monterosso, J., Lyubomirsky, S., White, K., & Lehman, D.R. (2002). Maximizing versus satisficing: Happiness is a matter of choice. *Journal of Personality and Social Psychology*, 83, 1178–1197.

Simon, H.A. (1957). *Models of man: social and rational*. New York: Wiley.

Sitzia, E. (2018). The ignorant art museum: Beyond meaning-making. *International Journal of Lifelong Education*, 37, 73–87.

Stanovich, K.E. (2013). Why humans are (sometimes) less rational than other animals: Cognitive complexity and the axioms of rational choice. *Thinking & Reasoning*, 19, 1–26.

Stanovich, K.E. (2016). The comprehensive assessment of rational thinking. *Educational Psychologist*, 51, 23–34.

Stanovich, K.E. (2018). How to think rationally about world problems. *Journal of Intelligence*, 6, 25.

Tversky, A., & Kahneman, D. (1974). Judgment under uncertainty: Heuristics and biases. *Science*, 185, 1124–1131.

Wallas, G. (1926). *The art of thought*. London: J. Cape.

7 Museums, the "Magic Box", and Neuroscience Tools

Annalisa Banzi

The brain is a very sophisticated and complex organ that needs our care and attention to function well. As mentioned at the beginning, the "magic box" is made up of 100 billion neurons, and it is divides into two hemispheres (right and left), which are composed of four main lobes (frontal, parietal, occipital, and temporal). The cerebral cortex, the outer surface of the brain, is made up of convolutions (gyri) that are prominent elevated areas. As we said, Brodmann identified 52 brain areas and produced a brain map that is currently being used by experts.

In the previous chapters, I have introduced some of the main topics related to psychology (primarily cognitive psychology), which can help us to understand human beings' ways and limits in acquiring, analysing, storing, retrieving, and using information in the museum environment.

I would now like to focus briefly on the science of the brain. Neuroscience is a branch of the life sciences that deals with the structure and function of the brain and the nervous system. Through these studies, it sheds light on our behaviour and learning. Robertson and Mack (2017) stated that the science of the brain is of key importance to the museum experience itself. They argued that the brain is the organ with which people cognitively and affectively process their museum experiences into unique and individual perspectives. Visitors vary enormously not only in terms of demographics and preferences, but also in their capacity to experience the museum and its contents based on their neurological capabilities. The researchers also pointed out that various elements of neuroscience can help optimise the visitor experience, especially in the case of an increasingly diversified audience. Children, teenagers, adults, the elderly, and people with special needs all have different neurological advantages and limitations, which means that their ability to interact and enjoy the museum can vary significantly.

Although some evidence and concepts provided by cognitive neuroscience are mentioned in these first seven chapters, at the moment I prefer to focus mainly on time-tested neuroscience tools.

DOI: 10.4324/9781003304531-7

Tools for Assessing Brain Activity

There are several non-invasive techniques to study brain activity. They allow us to detect, in real time, where and when specific cognitive processes occur in the living brain. They vary in terms of *spatial resolution* (which refers to how accurately they identify activated brain areas), and *temporal resolution* (which refers to how much the measured activity matches the timing of actual neural activity).

Some of them cannot be used in museum due to their size and cost, like *brain-imaging techniques*. They investigate areas and functions of the brain. One example is the *functional magnetic resonance imaging (fMRI)*, which is perhaps the best known. Others are suitable for the museum environment, such as *electrophysiological techniques* that record brain electrical signals. *Electroencephalography (EEG)* detects very small changes in the brain electrical activity, in several places, through the use of scalp electrodes. Its temporal resolution is very good. EEG is connected to computer, which displays and collects all this data.

EEG signals can be detected by the brain computer interface (BCI), created for the entertainment industry and now also used in scientific research. I have introduced these tools in the section "Attention, memory, and learning in museums" (chapter 4). A BCI device provides direct communication between the brain and a computer. For example, the *MindWave* is a light, wireless, low-cost device with high temporal resolution, and it is a very practical tool for museumgoers to wear. It records the brain frequencies grouped into rhythms: *alpha*, *beta*, *delta*, *theta*, and *gamma* waves. Each of these rhythms is related to specific functions. For example, *alpha rhythm* (frequency 8–12 Hz) dominates the electroencephalogram during quiet wakefulness such as relaxation, meditation, and contemplation. BCI devices allow us to investigate the art–brain relationship from the artist's standpoint during the creative process of an artwork, and from the museumgoer's standpoint while looking at the objects in the museum (Folgieri, 2017). These devices can be used to measure and evaluate the visitors' cognitive processes while they are involved in educational activities, tours, etc., designed with the help of psychology.

In the section "Attention, memory, and learning in museums" (chapter 4), I have already proposed a practical application of neuroscience tools in museums. The next two parts of this chapter introduce other experiments conducted in Italian and US museums. I will describe them to offer you some food for thought.

The US Case

The PEM (USA) is the first museum to announce that it hired a neuroscientist and made use of neuroscience in 2017[1]. The goals of PEM *Neuroscience Initiative* (https://www.pem.org/neuroscience-initiative) are to use neuroscience as a means to understand visitor engagement, and as a tool to propose new strategies to increase visitor engagement with artworks. Engagement occurs when one's attention is captured in a way that generates an emotional response and, consequently, a memory.

The PEM staff develops a technical approach to evaluate visitor engagement that allows them to measure each of the three key elements of engagement: attention, emotion, and memory[2]. They use a mixed-methods approach to measure visitor engagement, based on eye-tracking, physiological measurements of emotion, and self-report metrics. This mixed-methods approach is an iterative process in which they continue to refine their understanding of visitor engagement over time[3]. It employs techniques that collect conscious and unconscious behavioural and emotional responses.

These experiments take advantage of the eye tracker, which is a device that records fixations (i.e., the eye gaze stops in a specific position) and saccades (i.e., the eye movement from one position to another). The subjects wear a pair of eye-tracking glasses, and the data is recorded on a computer. This tool provides some information on the visitor's visual attention.

Visitor engagement is also assessed with the help of the galvanic skin response (GSR). These are electrodes that are applied on two fingers of one hand, and they record the continuous variation of the skin's electrical characteristics. The electrical conductivity of the skin is driven by the brain, it provides information about the extent of emotional arousal or the intensity of an emotional experience. The GSR monitors the visitors' emotional responses to artistic stimuli.

The results collected with these devices are completed by self-reports, such as exit survey or interview. In psychology, a self-report is any test, measure, or investigation that is based on an individual's account of their symptoms, behaviours, beliefs, or attitudes. Self-reported data is usually collected with paper-and-pencil or electronic format, or sometimes through an interview (Kristalyn Salters-Pedneault, 2020).

These self-reports have been used in the priming-based experiments (chapter 4), in the PEM experiments, and in the TSW experiments (as we will see in the next part). Depending on the experiment to be carried out in a museum, there are different tools (e.g., eye tracker and EEG) that can be used together or separately.

The Italian Case

In 2016, the TSW Experience Lab carried out some experiments in the temporary exhibition "2050. Breve storia del futuro" (2050. A brief history of the future), held in the Royal Palace in Milan (Italy). It was a cognitive and emotional impact study. TSW team's goal was to answer some questions such as:

- what happens when a person looks at an artwork?
- what is the itinerary that people spontaneously take when they visit a museum?
- what attracts attention and what is the emotional reaction during an exhibition?

Emotions and implicit responses are some of the mechanisms that determine people's behaviour. Analysing these aspects can help to design innovative experiences focused on visitors who are considered active spectators. The TSW team used the following wearable devices to assess psychophysiological and behavioural responses:

- the *Emotiv Epoc+* (which is a brain-tracker) to detect the EEG traces
- the *E4* (which is a wristband made by *Empatica*) to detect GSR traces, heart rate, inter-beat-interval, and temperature
- the *Tobii Pro Glasses 2* (which is an eye-tracker) to collect gaze data and detect the visual attention related to the user's visual field during the visit to the exhibition
- a webcam to film the scene in order to monitor visitor/artwork interaction

The TSW team took advantage of *Neuralya* (which is a software developed by *Qwince*) to identify three indexes (engagement index, motivation index, and impact index) that relate all the psychophysiological responses collected. Moreover, after 40 days from the end of the exhibition, the TSW team administered the interviews and the *Net Promotion Score* (NPS). Standard test results, user observation, and psychophysiological components were analysed together to get a better idea of the motivations that determine some human behaviours.

In 2018, Intesa Sanpaolo Innovation Center appointed the TSW Experience Lab to assess the emotional impact of some artworks exhibited at the Gallerie di Italia Piazza Scala-Intesa Sanpaolo (which is the cultural and museum centre of the Intesa Sanpaolo bank) in Milan. The ultimate goal of this research was to understand how to design the most engaging experience for museum visitors. Thirty participants were invited to view four works that are part of the Gallerie di Italia Piazza Scala-Intesa Sanpaolo collection:

- the "Martyrdom of Saint Ursula" by Caravaggio
- the "Martyrdom of Saint Ursula" by Strozzi
- the "Martyrdom of Saint Ursula" by Procaccini
- the "Last Supper" by Procaccini

Participants' psychophysiological responses—particularly eye movements and central and peripheral nervous system activity levels—were recorded by means of devices such as eye-tracking glasses, EEG, and SCL bracelets. According to the TSW team, the greatest emotional intensity was produced by the "Last Supper" (Procaccini) and the "Martyrdom of Saint Ursula" (Caravaggio). The former generated a high level of engagement, while the latter produced a pleasant experience. This is an example of data collected in the experiment that can improve contents that allow visitors to better understand the exhibits.

In 2019, Intesa Sanpaolo Innovation Center again involved the TSW Experience Lab to evaluate the impact on visitors of the "Last supper", by Leonardo da Vinci, located in Santa Maria delle Grazie Church (Milan)[4]. Particular attention was paid to analysing how some elements (e.g., light, panels, and type of itinerary) can positively or negatively influence the quality of the museum visit. Thirty-eight participants of different nationalities were involved in the experiment. They were divided into two groups: those who had already seen the painting and those who were going to see it for the first time. They were invited to visit the museum on two different days: when the museum was open to the public and when it was closed. In the latter case, each participant had the chance to enter alone and remain in the refectory of Santa Maria delle Grazie Church for 35 minutes.

The psychophysiological–behavioural assessment was carried out by means of:

- eye tracker glasses—*SMI ETG 2 W* 120 Hz
- electroencephalograph (EEG)—*Cognionics* 20 channel
- galvanic skin response (GSR) sensor—*Shimmer GSR+*

At the end of the visit, participants filled out a questionnaire which investigated the qualitative and subjective aspects of their personal museum experience.

The TSW team collected very interesting data. For example, the eye movement analysis showed that the characters' faces and elements above the table captured the visual attention. Moreover, the analysis of the time devoted to the observation of each character showed that Jesus and St. Thomas were the most fixated. Considering the opening or closing of the museum, the two conditions influenced people. Individuals typically focused on the central part of the painting when the museum was open, and widely observed all the characters of the "Last Supper" when the museum was closed.

How to Involve Visitors in Museum Experiments. Some Practical Advice

Once the experiment procedure has been decided, we need to gather the participants. Here are some practical insights into how museumgoers could be pleasantly involved in scientific research. These cues can be personalised by museums once verified.

The intended experiment could be presented to visitors on the museum's social media and website. In a simple and clear way, the museum staff invites museumgoers to participate in the experiment by introducing the tools of neuroscience, practical details (e.g., the days on which the experiment will take place, etc.), and the general objectives of the experiments.

I think it is also vital to focus on visitors' expectations by clearly explaining all the steps listed above. Visitors might appreciate this experience because they will feel like an essential part of the project and also because they should understand what they are doing.

Going back to the practical example, the next step is for museumgoers wishing to participate in these scientific activities to inform museum staff via email or social media.

On the day of the experiment, participants are welcomed and the practical instructions are repeated again. Once the experiment is over, it would be nice to offer an unannounced gift from the museum shop (as in the case of the Austrian Gallery Belvedere experiments).

As soon as the analysis of the data collected during the experiments is finished, it would be useful from a visitor's motivational point of view and satisfaction to provide feedback. For example, the museum can organise a meeting (open to all or only to participants in the experiment) in which the museum staff explains the collected data, or it can share a document on its website illustrating these results. Of course, it would be a tall order for a museum to provide feedback to each participant, it would be more practical to share the data of each of the three groups involved in the experiment (chapter 4).

As we have seen in this chapter, collaborating with psychologists and neuroscientists means producing more meaningful and effective results in the museum environment.

Additionally, the systematic measurement of visitors' cognitive skills by means of these devices is a tangible result of how museums can be considered virtuous and useful to society. These data could be used to *evaluate* museums and are as important as the number of tickets sold.

Notes

1 https://www.pem.org/press-news/pem-appoints-dr-tedi-asher-as-first-ever-neuroscience-researcher-at-an-art-museum accessed 22 June 2021.

2 https://www.pem.org/neuroscience-initiative/visitor-engagement accessed 18 June 2021.

3 https://www.pem.org/neuroscience-initiative/our-goals-and-approach-for-pems-neuroscience-initiative accessed 18 June 2021.

4 The project was originally conceived by the Polo Museale Lombardia, whose objectives were to test the effectiveness and validity of the artificial lighting and the itinerary.

References

Eysenck, M.W., & Keane, M.T. (2020). *Cognitive Psychology. A Student's Handbook*. Oxon-New York: Routledge.

Folgieri, R. (2017). Arte, cervello e tecnologia. In A. Banzi, C. Conci, & L. Scoppola (Eds.), *Raccontare le storie dell'arte. Educazione e capitale umano* (pp. 207–224). Milano: Franco Angeli.

Kristalyn Salters-Pedneault (2020). https://www.verywellmind.com/definition-of-self-report-425267.

Robertson, H.L., & Mack, H. (2017). Neuroscience and the museum experience. https://www.academia.edu/32386324/Neuroscience_and_the_Museum_Experience_MuseumsEtc_Ltd_pdf accessed 19 March 2021.

8 Museums

How They Foster Wellbeing. A Round-Up of Initiatives

Annalisa Banzi

Visitors' wellbeing is one of the outcomes that the BFM approach aims to achieve. Any wellbeing-related museum activity, inside or outside the museum walls, is extremely valuable for designing positive museum experiences.

This chapter seeks to give an idea of how museums are already promoting wellbeing inside and outside their spaces. The round-up of initiatives report experiences from different countries, demonstrating how museums are active and willing to improve wellbeing in their communities around the world.

I share some data on the impact of museums on people, and give a few examples to briefly explore art therapy, "slow looking" (Slow Art Day), and mindfulness (i.e., indoor activities). I also mention initiatives born from collaborations between hospitals and museums (i.e., external activities). Overall, it is a concise introduction of the state of the art.

What is wellbeing? According to APA[1], it implies a feeling of happiness and fulfilment, with low levels of discomfort, good physical and mental health, or good quality of life.

As Falk (2021) claimed, museums not only make people feel good, but also they make them feel good in a way that is fundamental and very rich in emotions. These "good feelings" transcend those offered by most contemporary recreational entertainment (e.g., theme and amusement parks), which satisfy everyone in their own way, support people's short-term expectations, and in most cases are at least momentarily memorable. However, only a few have the greater memorability of museum experiences that successfully support the most-deeply cherished and fundamental needs of the visitors.

In 2019, Fancourt and Steptoe published a study in the *British Medical Journal* stating that a dynamic cultural life, such as visiting museums, helps prolong life in older adults. The aim of the researchers at University College London was to investigate the links between different frequencies of arts engagement and mortality, over a 14-years follow-up period (the baseline data was provided in 2004–2005). It is an English longitudinal study on ageing, which evaluates a sample group of 6.710 adults in England, aged 50 years and over (53.6% women, average age 65.9 years). According to this research, people who participate in arts activities frequently have a 31% lower risk of death at any

DOI: 10.4324/9781003304531-8

point during the follow up, regardless of demographic, socio-economic, and health factors.

Chatterjee and Noble (2017) examined hundreds of museum interventions (research studies and best practice) in health and social care to understand if museum enhances wellbeing in its visitors. The authors concluded it can benefit museumgoers in different ways: developing new skills, reducing social isolation and negative emotions, improving self-esteem, and so forth. As stated in *A Second Report from the National Alliance for Museums, Health and Wellbeing* report (2018)[2], museums have recognisable merits as curative institutions incorporated into the broader healthcare landscape; this credit is linked to the inspiring qualities of the museum spaces and collections.

Museotherapy, Art Therapy, and Museums

The Montreal Museum of Fine Arts (MMFA) believes that art has a positive impact on physical and mental wellbeing and health, a new concept known as *museotherapy*. MMFA gathered many professionals from the medical world and the wider community to contribute with their experience to strengthen development in the area of museum therapy, especially through the MMFA's art therapy studio, the medical consultation room, and Art Hive[3].

There is a clear distinction between art education and art therapy. The latter helps people to explore and express their feelings and experiences through art. It is useful with people of all ages, living a variety of emotional or physical conditions.

The United Kingdom has a strong tradition of art therapy dating back to the 1940s. The British Association of Art Therapists (BAAT) explains that art therapy is a form of psychotherapy that uses art media as a primary modality of expression and communication. Art is not a diagnostic tool but a means to cope with emotional issues that can be confusing and distressing. Art therapy is aimed at children, young people, adults, and the elderly. It deals with a wide range of difficulties, disabilities, or diagnoses (e.g., emotional, behavioural or mental health problems, learning or physical disabilities, life-limiting conditions, neurological conditions, and physical illnesses). It does not require any previous experience or skill in art. Sessions can be group or individual, depending on people's needs. Art therapy can be enjoyable but is not a recreational activity or an art lesson[4].

According to De Gregori (2020), art therapy does not cure the pathologies, but helps people to work on their healthy side and their perspectives to create a better present and future through creativity. Art therapy uses non-verbal communication and focuses on four diagnostic areas: emotional, bodily, imaginary, and cognitive.

Art therapy, being based on non-verbal and mainly visual language and communication, offers a valid alternative to spoken and written words (Dalley, 1984).

Coles (2020) argued that when considering psychological therapies as a means of knowing oneself, then the museum, as a learning space, could be perceived as the appropriate environment for therapy. Coles also stated that greater recognition of the therapeutic value of museums would allow people to engage more deeply and strengthen the partnership between museums and art therapy. Jury and Landes (2015) referred to museums as a non-clinical, safe, and containing setting for art therapy.

In Italy, there are several museums that work with art therapists. For instance, Museion, a modern and contemporary art museum located in Bolzano, runs the *Alzheimer Circle* project, created in 2015 in collaboration with Firmian, which is a local long-term care centre. The project's name was conceived by Guido Morgavi, an occupational therapist who works for Firmian. The word "circle" underlines the idea that there are more and more people working on this project, which takes place not only in the long-term care centre. It is a permanent format of Museion and is aimed at people with Alzheimer's or other forms of dementia, their relatives, and their caregivers. The initiative has been expanded over the years and now involves several Italian- and German-speaking groups (Bolzano is a bilingual community). Some of the groups come weekly and use the Museion premises autonomously for regular therapy modules, others are accompanied once a month in interactive tours of the exhibitions.

The exhibitions allow participants to experience the emotional and communicative power of art in a pleasant, tolerant, and stress-free atmosphere. Before each meeting, Brita Köhler, head of visitor services and educational projects at Museion, and one of her therapy partners, select the appropriate artworks that can trigger memories; emotions; and physical, mental, and tactile experiences. The selection privileges objects that transmit positive contents. These exhibits are located in spaces that permit all participants to view them easily and are far from noisy areas. Since Alzheimer's can make the person forget letters and numbers, the most suitable artworks are those characterised by very simple colours, contrasts, and figures.

Different approaches, methods, and materials (e.g., an old suitcase, a photograph, a piece of fabric, or a melody) promote the enhancement of residual capacities, sensory stimulation, and psychomotor skills of people with Alzheimer's. Artworks are visually rich objects that facilitate the exploration of emotions, which are linked to memories. For example, in the Július Koller's exhibition, objects were made from different everyday life fabrics, so Köhler selected pieces of textiles with different colours, patterns, textures, and styles to stimulate the participants' senses. At the beginning of the session, the group observed the artworks that were typically selected according to specific criteria (e.g., colour and contrast are particularly stimulating as they are material aspects of the objects). Subsequently, the participants were asked to hold fabrics in their hands, which helped them to share emotions, episodes, and memories related to their personal life. Starting with the observation and description of the artworks is typical of the Alzheimer Circle format; the other initiatives of the Museion usually begin with the introduction and discussion of a topic that is related to the chosen exhibits. Stimulating the memory, the senses, the relationship between the participants, and the awareness of one's own body are some of the main objectives of the Alzheimer Circle. As mentioned, this format uses different approaches, methods, and materials. In the case of the Carla Accardi's exhibition, after the observation phase, the participants listened to a piece of music while looking at the exhibits. No debate was proposed. Each person was encouraged to draw on a piece of paper what the music and artworks inspired (Köhler, private communication, 2021).

This project, like the others that I will mention later, is based on the collaboration of experts from different fields and on the museum environment, which is a unique and invaluable place to carry out such initiatives.

The Bilbao Fine Arts Museum (BFAM) located in Spain has been running the *Let's Include the Museum* programme since January 2011. It aims to create a participatory meeting place for people at risk of social exclusion. This project is based on two aspects. First, the BFAM wants to be seen as a public space for the benefit of its community. It is also interested in encouraging centres working with people at risk of isolation to take advantage of art as a means of personal growth and integration. Second, the BFAM hired an art therapist in order to design and coordinate projects focused on the understanding of the individuals' emotional and inter-relational needs, and also the knowledge about art and its creative processes. Each meeting of two hours is made up of three steps: visit the gallery, contemplating a selected artwork on the bases of the characteristics of the group; carry out a creative-experiential workshop; and conduct a session giving time to share reflections and evoked feelings. The programme's objectives are:

- to enable individuals to discover the museum artistic heritage, and to allow them to interact with the artworks through their own artistic expressions
- to welcome participants' contributions concerning the displayed artworks
- to give people the opportunity to express feelings and opinions through the creative process during the workshop
- to encourage personal growth
- to foster the integration of these individuals in the community

The positive outcomes obtained by the three-month pilot project in 2011 has led the programme to thrive and to be expanded to many other groups, such as children living in foster families, women who have been abused, and people with intellectual disability (Lund, 2020).

In Russia, art therapy, as a profession, did not exist in the early 90s. During the time of Perestroika, American and European practitioners introduced clinical art therapy practices and training programmes, allowing Russians to start thinking about the use of art therapy in museums, to establish a clear distinction between museum education and museum-based therapy, and to advocate new ideas of museum art therapy as an evidence-based practice within the museum community. A project example carried out in that period is provided by the State Russian Museum (located in St. Petersburg) that established a partnership with an orphanage for children and adolescents with learning difficulties. The museum developed a one-year programme involving teenagers, their carers, and other specialists, to encourage social adaptation and creative rehabilitation. The sessions were based on a narrative approach, which helped the teens to focus on the artefacts and to maintain a sense of personal continuity. Gradually, adolescents began developing new types of behaviour in balance between being autonomous and being part of the group, and expressing their thoughts and feelings. They improved their concentration and attention span. They also increased their adaptability to new situations and their communication skills (Zhvitiashvili, 2020).

Can creative engagement in museums improve the mental health and wellbeing of people experiencing mental distress?[5] This is the title of a study carried out in 2012, by four museum sites in Anglesey, Gwynedd, Conwy, and Denbighshire (North Wales, United Kingdom). The goals of the research were to offer art sessions in museums and galleries to people who had mental health problems or were experiencing episodes of stress, and to explore the role of museums in improving the wellbeing of these people. The survey collected important findings related to change with immediate effects (such as enjoyment and relief from physical pain), related to long-term benefits (such as increased confidence, improved ability to accept praise, and fostered ability to deal with problems). Social interaction was one of the main topics that emerged from these results. Participants considered the museum setting as a stimulating and relaxing place; they found that there were a variety of objects to pique their interest. Many of them developed an increased awareness as a result of time spent in such a visually rich environment. The involvement with the museum collections gave the participants the possibility to create links between the past and the present, helping them orientate themselves, and acquire a sense of perspective. This study shows that museum activities have a positive influence on people affected by mental distress, and that also the museum setting contributes to this positive outcome.

Museums, Hospitals, and Healthcare

Cultural heritage and museums can also actively support hospitals and the healthcare system in their mission. *The Louvre in hospitals* is a project created by the museum in collaboration with the Assistance Publique-Hôpitaux de Paris[6]. The travelling library of artworks created by Louvre is made up of reproductions of artworks (casts and two-dimensional copies) that are exhibited every year in a different hospital (this project involves eight hospitals). The patients' rooms and the common areas in the hospitals host these reproductions. The initiative aims to foster a better life for hospital patients, reduce isolation and social exclusion due to illness and hospitalisation, and enrich the doctor–patient relationship. A targeted cultural programme focused on artworks, body and gesture was created for staff, patients, and their relatives. It included activities in the hospitals and tours within the museum specifically designed for this public. Over 2,000 people (patients, patient families, and staff) participated in this programme in 2015.

The Bethlem Gallery (United Kingdom), established in 1997, hosts artworks by patients of mental health services in South London. The gallery is located within the Bethlem Royal psychiatric hospital, and it is run by artists. It provides a supportive environment for artistic development as part of recovery and wellbeing. The Bethlem Gallery collaborates with the Bethlem Museum of the Mind, artists-in-residence, and arts organisations in, as well as outside, the United Kingdom. The gallery promotes access to the arts in healthcare facilities and engages the public in learning and debate about mental health and artistic practice[7].

By and large, the United Kingdom has been dealing with people's mental health and wellbeing for a long time. The first *Arts on Prescription* (AoP) programme was established in Stockport and dates back to 1994. These programmes, now spread across the country, allow British citizens to attend arts and cultural activities on the prescription of their family physicians. The projects are aimed at people with non-clinical and non-severe mental health problems or who are experiencing social isolation. The objective is to complement conventional therapies, helping people recover thanks to creativity and increasing social engagement. Although the projects vary in terms of approaches and settings, they share a reference process. Additionally, the creative activities take place in the community led by artists rather than therapists (Bungay & Clift, 2010).

Stickley and Eades (2013) carried out a follow-up study, reporting the results of interviews conducted with ten participants in an AoP programme two years after the first ones, in order to assess the levels of results obtained. The collected data indicating progress varied among interviewees. The unifying factors in the sample were predominantly related to *soft outcomes* (e.g., increased confidence and self-esteem), which facilitated *hard outcomes* (e.g., educational achievement and voluntary work). Poulos et al. (2018) carried out an evaluation of an AoP programme by means of pre- and post-course questionnaires, focus groups, and individual interviews. They collected data on 127 participants aged 65 and over and found that the AoP had a positive impact on them. On one hand, the quantitative results showed a statistically significant enhancement in the Warwick-Edinburgh Mental Wellbeing Scale (WEMWBS), an increase in the level of creativity, and a greater frequency of creative activities. On the other hand, the qualitative results pointed out that the programme provided inspiring art activities that created a sense of purpose and allowed personal growth and fulfilment, in an environment that favoured the development of meaningful relationships.

In 2018, the Montreal Museum of Fine Arts (Canada) and the Association of Francophone Doctors (MFdC) established a partnership. This agreement allows family physicians to prescribe free museum visits to their patients suffering from physical or mental health problems, as a complement to more traditional treatment options. MMFA has promoted research on art and health since 2016, and it has an *Art and Health Advisory Committee* made up of experts from different fields.

Recently, Belgium has developed a three-months pilot study, inspired by the Canadian example, to relieve stress, anxiety, and burnout due to COVID-19. Five public museums in Brussels covering from fashion to art have been involved in this pilot project. Patients treated for stress at Brugmann hospital are offered free visits to these institutions. The pilot study findings will be published at the end of the experiment with the hope that this initiative can be further implemented.

The Accademia Carrara, a museum based in Northern Italy, has developed two projects *La cura e la bellezza* (2018)[8] and *Opere in parole* (2020)[9] in collaboration with the Humanitas Gavezzani and Humanitas Castelli hospitals. In 2018, high-resolution copies of the Accademia Carrara artworks' details were hung on the walls of the two hospitals to welcome patients and their families. As stated by the organisers, beauty has the power to unleash emotions and gives some rest from worries and anxieties. The second project *Opere in parole* (2020) is even more engaging because some famous actors, musicians, writers, journalists, chefs, and cartoonists have created stories about the artworks, exhibited in the hospital, using their own artistic language. Booklets and podcasts are available for patients who wish to read or listen to these stories. This project contributes to fight loneliness in the Covid era, where relatives are not allowed to visit patients due to health restrictions. The Carrara-Humanitas model should be replicated because it benefits both institutions. Hospitals can offer a more welcoming environment while museums can promote cultural heritage. The high-resolution copies of museum objects also make it possible not to move the originals, thus avoiding conservation problems and improving the observation of museum objects details.

Patients and their families spend hours or days (in some cases even months) in hospitals. Their time can be more pleasant if they are involved in meaningful activities. This "slow" time gives people the opportunity to focus and observe (look at slowly) museum objects copies. People become familiar with these objects, especially when they are introduced through a medium we are used to (such as a story, or a comic made by contemporaries). This is a very important step: getting familiar with an object difficult to understand because it refers to visual and semantic codes that are no longer used, or are used only in specific fields (i.e., sailors knots in maritime museums). "Familiarity" can be facilitated by contemporary people who explain the museum objects using a contemporary code as in the example Carrara-Humanitas.

In 2012, the Medicine Tailored to the Woman's Foundation and the Castello di Rivoli, a contemporary art museum based in Northern Italy, carried out the *Cantiere dell'arte* (Art Workshop) project[10]. This foundation was established in 2009 to meet the needs of patients, their families, and the staff of the Sant'Anna Hospital (located in Northern Italy). The hospital spaces have been enriched with images and colours that evoke the pleasant atmosphere of a garden. Numerous artists, such as Michelangelo Pistoletto, Massimo Barzagli, and Franco Fontana, have donated their works to the hospital. *Nati con la Cultura* (Born with Culture) is another project launched in 2014 by the foundation and Palazzo Madama (an historic building that hosts the collections of the Civic Museum of Ancient Art in Turin, Italy), which aims to provide easy access to museums, since art is a powerful resource of wellbeing, regeneration, and creative empowerment for humans from the earliest years of life. Each child, upon discharge from the hospital, receives a "cultural passport", which gives the family the opportunity to visit the museum for one year without paying the ticket. In 2015, the project was expanded with the development of a network of Family and Kids Friendly Museums that guarantees families free access, for one year, to more than 40 museums in the Piedmont region (Northern Italy) and in some Italian cities (e.g., Brescia and Pavia). From that moment on, the families of the new-born Italian babies (even if they were not born in the city of Turin) can have the cultural passport, valid for one year (http://www.naticonlacultura.it/).

These examples propose different approaches to promote a fruitful collaboration between museums, hospitals, and the healthcare system. The beauty of these projects is that people, as human beings, are at the centre of attention and the museums' collection(s) are respected and appreciated.

Slow Looking and Mindfulness

Slow looking is a valuable skill that we should all take advantage of. The *Slow Art Day* (https://www.slowartday.com/) is a global event that occurs once a year with a simple objective: to help people to discover the joy of looking at and appreciating art. Regardless of the design, all events share the focus on slow looking and its transformative power.

In the last edition, there were more than 1,500 Slow Art Day events that involved museums and galleries from Africa to North America, from Asia to Europe, up to Antarctica. More than 100 volunteers over the years have helped build the global programme. Slow Art Day staff do everything they can to support the museum educators who are the backbone of the programme. They provide training, support, and community building. It has become a major event in the international artistic calendar.

This initiative was born out of a personal experience of the founder, Phil Terry. In 2008, he visited an exhibition at the Jewish Museum in New York, and he spent an amazing hour in front of "Fantasia" (painted by Hans Hofmann, 1943). After this episode, Terry decided to propose a similar experience to other people around the world. One day each year, people visit local museums and galleries to look at five pieces of art for 10 minutes each. After the tour, they have lunch together to share their experience. This initiative can be beneficial for our brain because it gives us time to get in touch with our emotions; it allows our cognitive processes, such as observational and attentional processes, to flow smoothly and to make connections between our personal past experiences, our knowledge, and artistic stimuli. There is also another important aspect. Slow Art Day is designed to connect people with the museum's objects while other visitors are involved in the same process: viewing slowly. A visitor may feel lost at first, but at some point, as Terry argues, people begin to feel comfortable in this relationship. This result may also be due to the power of the group.

Moreover, the Slow Art Day virtual events, held in April 2020, show the importance of art and museums especially during the COVID-19 pandemic. For example, the MOMus Thessaloniki Museum of Photography hosted a virtual session on the topics of personal and public spaces, and the meaning of home. During the zoom meeting, after slowly observing the images, participants shared opinions and ideas about the home and life during the COVID-19 lock-down in Greece. As the event was so popular, the museum organised a second virtual session. The Hafnarborg Art Museum, in Hafnarfjörður (Iceland), shared on Instagram a few sketches by Eiríkur Smith and Elías B. Halldórsson, for five days. This event aimed at helping attendees to relieve the stress of the pandemic. Viewers were asked to slowly look at the images and create sketches as a way to ground themselves in the present. The Fotomuseum in Antwerp (Belgium) provided a virtual slow-looking mindfulness exercise. Participants were invited to find a comfortable sitting position, and to choose an image, drawing, or photo to look at for five–ten minutes. The museum proposed a five-step meditative slow-looking activity: relax by paying attention to the breathing process, look at the artwork by answering some questions, focus again on breathing, look at the artwork a second time by answering some questions, and finally reflect on the exercise carried out. The National Gallery in London (United Kingdom) offered a five-minute meditation video on single artworks of the collection (still available on its website at the present time), focused on the different artwork details and enriched with sounds, favouring a slow look. Christina Bradstreet, course and events programmer at the National Gallery, claimed that instead of simply offering a slow looking experience, she is interested in adopting meditation techniques that link to the content of the paintings or the way they were created. In this way, art and meditation improve each other. For example, Bradstreet chose Rosa Bonhoeffer's "The Horse Fair" for a video, to explore the theme of the hustle and bustle of the busy horse fair as a metaphor for the overactive mind, and to reflect on how we might remain in a mindful state when dealing with the chaotic world around us[11].

Meditation helps awaken people from the sleep of automaticity and unconsciousness, thus making it possible to live their lives with access to the full spectrum of conscious and unconscious possibilities, as stated by Jon Kabat-Zinn (1994), the founder of the Mindfulness-Based Stress Reduction (MBSR) programme. According to Kabat-Zinn (2003, 2011), mindfulness is the awareness that arises through paying attention, on purpose, in the present moment, non-judgmentally, and open-heartedly to the unfolding of experience (which includes sensations, emotions, and cognitions) moment by moment. Harris claimed that mindfulness is a set of psychological skills to improve people's health, wellbeing, and lives. It is a kit of psychological tools that help people:

- to focus, and refocus, attention on the task or activity that is taking place and fully engage in it (focusing and engaging skills)
- to detach oneself from difficult or useless thoughts (unhooking or defusion skills)
- to be open to painful emotions permitting them to flow through you (acceptance or expansion skills)
- to savour, appreciate, and increase the satisfaction of pleasant experiences (savouring skills)

These skills have a common factor, which is paying attention in a particular way with openness, curiosity, and flexibility[12]. Bishop et al. (2004) considered mindfulness as a state of self-observation that makes room for a space or a pause between the phase of perception and that of the answer. Berila (2016) explained that a person who wants to train themselves to cultivate clarity, focus, and compassion does not have to embrace any particular religion. This practice allows participants to become aware of their experiences and thoughts. Mindfulness aims at paying attention by engaging our senses to notice the breath or any physical sensations occurring in the body and around us, in the present moment (here and now), without judging. There are clinical trials that confirm it has a positive impact on health.

Regarding the cultural heritage, Harrison and Clark (2016) argue that mindfulness allows us to further guide our observation of a work of art consciously. Several researches show that mindfulness allows visitors to establish a more distant view on their experiences, which generates reflection and impartial observation.

As written on the Manchester Art Gallery website, mindfulness protects and strengthens people's mental health by helping them manage stress better and thus reducing the risk of developing a mental health problem. This is very useful for city workers, but is also beneficial for other audiences such as children (who can build emotional resilience and self-esteem), and seniors (who can see life in a new way by becoming more aware of the curious, the strange, and the beautiful).

Echarri and Urpi (2018) investigated how mindfulness can be a contemplative technique to practice new ways of looking at artwork and generating meaning. In 2016, at the Museo Universidad de Navarra (Spain), the researchers proposed an educational activity that involved the contemplation of Rothko's painting "Untitled" (1969). The session lasted two hours and consisted of three phases: contemplation (i.e., a 20-minute mindfulness session), creative production (i.e., a 70-minute workshop in which each participant created an object based on the previous experience), and time for sharing experiences (i.e., a final 30-minute meeting in which participants had the chance to share ideas on the object made and on the experience of contemplation). At the end of the session, a survey was conducted with questions such as: *Could you tell us about your experience of contemplating the painting?* Overall, the responses emphasised its contribution to self-knowledge and a more conscious connection with the inner world. Based on the findings obtained, the researchers concluded that the technique can help focus attention on learning how to look carefully and contemplate. In this way, contemporary art has the opportunity to generate experiences in the inner world of people, improving the dialogue between the visitor and the artwork. The combination of mindfulness and artworks has two potential beneficial outcomes. On the one hand, mindfulness can enhance contemplation of the artwork. On the other hand, the artwork can improve the activity of full awareness.

In 2011, Massachusetts Museum of Contemporary Art (MASS MoCA), based in USA, developed a constructivist educational model based on conversational tours, mindfulness-based insight activities, and art-making exercises. This approach contributes to foster critical and visual thinking skills, and to apply them to art experiences and everyday life. Moreover, it enhances the museumgoers' ability for sustained observation, which is useful in art viewing. The MASS MoCA staff proposes guided visualisation, mindful eating, and slow walking tours.

There is evidence that mindfulness training has strong attentional and cognitive benefits. Two studies carried out by Zabelina et al. (2020) explored the role of mindfulness in art viewing and art making, in children and young adults. In study 1 (children), the mindfulness training was provided after the art viewing tour to examine the effects of mindfulness in memory retention. The children took part in an art tour of the Kid space gallery at the MASS MoCA. In study 2 (university students), mindfulness training was provided before art viewing to examine the effects of mindfulness on memory formation. In the art-viewing experiments conducted with children, the results were in line with those of the literature where mindfulness was linked to aesthetic preferences and improved long-term memory encoding. Findings collected in study 2 (young adults) also confirmed an increase in memory in art viewing. The researchers concluded that, in both cases, these findings suggest that mindfulness-based practices may provide a deeper art-viewing experience.

At the North Carolina Museum of Art (USA), Michelle Harrell, director of education, offered a 5, 4, 3, 2, 1 grounding strategy to activate senses and be grounded in the present moment. For instance, she focused on "The Garden Parasol" (1910), painted by Frederick Carl Frieseke. After taking a few slow deep breaths, Harrell invited to become more aware of the breathing and guided people to name:

- 5 things that observers can see in the painting
- 4 items that observers can imagine to touch in the painting
- 3 things that observers can imagine to hear in the painting
- 2 items that observers can imagine to smell in the painting
- 1 thing that observers can imagine to taste in the painting

From Harrell's experience as a museum educator, she has observed how works of art serve as a catalyst for discussion and reflection. Often, the discussion leads to a topic completely different than the artist intention or the historical significance of the work. Using a constructivist approach, viewers are allowed to construct their own meaning guided by the facilitator when appropriate. In this strategy, students practice a coping strategy as they observe a work of art. They may not remember the details within the work of art but the strategy is anchored in sensory experiences that can be recalled later to regulate emotions when flooded with stimuli or anxiety (Figure 8.1).

Here is a comment by Emily K. who was one of the parents in a virtual field trip where Harrell modelled the Mindful Moment with Monet to teach the 5, 4, 3, 2, 1 strategy. "My family took a day trip to the beach on New Years Day. It was cold and drizzly, but we went anyway. My son, who was 6 at the time, was both excited to be there and disoriented by this new experience of being at the beach. Usually it's warm and sunny and we skip around the sand in our bathing suits. Now we were bundled up and fighting the cold. He was also hungry and tired from waking up early. He began to sulk and wanted to go home. I could see my younger daughter having a grand time playing in the sand – even with her jacket and long pants – and didn't want to end it on account of my son. So I took him for a walk and used the 5-4-3-2-1 strategy I had seen Michelle Harrell demonstrate, to help bring him back to the present moment. We talked about one thing he saw, smelled, tasted, heard, and felt. That experience of grounding him in the moment, focusing on what was there instead of what wasn't, helped him. His attitude changed. He said yes to a snack. He said yes to playing in the sand. He still wanted to go home, but he was calmer and we could enjoy a couple more hours at the beach" (Harrell, private communication, 2021).

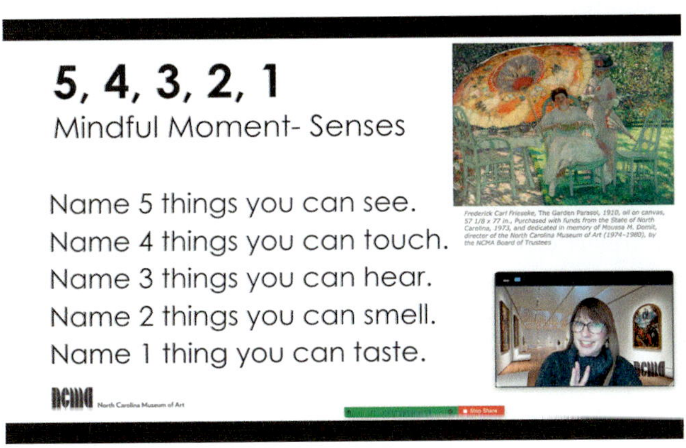

Figure 8.1 Mindful Moment at the North Carolina Museum of Art. The 5-4-3-2-1 Grounding Strategy. Courtesy of Michelle Harrell at the North Carolina Museum of Art.

The mindfulness examples listed in this chapter relate meditation to museum objects, so they are respectful of the cultural heritage and the museum mission. A museum can be an ideal place to explore mindfulness due to its unique atmosphere, which is associated with calm and contemplation, and because it is typically perceived as a safe space. However, it is not a gym and it is important to always link any activities to the museum's collection(s). I am taking this opportunity to propose the idea of a museum mindfulness session that I have in mind. It requires the involvement of an MBSR (mindfulness) teacher, a member of the museum staff, and a small group of participants (max. ten people, depending on the museum objects displayed in the room chosen for this meditation). The ideal museum room could be the one that can be isolated from large flows of visitors. Each participant should be invited to sit in a chair in front of a museum object (the perfect distance between visitor and object should be decided by museum staff). The allocation of the exhibits to participants should be decided by means of a draw to avoid discontent and waste of time. Here is a brief presentation of each phase:

- *introduction*: the MBSR (mindfulness) teacher should introduce mindfulness and the general rules of the session (how long it takes, the session programme, etc.), especially if visitors are beginners. Subsequently, there should be the allocation of the exhibits to participants. This step could take about 10/15 minutes
- *mindfulness*: this phase should be guided by the MBSR teacher who should invite participants to focus on the features of the exhibits previously decided with the museum expert. This part could last 15 minutes
- *discussion*: participants should be encouraged to share their experiences. At this point, the museum staff member should present each exhibit taking a cue from the participants' comments to trigger an artistic debate. This part could last 30/45 minutes
- *conclusion*: the MBSR teacher and the museum expert should end the session with their personal final comments. This step could take about ten minutes (five minutes to each expert)

This process could be a single one or can be repeated more than once with the same exhibits. It could be suitable for museums with different types of permanent or short-term collections. Naturally, it needs to be verified in the museum environment.

Initiatives, such as mindfulness and Slow art Day, give people the opportunity to explore museum objects without being an expert, simply by *experiencing* them, which can be the first step to get familiar with these types of "stimuli".

Shall we propose more wellbeing-related events with the help of the BFM approach? I think the answer is "yes". We could increase the proposals taking advantage of more psychological techniques and theories, and measuring the impact of these initiatives (also the ones already offered by museums) by means of the neuroscience tools introduced in chapter 7.

It could also be useful to create a digital archive that collects these experiences, methodologies, and findings which museums, interested in developing wellbeing projects, can freely access.

As stated by Falk (2021), museums are now widely seen as places where people willingly and proactively go with their family and friends. Research has demonstrated that practicing these pivotal types of soul-enhancing things (e.g., things that make people feel like they have used their time in a worthwhile manner) are all perceived as particularly precious and useful. In the end, as claimed by Falk, the word that best captures these positive perceptions of benefit is wellbeing.

Notes

1 https://dictionary.apa.org/well-being, accessed 30 September 2021.
2 https://museumsandwellbeingalliance.files.wordpress.com/2018/04/museums-as-spaces-for-wellbeing-a-second-report.pdf, accessed 24 March 2021.
3 https://www.mbam.qc.ca/en/education-wellness/art-therapy-and-health/, accessed 10 February 2021.
4 https://www.baat.org/About-Art-Therapy, accessed 12 March 2021.
5 https://arteffactproject.files.wordpress.com/2015/04/arteffact-final-report.pdf, accessed 23 March 2021.
6 https://www.aphp.fr/contenu/le-louvre-lhopital-rene-muret-ap-hp-la-visite, accessed 12 February 2021.
7 https://bethlemgallery.com/who-we-are/, accessed 11 February 2021.
8 https://www.lacarrarainhumanitas.it/video-la-cura-e-la-bellezza/, accessed 12 February 2021.
9 https://www.lacarrara.it/event/opere-in-parole/, accessed 12 February 2021.
10 This project is part of the interdisciplinary platform "Art, Health and Social Change", which aims to study how the arts positively benefit people. The platform involves more than 90 institutions including many museums. It creates tailor-made projects for the hospital. https://www.medicinamisuradidonna.it/images/Carla_Di_Grzia/13112019_BROCHURE_FONDAZIONE_ONLUS_SANTANNA_10x21cm_versione_inglese_bassa.pdf.
11 https://www.slowartday.com/slow-looking-meditations-with-the-national-gallery/, accessed 10 February 2021.
12 https://thehappinesstrap.com/what-is-mindfulness/, accessed 10 February 2021.

References

Berila, B. (2016). *Integrating Mindfulness into Anti-Oppression Pedagogy.* New York: Routledge.

Bishop, S.R., Lau, M., Shapiro, S., Carlson, L., Anderson, N.D., Carmody, J., Segal, Z.V., Abbey, S., Speca, M., Velting, D., & Devins, G. (2004). Mindfulness: A proposed operational definition. *Clinical Psychology: Science and Practice*, 11, 230–241.

Bungay, H., & Clift, S. (2010). Arts on prescription: A review of practice in the UK. *Perspectives in Public Health*, 130, 277–281.

Chatterjee, H., & Noble, G. (2017). *Museums, Health and Well-Being*. London: Routledge.

Coles, A. (2020). What do museums mean? Public perceptions of the purposes of museums and implications for their use in art therapy. In A. Coles, & H. Jury (Eds.), *Art Therapy in Museums and Galleries: Reframing Practice* (pp. 26–43). London: Jessica Kingsley Publishers.

Dalley, T. (1984). *Art as Therapy*. London-New York: Tavistock Publications.

Echarri, F., & Urpi, C. (2018). Mindfulness in art contemplation. The story of a rothko experience. *Journal of Museum Education*, 43, 35–46.

Falk, J.H. (2021). *The Value of Museums: Enhancing Societal Well-Being*. Lanham, MD: Rowman & Littlefield.

Fancourt, D., & Steptoe, A. (2019). The art of life and death: 14-year follow-up analyses of associations between arts engagement and mortality in the English Longitudinal Study of Ageing. *The British Medical Journal*, 367, 1–10.

Harrison, N.R., & Clark, D.P.A. (2016). The observing facet of trait mindfulness predicts frequency of aesthetic experiences evoked by the arts. *Mindfulness*, 7, 971–978.

Jury, H., & Landes, J. (2015). Museums and galleries—re-viewing museums: Innovative art therapy practice in museums and art galleries. *British Association of Art Therapists Newsbriefing*, 4, 26–28.

Kabat-Zinn, J. (1994). *Wherever You Go There You Are*. New York: Hachette Books.

Kabat-Zinn, J. (2003). Mindfulness-based interventions in context: Past, present, and future. *Clinical Psychology: Science and Practice*, 10, 144–156.

Kabat-Zinn, J. (2011). Some reflections on the origins of MBSR, skillful means, and the trouble with maps. *Contemporary Buddhism*, 12, 281–306.

Lund, K. (2020). Art therapy at the Bilbao Fine Arts museum. A gaze through emotions, culture and social integration. In A. Coles, & H. Jury (Eds.), *Art Therapy in Museums and Galleries: Reframing Practice* (pp. 202–221). London: Jessica Kingsley Publishers.

Museion, L'arte che cura, 24 November 2020, Achille De Gregori, https://www.facebook.com/museion.bozen/videos/1073392949751873/accessed10.03.2021.

Poulos, R., Marwood, S., Harkin, D., Opher, S., Clift, S., Cole, A., Rhee, J., Beilharz, K., & Poulos, C. (2018). Arts on prescription for community-dwelling older people with a range of health and wellness needs. *Health and Social Care in the Community*, 27, 483–492.

Stickley, T., & Eades, M. (2013). Arts on prescription: A qualitative outcomes study. *Public Health*, 127, 727–734.

Zabelina, D.L., White, R.A., Tobin, A., & Thompson, L. (2020). The role of mindfulness in viewing and making art in children and adults. *Mindfulness*, 11, 2604–2612.

Zhvitiashvili, N. (2020). From isolation to relation. Reflections on the development of museum-based art therapy in Russia. In A. Coles, & H. Jury (Eds.), *Art Therapy in Museums and Galleries: Reframing Practice* (pp. 82–107). London: Jessica Kingsley Publishers.

Video

Accademia Carrara—Opere in Parole, https://www.youtube.com/watch?v=hpoAvBvObkc.

Accademia Carrara—La cura e la bellezza, https://www.youtube.com/watch?v=1q597US1m6U.

Michelle Harrell, North Carolina Museum of Art (NCMA), grounding with 5, 4, 3, 2, 1 strategy, https://www.youtube.com/watch?v=QRRbjvu8Wko.

9 Parallel Worlds

Popular Education Through Neuroscience and the Fine Arts

Cristian Zaelzer and Stephen Legari

Museums by their very nature are designed to educate, reveal, inspire wonder, and bring the reaches of the known universe to the senses of the visitor. While the fine art museum might be more readily associated with teaching the history of art, world history, theory, and philosophy, the fine arts have been increasingly employed to describe even the most of complex of scientific phenomena. Indeed, one only need to browse the drawings of Leonardo da Vinci to appreciate that the arts and sciences have enjoyed a long and braided history of discovery and inquiry rather than being relegated to the specialised silos of practice of our modern time. Fortunately, both scientists and artists are seeking to bridge this divide towards mutual enrichment and museums have been positioned as a nexus for these exchanges.

For neuroscientists, these exchanges have become highly relevant, especially considering that just a fraction of the scientific knowledge produced in their laboratories reaches a lay audience. Communication with the public gets lost in translation because of differential exposures to scientific and critical thinking, discrepancies with social narratives, and a training that avoids emotional aspects of communication to offer the most rigorous and unbiased understanding of the facts. In this context, effective communication requires the use of emotions and the use of familiar elements, such as the use of popular language, to which the public can feel connected to and represented by. Those elements, in exchange, install a greater trust in what is being communicated no matter the complexity (Zaelzer, 2020).

When encountering the visual arts in a fine art museum, one is often confronted with the question, what am I seeing? But of equal importance is the question, how am I seeing? A recent and innovative collaboration between the Montreal-based Convergence Initiative and the Division for Education and Wellness of the Montreal Museum of Fine Arts (MMFA) endeavoured to explore both these questions. The "Parallel Worlds" project sought to bring together the worlds of neuroscience and the fine arts to explore phenomena and knowledge of visual perception and present it to the public in a popular fashion. The ultimate goal was to create a series of events that privileged the transmission of knowledge that could be engaging to specialists and lay-people alike and encourage discussion and new understanding.

DOI: 10.4324/9781003304531-9

This chapter describes the Parallel Worlds event series from conception to delivery. Included are the neuroscientific and artistic phenomena explored throughout the project and the bridges between them, the roles of the presenters, the formats of the events, and the dynamic exchanges with the attendees. While originally slated to be experienced live in the galleries and studios of the MMFA, the chapter will illustrate the various adaptations employed to rework the project for the virtual environment necessitated by COVID-19 restrictions. While the advantages of experiencing the fine arts and education live cannot be disputed, the virtual format of Parallel Worlds presented several advantages, which will be discussed.

Parallel Worlds is supported by the Brain Repair and Integrative Neuroscience Program (BRaIN) of the Research Institute of the McGill University Health Centre (RI-MUHC), Concordia University Faculty of Fine Arts, The Canadian Association for Neuroscience (CAN), and a Knowledge Mobilisation grant from McGill University's Healthy Brain, Healthy Lives Program (HBHL), made possible by a Canada First Research Excellence Fund (CFREF).

Scientists and Education

Most scientists disseminate their findings only to peers doing minimal outreach, mainly focusing on school children, and implicitly adopting the *deficit model,* the notion that the public has a knowledge gap, and those scientists or educators only need to fill this gap through education (Aikenhead, 2006; Besley et al., 2015; National Academies of Sciences, 2016; Rainie et al., 2015). Researchers in the field of science communication have repeatedly found the *deficit model* to be futile and useless in dealing with the "*confirmation bias*" (Gorman & Gorman, 2017; Lord et al., 1979; Mercier & Sperber, 2017; Sloman & Fernback, 2017). Effective evidence-based decisions require continuous reassessment of information by policymakers. Dynamic engagement between knowledge-producers and individuals, communities, and societies is necessary for successful knowledge translation. Therefore, the *deficit-model* is outdated, and scientists must embrace communicative practices that gives the public a voice throughout the scientific process. Such practices can be found in the *two–way engagement model* (Cooper, 2016). The participatory nature of *two–way engagement* can foster public interest and community engagement by "pulling in more voices, building support for science, growing interest among youth, encouraging science careers, improving science knowledge, and boosting the overall value of science to society." (Council of Canadian Academies and Expert Panel on the State of Canada's Science Culture, 2014). The horizontal didactic techniques practiced in two-way engagement not only help the public to better understand specific scientific issues, but also encourages the audience to realise their active role in advancing scientific knowledge (Bonney et al., 2009; Hallmann et al., 2017; Seibold et al., 2019; Vogel, 2017). The *two-way engagement* ensures a more comprehensive practice of diversity and inclusion by allowing unprivileged and minority voices to be added to the opinions of those constructing and practicing science (Singer et al., 2015; Steering Committee for a National Science Communication Strategy (Australia), 2010; Wilsdon et al., 2005). Longer engagement periods create more opportunities for the public to participate in the process. The participation gives the public a chance to challenge and be critical of the science generating more interest and understanding of the specific question, the scientific inquiry, and the collaborative process. The longer engagement also helps the scientists to understand better the needs from those involved by spending more time and interest with those whom the science could benefit (Powell & Colin, 2008). *Two-way engagement* reaches the public at a personal level, building trust and reciprocity that is essential when communicating a scientific message (National Academies of Sciences, 2016). Museum tours, workshops, and programmes that are constructed over themes and are available for people to explore over weeks or months offer a compelling entrance into *two–way engagement* with the community.

The Partnership

The project was the brainchild of the Convergence Initiative, an independent Canadian non-profit organisation dedicated to advancing the knowledge of neuroscience and art and promoting the cross-pollination between these two disciplines. The organisation's goals are to advance the education of neuroscience and art, to promote the intersection between these two disciplines, and to influence people's perspectives about neuroscience and the arts. Towards this end, Convergence fosters collaboration, trans-disciplinary thought, and knowledge sharing. The project was proposed to the Division of Education and Wellness of the MMFA in 2019. The MMFA enjoys a long history of collaboration with community and clinical organisations and engages in research to better understand the contribution of the fine arts and a fine art museum in the service of public well-being of which education is believed to be a primary tenet. The ultimate goals of the project were mutual: the transfer of knowledge about colour and visual perception between communities of neuroscientists, artists, educators, and the public and to bring diverse audiences together, expose them to advances in neuroscience, and develop novel methods of teaching both neuroscience and art.

Parallel Worlds

At the proposal stage, the framework for the Parallel Worlds project was already well-developed by the Convergence Initiative team and the response from the MMFA was enthusiastic. Initial meetings took place on-site at the MMFA and included visits to galleries and brain-storming sessions. The COVID-19 world pandemic obliged a change in strategy to overcome the multiple lockdowns and public health guidelines, not to mention museum closures, and adapt to an online format using Zoom and social media. The project was ultimately re-conceived to include all of its original elements including co-presentations from neuroscientists and museum guides, public discussions, creative workshops, and an online tour.

From April to August of 2021, Parallel Worlds was offered for free to the general public in the form of three monthly events. These included a live online colloquium where a scientist (usually a neuroscientist) and a fine art museum guide (docent) discussed a topic related to one aspect of vision, colour, and art. The second event took the form of an online art-science workshop linked to the colloquium. And finally, a permanent virtual tour was made available that included artworks selected for their scientific, historical, technical, and aesthetic value concerning the study and appreciation of the visual system and the brain circuitry involved in the health and disease of it. Each online session was broadcast live on Zoom and Facebook Live allowing a diverse Canadian and international audience to get together and explore the advances in visual neuroscience and the impact and influence of art on those advances. While most of the events were delivered as synchronous, all of them were recorded and kept online to be experienced as well in asynchronous form.

The programme aimed to explore the intuitive understanding of image perception executed by artists centuries before neuroscientists could test it in the laboratory. The lessons learned from earlier observations in the lab were discussed and the notions of how science has become a source of inspiration for artistic inquiry and research were proposed (Cavanagh, 2005). The colloquiums and workshops examined subjects like why we imagine shapes in the clouds? What is the first thing that our brain processes when observing images? How can colour be a socio-psychological construction? Or how some pigments in paintings can be dangerous while others allow us to reveal invisible things in the brain. Discussions about abstraction and Gestalt, neurons firing together, and the sources of imagination were explored with equal enthusiasm.

The project was organised around five themes. Each theme was assigned a colour and an eye-catching title in order to spark interest in a specific topic in neuroscience, art history, and creativity. Each monthly event began with a colloquium that allowed for the cross-dissemination of knowledge in visual perception or visual disorder in the realm of neuroscience, and artistic developments in technique, motif, material, and narrative relative to art history. These same themes were then taken up by five artists who developed creative workshops for the general public to be delivered live online a week following each of the colloquiums. The tour was hosted on the Convergence Initiative's website and was comprised of artworks from the MMFA's collection with audio provided by the museum's guides.

The Colloquiums

While the topics were diverse, each colloquium followed a similar format and were a total of 90 minutes in length. The presenters were introduced and each was invited to speak for no longer than 30 minutes to avoid Zoom fatigue, recorded, and posteriorly subtitled in English or French to include audiences with hearing impairment. Each event began with a tour of artworks selected from the permanent collection of the MMFA. At each stop along the tour, the guides discussed the artistic practice and techniques involved in the piece. This information was put it the larger context of the colloquium's themes be it visual perception, use of colour, distortion and abstraction, material innovation, etc. Just as in a live situation, the guides worked to invite the visitors into the work by posing open questions designed to invite personal reflection and observation. These tours were also meant to allow museum visitors to make associations between neuroscientific and artistic principles while fostering awareness of the importance of neuroscience and mental health in their daily lives.

Following the guided-tour, the guest scientist presented relevant evidenced-based data on the theme of the day but tailored for public and popular delivery. Each presentation might include principles of neuroanatomy, visual perception, and mental health relevant to the phenomenon being discussed.

Starting with a popular pigment or dye used nowadays in art or science, the names of the colloquium were: Vanta Black, chosen to speak about visual perception without the use of colour; Crimson, to explore colour as a social construct; Uranium Yellow, to discuss the toxicity of certain dyes and pigments used in art and their effects on the brain; YInMn Blue, to guide a journey through the phenomena of pareidolia; and, Alexa488, where we discovered the advances of fluorescent dyes and technology of new materials to study the brain and produce new expressions of art. The following provides an overview of each of the talks with two examples exploring how an artwork was used. The reader is encouraged to visit the project's website for the full experience.

The Talks

Vanta black—a world without colour (disorders in the perception of colour)

In this colloquium, our invited neuroscientist, Dr. Patrick Cavanagh, together with our museum volunteer guide, Marie-José Daoust, discussed the ability of artists to create impressions of depth and light from pigments on a flat surface. Capturing scenes with almost no light on night-time scenes and depicting volumes and space using lines in the absence of any sense of light. We looked at shadows where the absence of light helped convey the depth in a scene and learned to detect the shortcuts taken by artists, like impossible shadows, that break the rules of physics to achieve a more effective painting. All to explain how our brain takes shortcuts to perceive the world through vision, shortcuts that artists have discovered in their practice for millennia (Figure 9.1).

Parr's artwork shows the graphic impact of black on white, and a composition that invites the viewer to a narrative and participate in meaning-making. The absence of colour is not a limit for the brain to infer a story. Black, white, and abstraction are used by the brain to infer a model from reality. A dark patch is more visible than a white patch on the same work. The

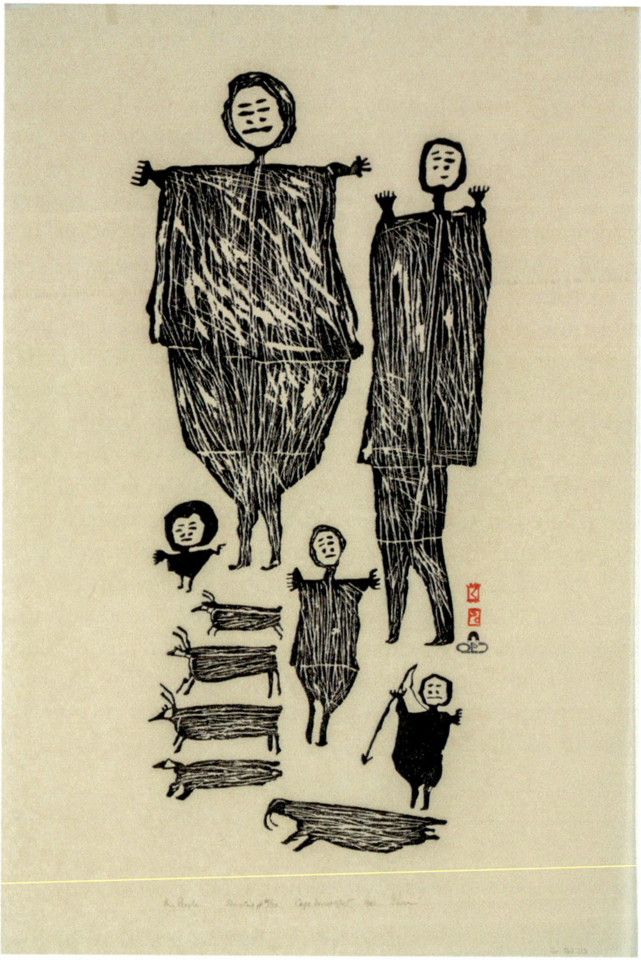

Figure 9.1 Parr (1893–1969, Tessikjakjuak, in Present-Day Nunavut) My People, 1961, 76.3 × 50.7 cm, Stonecut, Montreal Museum of Fine Arts.

brain only needs so much information to infer a story. Edges are extremely important, and edges may be processed first and later "filled-in". These figures are similar to how the brain discerns shadows and silhouettes as well. The fact that a simple line drawing can give a vivid impression of life links into the idea that our vision also works in general by extracting from these sorts of outlines.

Crimson—the colour of passion (colour as a social construct)

The importance of colour is prevalent in society, from the colours meticulously chosen for countries' flags to the clothes that we wear in our day-to-day lives.

Colour is embedded with many connotations that we utilise to understand our world. Colour preferences can be seen individually and collectively and differ across cultures. The question aesthetic scientists ask is, why? In this talk, Neuroaesthetician Dwaynica Greaves and MMFA volunteer guide Louise Gauvreau discussed colour theories within Aesthetic Science to understand the approaches taken to find out why we have colour preferences and how they shape our social world.

Uranium yellow—poisoned by colour (neurotoxicity and dyes)

Probably art would not be included among high-risk jobs. However, when a close examination of some artists' material choices is done, the story changes. Lead white, vermilion, Scheele's green, chrome yellow, Naple's yellow, and many other pigments include toxic elements such as lead, chromium, arsenic, mercury, or antimony that can cause severe diseases.

This colloquium explored the palette of old masters such as Titian, Greco, or Vermeer. It discussed the chemical composition of the poisonous pigments used to create some of the most famous paintings in the world: Sunflowers, Girl with a pearl earring, The Scream. Masterpieces of art history also fascinating from a toxicological point of view. In this aspect, we will see some of the most relevant poisoning cases that might be attributed to artistic materials, including those of Van Gogh and Goya. Chemist, Oskar Gonzalez Mendia, Chemist, and MMFA volunteer guide, Christiane Hudon, discussed here that while pigments are beautiful, they can be dangerous too (Figure 9.2).

This painting was chosen for its generous use of red, often associated with power and powerful feelings. Here, the painter uses colour and stylised shape to add a symbolic dimension to the halberdier. The scarlet hue of the uniform enhances the man's presence. It is the violent red of warriors who face death in battle. Given the paintings date, it is likely vermilion red and was originally made by powdering cinnabar, a bright scarlet to a brick-red form of mercury sulphide mineral. Methods for its extraction and knowledge of its toxicity go back as early as around 350 BCE. The cause of poisoning associated with vermillion is mercury, because its primary mechanism of toxicity involves the complete shutdown of proteins responsible for the natural recycling of vitamins C and E to their active forms and linked to potential brain damage. Later, vermillion red would be replaced by cadmium red.

YInMn blue—images in the clouds (pareidolia)

Pareidolia is the integration of ambiguous stimuli into meaningful representations, like when you look at a cloud with no particular shape and your brain extracts forms from it. Pareidolia has been linked to creativity; in YInMn Blue, Karim Jerbi, Cognitive Neuroscientist, and Sylvie Douyon, MMFA volunteer guide, examined visual and superstitious/divergent perception,

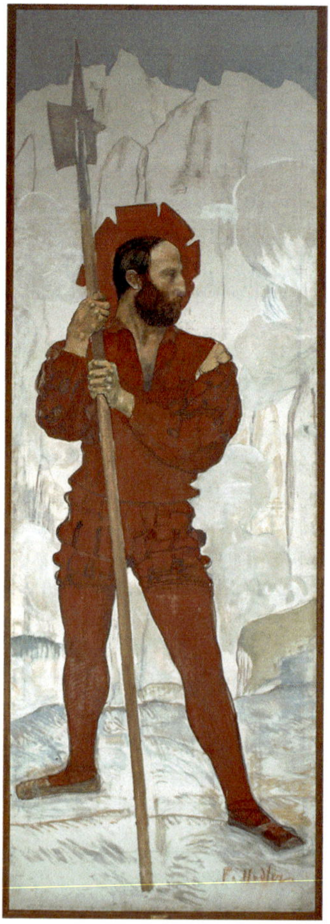

Figure 9.2 Ferdinand Hodler, Halberdier, 1895, 327 × 108.3 cm, Oil on Canvas, Montreal Museum of Fine Arts. Gift of Mr. and Mrs. Michal Hornstein.

abstraction and Gestalt, and the links of those phenomena to creativity and colour in the brain.

Alexa488—a fluorescent ghost (the use of fluorescent molecules in neuroscience)

In Alexa488, Melina Jaramillo Garcia, Molecular and Cellular Microscopy Douglas Research Centre Platform Coordinator, and Madeleine Colaco MMFA volunteer guide, discussed how fluorescence microscopy has been used to find markers for neurodegenerative diseases and how the exploration of new ideas and technological advances have pushed the fields of art and neuroscience.

The Workshops

Due to COVID-19 public health emergency and social distancing measures, hosting workshops was impossible during 2020 and a big part of 2021. To solve this issue, an online programme was developed where attendees benefited from an interactive activity that approached the experience of a presential workshop in the museum.

Each workshop was based on the two-way engagement model of education, where the participants see themselves immersed in the activity, having a voice and an informed opinion of what is happening instead of being a mere observers. By being involved in these interactive workshops, the participants were able to apprehend and assimilate/integrate/absorb scientific concepts in a more intuitive approach. The workshops consisted of several short explanatory instructions delivered by the guide that allowed the participants to develop the activity at their own pace.

Vanta black—a world without colour (disorders in the perception of colour)

How does a portrait capture the essence of the self? When does your own face become that of a stranger? In this workshop, participants explored how shadow, line, contrast, and motion alter our understanding of the human face. Participants experimented with pencil and charcoal on paper, smartphone photography, simple digital image editing techniques, and web-based artificial intelligence (AI) to create a series of iterative self-portraits. The portraits examined how we typically perceive light and darkness but also investigated non-normative ways of seeing faces, such as prosopagnosia (face-blindness) and akinetopsia (motion-blindness). The workshop included short presentations by the workshop leader—Ms. Bettina Forget, MA ArtEd.—group discussion, individual art-making, and collaborative work.

Crimson—the colour of passion (colour as a social construct)

This workshop examined our linguistic connections with colours and the sensory evocations between words and vision. The participant explored how naming can alter or reinforce our perceptions of colour. Such linguistic links with colours have sparked controversy through the centuries, revealing that, ultimately, the meaning of colour is socially constructed. Participants added their own personal perspectives to the lexicon of colours. Employing the Adobe Colour Wheel, each participant chose a colour that speaks to them. Then, the instructor—Darian Goldin Stahl, PhD—guided the participants through a sensory naming exercise in an attempt to encapsulate the feeling of the colour. Finally, the participants submitted their colours and titles to the Convergence website. This experiment's results illuminated the influence of naming on our shared or disparate perceptions of colour.

Uranium yellow—poisoned by colour (neurotoxicity and dyes)

As artists and art lovers, we are really concerned about beauty. As humans, we are really careful about what we put inside our bodies. But is it worth it to ask ourselves how our creative practice could be impacting our bodies and those around us? We can easily forget about the by-products of ours and other creations, ignoring the hidden poisons in beauty. How can we develop an artistic path that positively impacts the world around us and our bodies? How can we avoid the beauty of colour becoming poison for us or those (humans and no humans) around us? Even though not all paints are harmful to our bodies and the environment, in this workshop, designer Laura Rosero helped participants explore how colours are hidden in their home, in the form of waste and products in in their kitchen. Paint was created using unusual material, recursiveness, and imagination.

YInMn blue—images in the clouds (pareidolia)

Pareidolia is the fascinating phenomenon of seeing meaningful patterns or connections in ambiguous images, like recognising a dragon or a space rocket in a cloud. This phenomenon emerges from our tendency to seek patterns in the face of uncertainty.

In this workshop, neuroscientists and artist Antoine Bellemare Peppin interactively related the science behind pareidolia with practical, creative applications. The participants explored different ways of experiencing pareidolic perception while learning about fundamental gestalt mechanisms enabling its emergence. Participants were invited to develop creative ideas by constructing their pareidolia, with a specific focus on storytelling. Furthermore, a dialogue between human and machine creativity was initiated through the use of tools derived from artificial intelligence exploring the intrinsic relation between pareidolia and creativity, the benefits of paying attention to your environment as a creativity trigger, and the emerging role that artificial intelligence could play on those relations.

Alexa488—a fluorescent ghost (the use of fluorescent molecules in neuroscience)

In this workshop, artist and educator Jihane Mossalim explored the red, green, and blue (RGB) colour code used by both modern coloured screens used every day and the main fluorescent dyes employed to reveal the different brain components in contemporary science. Participants created their own "brain structure inspired art piece" using a coloured drawing developed during the workshop, hiding a word, a shape or a sentence within the drawing and then using the different features of an application or the filter properties of transparent coloured paper to make it appear.

Using the Green Fluorescent Protein (GFP) as an example, the participants explored the use of colour as a tool to detect elements that might be very difficult or impossible to see with the naked eye. Emulating that process, participants developed a better understanding of fluorescent colours in science and transformation, contrasts, and the use of the RGB model in computers and cell phone screens.

The tour

When Parallel Worlds was originally conceived to be presented on-site at the MMFA, works from the permanent collection on display, as opposed to a temporary exhibition, were chosen to illustrate the themes of the colloquiums. These choices were pragmatic in that artworks on display in galleries tend to be relatively stable in terms of curatorial change and the galleries often lend themselves to group discussion more easily that major exhibitions. For Parallel, Worlds, the pavilion housing the MMFA's Inuit, Canadian, and Quebecois collections was selected for its breadth across time and diversity of styles while celebrating the history of art from this country. As the project was re-conceived for on-line delivery due to COVID-19 constraints, copyright of artworks had to be considered and the choice of artworks to share was limited.

Each artwork selected appeals to some point in art history and technique development while demonstrating an impressive advancement in the understanding of brain perception of image and its reproduction in 3D or 2D. It is important to point out that much of what we know today from neuroaesthetics and brain science related to vision comes from these observations previously done by artists.

The tour, housed on the Convergence Initiative website features high-resolution images of the artworks and accompanying text in explaining the neuroscientific and the artistic aspects concerning the selection of the work for the tour. Additionally, audio was recorded by the volunteers guides in English and French for those who prefer to listen to the information.

The curatorial work was developed by Cristian Zaelzer, PhD, Sciences, Bettina Forget MArtEd, and Stephen Legari Msc, MA, with commentaries in the content from Vision Neuroscientists Janine Mendola, PhD and Alex Baldwin, PhD.

Discussion

The COVID-19 pandemic prevented the Parallel Worlds project from enjoying the rich environment of the galleries of the Montreal Museum of Fine Arts and the vibrant exchange that comes from encountering the fine arts directly and in connection with others. However, the virtual format that this project took proved to have several advantages that could not necessarily have been realised in a live format. Most notably of these was the opportunity invite scientists and specialists from diverse backgrounds from around the world and ensuring a gender balance in the delivery of the project. This allowed the project to align with commitments to equality, diversity, and inclusion. The online format also permitted attendees to join from anywhere in the world, free of charge. Parallel Worlds offered as well an unprecedented venue for participating scientists to reach a lay audience and improved appreciation for the scientific endeavour, increased public trust in science, and allowed people a familiar contact with those who produce science nowadays. The museum setting facilitated a new exploration and construction of bridges between science and art, not only as a static piece belonging to a collection, but also as a dynamic system where different stakeholders share views and feed each other in a process that foster the acquisition of new knowledge and create new bonds among professionals of different fields.

All elements of the Parallel Worlds project can be viewed at: https://www.convergenceinitiative.org/parallel-worlds-en

References

Aikenhead, G.S. (2006). *Science Education for Everyday Life: Evidence-Based Practice.* New York: Teachers College Press.

Besley, J.C., Dudo, A., & Storksdieck, M. (2015). Scientists' views about communication training. *Journal of Research in Science Teaching*, 52, 199–220.

Bonney, R., Cooper, C.B., Dickinson, J., Kelling, S., Phillips, T., Rosenberg, K.V., & Shirk, J. (2009). Citizen science: A developing tool for expanding science knowledge and scientific literacy. *BioScience*, 59, 977–984.

Cavanagh, P. (2005). The artist as neuroscientist. *Nature*, 434, 301–307.

Cooper, C. (2016). Scientists should talk to the public, but also listen. *Scientific American Blog Network*, https://blogs.scientificamerican.com/guest-blog/scientists-should-talk-to-the-public-but-also-listen/, accessed 10 September 2019.

Council of Canadian Academies and Expert Panel on the State of Canada's Science Culture (2014). *Science Culture: Where Canada Stands.*

E. National Academies of Sciences (2016). *Communicating Science Effectively: A Research Agenda.* 10.17226/23674.

Gorman, S.E., & Gorman, J.M. (2017). *Denying to the Grave: Why We Ignore the Facts that Will Save Us.* Oxford New York: Oxford University Press.

Hallmann, C.A., Sorg, M., Jongejans, E., Siepel, H., Hofland, N., Schwan, H., Stenmans, W., Müller, A., Sumser, H., Hörren, T., Goulson, D., & de Kroon, H. (2017). More than 75 percent decline over 27 years in total flying insect biomass in protected areas. *PLoS ONE*, 12. 10.1371/journal.pone.0185809.

Lord, C.G., Ross, L., & Lepper, M.R. (1979). Biased assimilation and attitude polarization: The effects of prior theories on subsequently considered evidence. *Journal of Personality and Social Psychology*, 37(11), 2098–2109.

Mercier H., & Sperber, D. (2017). *The Enigma of Reason.* Cambridge, Massachusetts: Harvard University Press.

Powell, M.C., & Colin, M. (2008). Meaningful citizen engagement in science and technology: What would it really take?, *Science Communication*, 30, 126–136.

Rainie, L., Funk, C., Anderson, M., & Page, D. (2015). *How Scientists Engage the Public.* Washington, DC: Pew Research Center, accessed 23 April 2020.

Researchers should reach beyond the science bubble. (2017). *Nature*. 542, 391, 10.1038/542391a.

Seibold, S., Gossner, M.M., Simons, N.K., Blüthgen, N., Müller, J., Ambarlı, D., Ammer, C., Bauhus, J., Fischer, M., Habel, J.C., Linsenmair, K.E., Nauss, T., Penone, C., Prati, D., Schall, P., Schulze, E., Vogt, J., Wöllauer, S., & Weisser, W.W. (2019). Arthropod decline in grasslands and forests is associated with landscape-level drivers. *Nature*, 574, 671–674.

Singer, J., Bennett-Levy, J., & Rotumah, D. (2015). You didn't just consult community, you involved us: Transformation of a "top-down" aboriginal mental health project into a "bottom-up" community-driven process. *Australas Psychiatry*, 23, 614–619.

Sloman S., & Fernback, P. (2017). *The Knowledge of Illusion: Why We Never Think Alone*. New York: MacMillan.

Steering Committee for a National Science Communication Strategy (Australia), Australia, and I. Department of Innovation Science and Research (2010). *Inspiring Australia: A National Strategy for Engagement with the Sciences*. Canberra, A.C.T.: Dept. of Innovation, Industry, Science and Research.

Vogel, G. (2017). Where have all the insects gone? *Science*, 356, 576–579.

Wilsdon, J., Wynne, B., & Stilgoe, J. (2005). *The Public Value of Science (or How to Ensure that Science Really Matters)*. London: Demos.

Zaelzer, C. (2020). The value in science-art partnerships for science education and science communication. *eNeuro*, 7. doi: 10.1523/ENEURO.0238-20.2020

10 The Museum and Quality of Life

Vincenza Ferrara

The museum is considered a learning environment and the multiplicity of meanings that a museum object can represent makes cultural heritage a valid tool for educational activities, including trans-disciplinary ones. The European Council recommendation of 1998[1] concerning heritage education says that heritage education should be promoted through the medium of different school subjects at all levels and in all types of teaching. This is because heritage education is based on active educational methods with cross-curricular approaches.

To achieve learning, it is necessary to develop useful skills and abilities in order to obtain cognitive tools for personal fulfilment and quality of life. We are talking about soft skills that represent being autonomous, having self-confidence, having resistance to stress, organising and planning, learning permanently, knowing how to achieve goals and manage information, being enterprising, having a spirit of initiative, communicating, practicing problem solving, knowing how to work in a team, and possessing leadership skills. Soft skills can be declarative (knowing), procedural (knowing how to do), and pragmatic (knowing how to do in practice)[2].

Another important reference to the development of skills is the World Health Organization (WHO), which considers them *life skills*[3]. With this terminology, we mean all those skills that you need to learn to be able to relate to others and to deal with the problems, pressures, and stress of everyday life. The lack of such socio-emotional skills can in fact cause, especially in young people, the establishment of negative and risky behaviours in response to stress. The WHO invites *educational institutions* to introduce specific projects in schools or other places dedicated to learning (why not museums?), or all the places where basic training is carried out. This is accompanied by the need for continuous training since it is necessary to cultivate these skills and competences as resources for one's own fulfilment and wellbeing throughout one's life. Life skills are the skills that lead to positive and adaptive behaviours that make the individual capable of effectively coping with the demands and challenges of everyday life. They can be grouped according to three macro-areas:

DOI: 10.4324/9781003304531-10

1 EMOTIVE (self-awareness, emotion management, and stress management)
2 RELATIONAL (empathy, effective communication, and positive relationships)
3 COGNITIVE (problem solving, decision making, critical thinking, and creative thinking)

The modern museum can play an important role in society precisely in the areas of learning and health. Studies in this sector can collaborate to design or re-design new activities within museum structures or make their heritage available in other contexts to promote actions capable of relating to the world of education on the one hand and on the other acting as a learning environment, informal and non-formal throughout life. To achieve this goal, it seems useful to refer to the application of pedagogical methods that use the museum object as a tool for the development of cognitive activities. Studies have shown how much the impact of some activities is positive for learning and wellbeing. Among these methods, we find Visual Thinking Strategies (VTS). This is a method, which, using art, achieves cross-cutting objectives to improve learning and relationships. It was structured in the late 1980s in the United States by cognitivist psychologist Abigail Housen and by Philip Yenawine, at that time head of educational activities at the Museum of Modern Art (MoMa) in New York. Starting from studies on the different reactions of the public to artworks, Housen identified and described the breadth of types of thought that art is capable of arousing. Housen and Yenawine therefore understood the potential that observation of the artwork can have in the development of important skills and proposed a method with an important pedagogical value (Housen, 2007; Yenawine, 2013).

The VTS method was first applied in schools; subsequently, its value for the development of transversal skills revealed its usefulness for training also in other sectors such as, for example, that in the health professions and the wider field of care[4]. This experience has also been applied to museum objects not related to the visual arts or photos. An example concerns an experience carried out a few years ago in Rome with a proposal for a multi-disciplinary path for teachers by visiting museums of different disciplines. Activities were carried out within the Civic Museum of Zoology, stimulating discussions with the VTS method. The proposed images concerned among others a gray stork represented with some elements that the taxidermist considered useful to insert next to the bird to represent the story of the stork that, in migration, was wounded near Castel Porziano and taken to a centre of wildlife recovery. This image was considered part of a path that went through other institutions such as the Capitoline Museums where attention was placed on the statue of Leda with the swan, from the original by the sculptor Timotheos (360 BC), or the Museum of Rome of Palazzo Braschi where we find some swans represented in the portrait of Elisabeth Brancaccio with her children, by Francesco Gai. During the path built with museums of different disciplinary origins, the learning process can also include science subjects where the museum objects contribute with their own stories and meanings. Other VTS experiences have shown the interest of science museums in this approach (Downey, 2018).

But, how does this approach work? The practice of VTS takes place in small groups of peers, both for knowledge and basic culture, in front of a work of art, an image, or a museum object. An experienced facilitator will use only three questions to lead the discussion. The questions asked by the facilitator must always be the following:

1 What is going on in this picture?
2 What do you see that makes you say that?
3 What more can you find?

We have to follow simple but fundamental rules: choosing an image unknown by participants, asking them to observe it in silence for enough time, then requiring the participants to raise their hands in order to have the floor and express their hypothesis in relation to the questions posed. Stimulating listening to the opinions of others is very important, since the contribution of each participant will serve to enrich the observations of others in the group, creating a sort of *collective consciousness*. It is also essential that the observations and opinions of the participants are always substantiated by visual elements. This apparently simple transition progressively brings to consciousness the mechanisms of recognition of reality that each one unconsciously implements on the basis of their own previous experiences. The last question will also lead to an increasingly in-depth observation, which will often be able to intrigue the participants, for example, by enhancing the wealth of details and meanings contained in every artwork. The facilitator leads the VTS discussion summarising the opinions expressed and stimulating the intervention of participants.

At the end of the activity, the facilitator will reveal the details and the meaning of the image that was the subject of the discussion. In the case of an artwork, he will therefore be able to cite the title and the author and describe the object of the observation trying to refer to the hypotheses put forward by the participants. Participants stimulated by the previous discussion will be more willing to listen to what the facilitator has to say, and the cognitive elements will more easily become part of their personal cultural baggage.

The experience of observing the image with the VTS method stimulates the participants' awareness of how perception works. At the beginning, we have an overview, we identify details that, based on our knowledge and experience, lead us to an elaboration of the perceived information, assigning a meaning to the whole. The subsequent observation and listening to other possible interpretations, based on their different details or meaning guide the participants in a further elaboration of content observed activating a problem-solving process. This experience also suggests to us the need to take some time when we are in front of an image in order to understand its meaning. This exercise then allows us to reflect on the multiple interpretations that the same image can suggest, leading to greater awareness and acceptance of the ambiguity of perception related to our (and others') knowledge. Finally, it should be noted how peer group discussion allows improvement of each participant's communication and listening skills. Important educators in the world of pedagogy are important references of the VTS method such as John Dewey, who indicated in observation and consequent reflection a useful area for applied intelligence. No less important is Howard Gardner's contribution with his invitation to use visual intelligence and respect for the different learning approaches of people (Gardner, 1983). Judith Rich Harris was another guide for designing the method. Important is her theory that explains how peers exert a greater influence than parents on the education of young people by sharing hypotheses proven by experimentation and the support of other data such as the meaning given to visual elements (Harris, 1998).

The method also responds to what Lev Vygotskij argued in the volume "Thought and Language" where he underlined the social nature of human learning. Once again, it emerges that the primary competence is of a social order, which then structures itself as an individual competence (Vygotskij, 1962). Learning would therefore result from interactions with the surrounding environment, including those with the people who populate it. Understanding, therefore, is never passive, but implies an active construction through exploration and reflection. The *VTS* method shows how the image of a cultural heritage object can respond to the constructivist approach of learning and be used in this context. Starting from the assumption that all knowledge is personal knowledge, and it is the result of the personal reconstruction and experiences of the individual, we cannot fail to consider some studies on images and their reading. An important reference is the research of Rudolf Arnheim and his consideration that what we see corresponds, in reality, to an act of cognition that activates and stimulates the search for solutions in order to assign a meaning to what is observed which represents something known for the observer (Arnheim, 1954). The surprising thing about the reaction of the participants to this method is that after a few meetings their approach to a proposed image changes because of the activation of the problem-solving process, of communication, and of respect for the other's thinking and for collaborative work. It is as if the mind changes its functioning by conditioning the activities. And then, one wonders: why is it said that VTS *open the mind?* There are many studies on the learning and activation of certain brain areas and not least those related to the functioning of the neural networks to which reference can be made. Research indicates that learning involves changes in the connections that are established between neurons and that effective teaching directly affects the functioning of the brain, modifying its connectivity (Owens & Tanner, 2017; Goswami, 2004). Didactic activity is important to modulate and stimulate the functioning of the cognitive system in order to improve the quality of the processing of meanings that allows for the addition of new knowledge. What are the mechanisms that are activated by the VTS method to activate extremely positive reactions on the part of the participants, one wonders? Interesting is the Van Leewen's study for the development of new neuro-scientific knowledge on the perception of art and the complex thought processes underlying the VTS method[5].

The VTS method was formulated as a way to help students develop and recognise *visual literacy* by observing art and discussing the meaning and evidence of each meaning in small groups. But, the VTS method also helps in the development of some basic skills and somehow makes the mind more open and flexible. Why? We will try to record some reflections on this issue. When a group is guided in the VTS practice, one notices a predisposition to concentration, greater ability to observe, and ease in communication, and one wonders what mental processes are involved to achieve these abilities. We know that each of us works very differently and that the learning process is intimately related to personality and social context. We also wonder how art used as a tool stimulates our mind in an extremely positive way for everyone. In the people involved in the VTS process, whether they are facilitators or participants, observation, concentration, thought, and expression are activated. This happens because neural networks related to cognitive aspects are activated during the practice. The involvement of these areas is linked to the process of *actions* of thought that are activated.

Philip Yenawine, as educator at MOMA, and Abigail Housen have flipped the classic museum visit. Instead of speaking to the public about the work of art, the museum educator assumed the role of facilitator/moderator by stimulating the discussion of the participants allowing them to make sense and create meaning starting from their personal observations.

The moderator carefully follows the progress of the discussion and asks participants to identify the visible references related to their opinions. The moderator helps the process of reaching a shared position with respect to the work by underlining the elements and paraphrasing each comment in a neutral way, before linking this to the ongoing debate. The unveiling of the meaning that the artist wanted to represent appears as another point of view. This activity makes the participants curious and available to listen, and therefore to actively learn the knowledge that the facilitator (museum operator, teacher, and facilitator) deems useful to share (Yenawine, 2016). This method, as described, has achieved widespread international success in museums, in art academies, in primary and secondary education sectors, in medical schools, in neuro-rehabilitation schools, and also in many companies. The effectiveness of the VTS method has also been confirmed and reported in numerous studies and scientific publications. VTS has been shown to improve written and spoken language skills as well as social relationships, observation, and critical thinking skills. These results are a strong indication of the link between VTS practice and the activation of specific neural networks for learning. In top-down educational models, the teacher is the expert who shares their knowledge with the students. Such a learning model places a strong emphasis on storing and reproducing this information, rather than exploring the students' personal meaning, social and cultural context, and objective value of interpretation. This traditional model encourages students to enter a guided "performance" mode that limits their ability to think about multiple interpretations or to find alternative solutions to an issue. In contrast, the VTS method focuses on the process that allows pupils to find and organise meanings and divergent thinking. In this way, personal perceptions are inserted in a social and cultural context and considered for their objective value and therefore recognisable by others. Divergent thinking is very important since it is a way of evaluating reality by trying to adopt different points of view and finding alternative solutions to problems. However, all solutions must be evaluated and such thinking is linked to creativity. This allows students to engage personally and with others in search of the meaning of the image been observed. The VTS method represents all these aspects by activating the group discussion centred on *protagonism* in the learning process of each student in front of the artworks, museum objects, or other kind of images that have been selected to satisfy the interests of the participants. One of the skills that the VTS method stimulates is the awareness by the participants of which capacities this activity improves.

The role of visual arts and their usefulness for therapy, for the promotion of wellbeing, and for the development of clinical skills, are highlighted by the report of the European section of the WHO[6]. Furthermore, exposure to arts or exercising artistic activities can be *therapeutic*, lowering cortisol levels and therefore limiting stress (Grossi et al., 2019; Bolwerk et al., 2014). This makes us think that the method of VTS and others that use the arts create a comfort zone for participants which stimulates them to repeat the experience. The results of these experiments explain why this and other methods useful for cognitive development can be important for museum institutions. The museum supports training institutions by qualifying itself as a learning environment. This cultural institution can promote the cultural heritage by engaging visitors in stimulating activities. Indeed, the visitors should be satisfied and they will therefore want to return to the museum for further experiences. These considerations are the result of the project that has been developing in Italy since 2014. It has applied the VTS method and other artistic practices as tools for learning in different contexts with extremely positive results that indicate how much the study of cognitive approaches can be useful for heritage promotion, learning development, social inclusion, health, and wellbeing promotion. These experiences were carried out in the field of medical education, schools, studies related to neurological rehabilitation, and for the improvement of the team in hospital care departments. Courses linked to VTS in the curriculum of medicine and nursing sciences, with the collaboration between the Sapienza University and some museums in Rome, has allowed the introduction of these activities into the field of medical education (Ferrara, 2020). It also has permitted the validation of a grid to measure the impact of this method and art activities on the development of soft skills (Ferrara et al., 2020). Interesting results have shown how these activities improve the soft skills important for the health profession and for the realisation of personal wellbeing. Experiences in school since childhood have also stimulated positive reflections on the part of teachers who have used this method in the classroom. The students who were able to find the artworks analised at school in the museums they visited, showed a particular familiarity with the place and the desire to repeat the museum experience. During the research conducted in Italy, questionnaires were administered in schools, universities, or workplaces to analyse the impact of VTS on the participants. It is interesting to read some comments from participants recorded at the end of a meeting or a cycle of activities. All the feedback is very positive.

We report some of the comments of participants:

Results of High School Students

The activity of VTS for me was:

1 Educational, and a way to "have fun" by continuing to learn without making the lesson boring.
2 I start from the consideration that history of art is my favorite subject; but, done in this way, it is something fantastic for me, because we can confront each other and exchange opinions. For me, art is this!
3 I found the VTS activity really interesting, and I didn't think I would let myself be carried away by curiosity in describing the painting, but I was.
4 The activity was useful for me to analyse with my eyes and taught me to discuss a topic intelligently with my classmates.

Would you Like to Repeat this Experience Again?

1 Yes, because it was a way to learn more and better than we already had in our regular art lessons.
2 Yes, I liked it a lot. When you describe a painting, there is no right or wrong answer, so you are free to think and express the emotions that the painting has aroused.
3 Honestly, I really like starting the discovery of a new artwork in this way, because before hearing the opinion of someone who knows more than me, I would like to try to give my own interpretation. Once this is done, it is interesting to learn through the words of an expert.
4 Yes, I think it would be nice to repeat this experience, since in my opinion this is a good way to learn, in particular because it is not boring.

Results of Medicine Students

Leave a Comment on this Course

1 It was a very positive experience. I learned how important the study of art also is in my course. I found it interesting how this can allow me to improve patient observation and develop empathy, through the interpretation of images.
2 I found it a very interesting and constructive experience, because it pushes us to think and have our own individual vision of things and not simply "imposed" as done in schools. It is also useful for teamwork because through observation and comparison of all ideas, we arrive at a common vision, and each of us can enrich the others by demonstrating their ideas.
3 I am happy to have had this experience, which certainly enriched my course of study and gave me an extra tool, as an alternative to traditional teaching.
4 Certainly, it is a positive experience, which is unusual in a medical course and enriches the baggage of clinical methods.

What I Have Learned

1 This course has taught me that a lot of information can be gained from careful and critical observation.
2 Careful observation can help me in diagnosis.
3 Observation was one of the most interesting things, especially because it allowed me to put into practice my critical and *investigative* skills.
4 I learned to observe carefully and critically, to formulate hypotheses by consulting with others. and to integrate different ideas and knowledge.
5 From this practical activity, I learned how important it can be to carefully observe and pay more attention to single details in order to be able to grasp the general sense of a context, without relying too much and exclusively on one's first impressions (sometimes misleading). It was also useful to be able to question oneself, listen to the opinions of others, and be open to discussion.

Result of Nursing Students

What I Have Learned

1 Observe, evaluate, and reflect.
2 At first, I thought it was a waste of time, but I had already changed my mind from the second lesson on, which made me think a lot. I have learned that in every situation the details make the difference and that you should never look superficially.
3 Active listening, not dwelling only on the evidence of appearance, but making further considerations.
4 I learned to put my ideas and those of my peers together in order to achieve a common result.

The experiences in museums with VTS can regard the possible positive consequences on neurological rehabilitation such as those related to some kinds of Alzheimer and Dementia (MacDonald, 2021). The VTS method has been applied in some rehabilitation centres with interesting results for cognitive improvement in brain injuries (Snoek et al., 2019). A particularly interesting result was obtained with activities carried out as part of a project for an experimental thesis in Medicine and Surgery. This regarded the evaluation of possible influences of the visual arts in the modification of sectors of emotional intelligence with patients affected by Lupus Erythematosus (LES) at the Sapienza University of Rome Neurology Department (Perrone, 2020–2021).

The application of the VTS method has allowed us to understand how this can help improve cognitive ability in patients, implementing critical thinking, problem solving, promoting empathy, improving tolerance to ambiguity, and relational skills. The results showed how much the activities with the visual arts can contribute to improve the emotional intelligence quotient and enhance empathy, understanding, and interpretation abilities of oneself and interlocutors' emotional states. The experiences carried out show how the VTS method appears effective in improving the skills of medical-health personnel, guardians, and empathic authors of medical acts intended as diagnosis and therapeutic alliance. Patients can also benefit from it in the fighting of the silent burden of anxiety, which is very widespread in SLE. It can also be a non-pharmacological therapeutic support useful for improving the patients' quality of life, in line with a WHO study on the use of the arts, and therefore also of the visual arts for the development of wellbeing and health promotion.

An interesting experience involved the introduction of these activities within a hospice, in particular by proposing meetings in which the Palliative Care Team participated. The results obtained from a qualitative assessment by the participants made it possible to consider the use of the method as an excellent tool for developing a series of skills that should belong to every health worker, and even more so to those who work in the time of end of human life. Furthermore, VTS has also proved to be a mode of excellence for defining moments of abstraction from the *here and now* and producing that psychophysical wellbeing attributable to the creation of a comfort zone (Ferrara et al., 2021).

The results of these experiences, also by neuroscience studies, indicate cultural heritage as an important vehicle for stimulating our cognitive abilities for learning or for emotional stimuli useful for modifying the activities of our neural areas and promoting our psychophysical wellbeing. It is no coincidence that in some countries (United States and Canada) exposure to and activities with the arts are indicated by physicians for personal care. In other countries, the idea of including these activities in the process is also starting to be promoted as a non-pharmacological intervention. Museum environments can be considered useful for learning and wellbeing, and operators can build relationships with the various sectors of education and health in order to create teams capable of designing useful applications. Many studies have underlined the importance of neuroscience experiments to analyse how the observation of museum objects can influence the neural system. Following this goal, researchers of Sapienza University and Duke University in collaboration with the National Etruscan Museum of Villa Giulia have designed a study to analyse the impact of the vision of artifact on visitors' perception and cognitive reactions. The NeuroArtifact project aims to investigate and evaluate the cognitive impact of archaeological data (empirically and digitally reconstructed) at different scales (site and landscape) and through different technologies. Furthermore, the goal is to measure the neural reaction during a narrative approach (i.e., application of the VTS method) to verify how much the introduction of some activities can help in the cognitive development and in the involvement of the participants[7]. Neuroscience and neuropsychology studies give some indications that can help the understanding of perceptual reactions by helping cultural institutions, on how art is understood, and healthcare institutions, on how to use it as a treatment tool (Chatterjee et al., 2010; Iosa et al., 2021).

It seems to be increasingly useful to create alliances between research, educational, and cultural institutions to find new ways and new strategies for the promotion of cultural heritage and to redefine its important role in society. The results of neuroscience and pedagogical research can be useful for cultural institutions enabling them to understand how to redesign museum spaces. They also help to define new approaches to heritage in order to engage visitors, improve their learning, and their quality of life.

Notes

1 RECOMMENDATION No. R (98) 5 CONCERNING Heritage Education. https://rm.coe.int/16804f1ca1, last accessed 15 December 2021.

2 RECOMMENDATION No. C (198/01) CONCERNING on key competences for lifelong learning 2018. https://eur-lex.europa.eu/legal-content/EN/TXT/PDF/?uri=CELEX:32018H0604(01)&rid=7, last accessed 14 January 2022.

3 World Health Organization. Division of Mental Health (1994). Life skills education for children and adolescents in schools. Pt. 1, Introduction to life skills for psychosocial competence. Pt. 2, Guidelines to facilitate the development and implementation of life skills programmes, 2nd rev. World Health Organization. https://apps.who.int/iris/handle/10665/63552, last accessed 15 December 2021.
4 https://vtshome.org/research/, last accessed 15 January 2022.
5 https://www.thinkingeye.org/shaping-open-minds, last accessed 19 December 2021.
6 Report 67. What is the evidence on the role of the arts in improving health and well-being? A scoping review (2019). World Health Organization, WHO Regional Office for Europe, WHO Europe. 2019. Available from: https://apps.who.int/iris/bitstream/handle/10665/329834/9789289054553-eng.pdf, accessed 17 May 2021.
7 https://neuroartifact.org/, last accessed 13 January 2022.

References

Arnheim, R. (1954). *Art and Visual Perception. A Psychology of the Creative Eye*. Berkeley and Los Angeles: University of California Press.

Bolwerk, A., Mack-Andrick, J., Lang, F.R., Dörfler, A., & Maihöfner, C. (2014). How art changes your brain: Differential effects of visual art production and cognitive art evaluation on functional brain connectivity. *PLOS One*, 9. 10.1371/journal.pone.0101035

Chatterjee, A., Widick, P., Sternschein, R., Smith W.B. II, & Bromberger, B. (2010). The assessment of art attributes. *Empirical Studies of the Arts*, 28(2), 207–222.

Downey, S. (2018). *The Role of Visual Thinking Strategies for Object-Based Learning in Science Education*. In American Geophysical Union Fall Meeting Abstracts (Vol. 2018, pp. ED23E–0952).

Fancourt, D., & Finn, S. (2019). *Health Evidence Network Synthesis Report 67. What Is the Evidence on the Role of the Arts in Improving Health and Well-Being? A Scoping Review* (Report No. 67). WHO Regional Office for Europe. https://apps.who.int/iris/bitstream/handle/10665/329834/9789289054553-eng.pdf

Ferrara, V. (2020). *L'arte come strumento per la formazione in area medica e sanitaria*. Aracne ed.

Ferrara, V., De Santis, S., & Melchiori F.M. (2020). Art for improving skills in medical education: The validation of a scale for measuring the visual thinking strategies method. *La Clinica Terapeutica*, 171(3), 253–259.

Ferrara, V., Vecchi, R., & Pascoli, E. (2021). Visual thinking strategies: Un'altra formazione in cure paliative. In *Si Cura Meglio dove si fa rete – XXVIII Congresso Nazionale SICP* (pp. 327–328). http://sicp2021.com/wordpress/wp-content/uploads/SICP2021_AbstractBook_%20E-PRESENTATION.pdf (last accessed 13 January 2022).

Gardner, H. (1983). *Frames of Mind: The Theory of Multiple Intelligences*. New York: BasicBooks.

Goswami, U. (2004). Neuroscience and education. *British Journal of Educational Psychology*, 74, 1–14.

Grossi, E., Tavano Blessi, G., & Sacco, P.L. (2019). Magic moments: Determinants of stress relief and subjective wellbeing from visiting a cultural heritage site. *Culture, Medicine and Psychiatry*, 43(1), 4–24.

Harris, R.J. (1998). *The Nurture Assumption: Why Children Turn Out the Way They Do*. New York: Free Press.

Housen, A. (2007). Art viewing and aesthetic development: Designing for the viewer. In P. Villenueve (Ed.), *From Periphery to Center: Art Museum Education in the 21st Century*. Reston, Va.: National Art Education Association.

https://neuroartifact.org/, last accessed 13 January 2022.

https://www.thinkingeye.org/shaping-open-minds, last accessed 19 December 2021.

Iosa, M., Aydin, M., Candelise, C., Coda, N., Morone, G., Antonucci, G., Marinozzi, F., Bini, F., Paolucci, S., & Tieri, G. (2021). The Michelangelo effect: Art improves the performance in a virtual reality task developed for upper limb neurorehabilitation. *Frontiers in Psychology*, 11. 10.3389/fpsyg.2020.611956

MacDonald, S. (2021). Using VTS to Build Conversations with People Living with Dementia. https://vtshome.org/2021/06/22/using-vts-to-build-conversations-with-people-living-with-dementia/, last accessed 13 January 2022.

Owens, M.T., & Tanner, K.D. (2017). Teaching as brain changing: Exploring connections between neuroscience and innovative teaching. *CBE—Life Sciences Education*, 16(2). 10.1187/cbe.17-01-0005

Perrone, M.E. (2020–2021). *Intelligenza emotiva nel LES scienza e arti visive: binomio o dicotomia? studio pilota* (Unpublished thesis). La Sapienza University of Rome, Rome.

Snoek, A., Van der Werf, S., & Horst, R.T. (2019). Het effect van Visual Thinking Strategies op visueel neglect, kritisch denken en associatieve gedachteprocessen bij niet-aangeboren hersenletsel: Een N= 1-studie. *Tijdschrift voor Neuropsychologie*, 14(1), 41–49.

Vygotskij, L.S. (1962). *Thought and Language*. Cambridge, MA: MIT Press.

Yenawine, P. (2013). *Visual Thinking Strategies: Using Art to Deepen Learning across School Disciplines*. Cambridge, MA: Harvard Education Press.

Yenawine, P. (2016). *Theory into Practice: The Visual Thinking Strategies*, Conference Paper, https://vtshome.org/wp-content/uploads/2016/08/9Theory-into-Practice.pdf, last accessed 20 December 2021.

11 Unlocking Value in Museums and Art Galleries Through Measuring Wellbeing

Robert M. Sadleir

Public policy makers are struggling to develop a new economic model suited to our "Limits to Growth"[1] world. *Circular economy, ecological economics, natural capitalism, doughnut economics,* and a *new green deal* have been touted as some of the alternative solutions. Such approaches find the legacy measure, gross domestic product (GDP)[2], and its focus on economic inputs or outputs, is a very limited way to estimate the level of prosperity or wealthiness of economies. By focusing on economic inputs and outputs, it fails to consider the cost of externalities to production such as air or water pollution, CO_2 emissions, and broader environmental degradation arising from a culture of consumption and disposal. New, emerging approaches seek to better recognise success and deficits in sustainability through stronger linkages between economic activities to environmental and social contexts. Such approaches have encouraged a rethinking amongst more conservative institutions, such as the OECD to rethink how prosperity might better be measured. A significant development in reshaping the capitalist growth model is the decision by the Organisation for Economic Cooperation and Development (OECD)—the policy think tank for the 38 leading market economies—to take a more holistic approach to measuring national productivity.

At the heart of boundary economics is the usage of resources proportionate to our planet's ability to replenish[3]. Ensuring resource allocation is fair within constraints requires increasing emphasis on local decision making and individual experience sensitive to a hierarchy of needs. The OECD's new approach acknowledges this, adopting a *wellbeing* framework that considers the "functioning of the economic system but also … the diverse experiences and living conditions of people and households"[4]. Two countries, Iceland and New Zealand, have already adopted the OECD framework to measure national performance. Additionally, the New Zealand government established in 2019 a *Wellbeing Budget* where wellbeing is the cornerstone of government policy (NZ Treasury, 2019)[5].

The implications for Museums and Art Galleries (MAGs) will be wide ranging; not just in terms of the measure of performance; but the fostering of wellbeing will shift perceptions overtime, redefining the shape and purpose of cultural institutions and their responsibilities to existing and new stakeholders.

DOI: 10.4324/9781003304531-11

The scope of this chapter is to provide an overview of this context and possible outcomes to MAGs. For example, how the broader parameters of wellbeing will shape MAGs fit with communities and cities as well as the obligations to mitigate the culminating anxiety and stress faced by citizens during this age of transition. Such a context suggests MAGs will become an important component of well-being infrastructure in future—SMART(er)—cities. It also suggests from a brain science perspective that MAGs, as a source of wellbeing generation, can foster brain capital since stress-related emotional behaviour can be shifted from a fight or flee response of the amygdala to the intelligence, fertile imagination, and awareness that form the mind (New Scientist, 2017).

Wellbeing and Existing Performance Measurement

The OECD framework of indicators laid out in Table 11.1 offers a more comprehensive approach to measuring national performance. With MAGs being a part of the national economy, it is worth understanding these measures and how they might be considered when determining the value of museums and other cultural institutions and their impact.

Currently, most MAGs do not directly consider all these indicators though some may be measured by proxy. The baseline tool for measurement of museum outcomes are mostly related to their collections and audience or visitor surveys, some measures of environmental impact have been introduced in recent years. In relation to visitors, key performance indicators are often still rather crude such as: visitor foot fall, visitor profiles, revenue from exhibits, cafés, shops, or economic impact studies[7]. Although impact is much discussed, the focus of measuring tends to be on growth rather than impact and its type, and does often not consider the full costings of growth. Moreover, such indicators "privatise" the benefit value of museums, internalising value generated by MAGs and neglecting the broader benefit (or cost) to surrounds, communities, and cities. In many ways, MAGs are measuring their own domestic productivity rather than wellbeing generation. Focussing on such a limited ecosystem for cultural institutions is myopic and in a manner that is no longer aligned with the development of a sustainable economy. It suggests a zero-sum (win/lose) approach to resource sharing.

Table 11.1 OECD lead indicators: Current wellbeing[6]

Income and wealth	*Health*
Work and job quality Environment Housing Safety Subjective wellbeing	Civic engagement Work–life balance Knowledge and skills Social connections

Furthermore, such approaches are not so good at measuring "intangibles" and developing proxies to capture these benefits. Partially, this is due to the manner in which data is captured and how it is interpreted to manage and develop museums. An example of this is audience surveys. These surveys are designed to capture the visitor experience; however, the methodology and approach of audience research firms is often constrained by industry norms such that surveys are designed in a way to capture a point in time. A dynamic approach would recognise the compounding utility (or disutility) from a flow of activities undertaken during a visit and capture the participants emergent experience. As well, many questionnaires are less good at measuring *impact* of an experience, making it more difficult for *machine learning* and *deep Learning* modelling approaches to derive predictive outcomes and, in my opinion, deny MAGs a better opportunity to mitigate risks, reduce uncertainty, and realise opportunities.

The challenge lies in measurement, the methodologies, and realising the value-added arising is not static nor discrete. By using data and algorithms, we can develop pathways to wellbeing within museums and galleries that enhance the wellbeing of its visitors, as the author is currently exploring in a pilot project.

Case study: Measuring Wellbeing via Activity Flow: Christchurch Art Gallery Te Puna O Waiwhetū, New Zealand

To address this challenge and understand better pathways to wellbeing, QWB Limited,[8] a New Zealand company, developed an approach measuring wellbeing generated by interaction between visitors and art gallery resources. Modelling existing audience survey data from *Christchurch Art Gallery Te Puna O Waiwhetū* in New Zealand (CAGTPOW), the firm sought to understand how visitor actions and activities created wellbeing during visits.

Thorough analysis of over 4,000 museum visitors to the gallery in 2020–2021 CAGTPOW was shown to increase a sense of wellbeing by engaging visitors in a series of interconnected activities[9]. For example, if visitors attended an exhibit and then visited the museum shop, their sense of wellbeing increased by 12%. If they also spent time in the gallery's café, then they could increase their overall sense of wellbeing to up to 48% per visit. The yardstick for wellbeing measurement was a proxy statement: "My day feels very satisfying". Those that responded positively, were more likely to have undertaken a series of activities rather than one isolated act.

As the audience surveys used in the analysis were not designed to measure wellbeing, understanding the underlying cause(s) of wellbeing is unclear. Could it be that the utility brought about by visiting the café was due to the quality of the food and/or drink? A social connection? A special moment? From the data available, we simply don't know. But, suggesting buying a trinket at the shop contributes to a heightened sense of wellbeing is highly possible. After all, the word *souvenir* in French means "memory" and anecdotal observation of the pricing of souvenirs (such as postcards, calendars, T-shirts, mugs, books, and keyrings) suggests the majority reflect visitors are prepared to pay a small, incremental margin for a keepsake. So, our findings are nominally validated by market prices!

From a macro perspective, a question arises: can the wellbeing generated by the MAGs be distributed to the broader community, cities, regions, and states?

Generating Wellbeing to Unlock Value

Wellbeing is "wealth"—a store of value—to society enhancing its resilience and contributes to return on investment on social impact infrastructure such as MAGs. Wealth is synonymous with wellbeing. Indeed, the word stems from the Saxon word "*Weal*" akin to "well" (The Annals of the American Academy of Political and Social Science, 1891).

So, the aim is to recreate a *commonweal*—a general welfare—building *healthy* community, and cities, where MAGs can foster wellbeing for individual visitors and the broader community to facilitate resilience and human flourishing. Whilst MAGs may only be able to measure their wellbeing benefit at the scale of community or city, the benefit could be aggregated to a regional or nation-state level depending upon the number of MAGs engaging the wellbeing framework. Value is not just limited to economic productivity such as jobs and income, but wellbeing can unlock value through identifying indicators such as social connections, environment, civil engagement, education, time-life balance, and safety that may have been neglected, undervalued, or under-resourced in the past to more comprehensively increase overall benefit. The OECD has thereby created a process for unlocking greater potential and wealth for museums that is currently under exploited. In the process, MAGs may engage new stakeholders whose attributes may complement wellbeing measures. For example, MAGs may look to extend relationships with local parks as studies show a link between nature and outdoor activity and improved health (Hardman, 2021). Will they maintain their existing profile or embrace new insights that may adapt their character?

Will Museums and Art Galleries Become Living Rooms?

To comprehend how MAGs could change, let's explore further one of the OECD's indicators: *housing*. Housing, hitherto, has been marginal to art galleries core mission. How can an indicator like housing be conceptualised to add value to MAGs? In the context of the last 20 years, we have seen a rapid rise in housing prices in the urban areas of most OECD economies further exacerbated by COVID-19. In the last 12 months, the average annual price change in houses across 55 countries was 9.2% (Romei, 2021). This is leading to a housing cost overburden where at least 20% of household income is spent on housing needs[10]. The rising cost of housing is also reflected in the average home shrinking in size[11]. MAGs can offset some of this burden through the provision of accessible public space in urban areas where families can escape cramped living conditions by temporarily accessing space and, moreover, facilities to provide additional wellbeing benefits.

This benefit is not seen as a primary mission for MAGs today. However, accessing public spaces in MAGs could reduce energy usage in homes and through provision of reliable Wi-Fi, could enhance social connection activities such as VOIP[12] calls to friends and family, and provide infrastructure (lighting, heating, Wi-Fi, etc.) for students to do homework, thus benefitting their education. This in turn can reduce expenditure on utilities improving families disposable income. In short, families can transfer some of the burden of housing costs to MAGs. It should be added that museums with their security and monitoring systems and health and safety protocols are relatively safe spaces. This offers questions of reappraising and prioritising resources in the arts and culture sector and what it means for a MAG as an urban stakeholder. This provides an opportunity to reframe and increase the perceived value of MAGs not just for individuals, but for the wider community, and to explore how this could open up new funding and resourcing avenues. It also opens up the prospect of developing wellbeing management systems within cultural institutions[13]. It also means by providing such benefits MAGs can have greater claim to budget funding beyond that allocated to the arts and culture sector.

Directors of MAGs may be circumspect about their buildings being perceived as "living rooms" but here its worth remembering the French composer, Erik Satie, who treated music as "furniture" and composed as such. The legacy of his *furniture music* can be found in elevator music and "on-hold" music on telephones bringing music to spaces previously unimagined[14]. It also changed perceptions as to what constitutes music and in the longer term may have contributed to the evolution of new music genres and enhancing the accessibility of music to both a broader audience and musicians.

How will MAGs evolve within the setting of wellbeing? Charles-Édouard Jeanneret—Le Corbusier—the Swiss-French architect once described the house as *a machine*[15]. Perhaps, we may view MAGs in the future as: "incubators of wellbeing for living in" and think of connecting MAGs to a wellbeing grid within cities, offsetting some of the negative externalities (stress) of urban life.

MAGs and a Healthier SMART City

Historically, MAGs in urban locations are components of cities and can, if properly integrated, regenerate urban environments. The *exemplaire* is the Guggenheim Museum in Bilbao, which through its design, shifted the perception of Bilbao as a post-industrial city in decline to a modern tech hub. Similarly, wellbeing can build *resilience* that can be harnessed by SMART cities enabling them to maintain functionality in a changeable world[16] (International Standards Organisation, 2019). This is not just about integrating transport networks but also enhancing responsiveness and interaction between citizens and administrators and addressing social and health matters. For example, in

New Zealand, an early adoptee of OECD wellbeing guidelines, about 80% of the population over 15 years old have experience of mental distress personally or among people they know (Kvalsvig, 2018). The *Health Promotion Agency* in New Zealand is looking into how "wellbeing" can offset or reduce mental distress and the Government has made mental health a priority in its wellbeing budget.

Chapter 1 discussed a range of museum initiatives that benefit health with examples of art therapy, art on prescription, "slow looking", and mindfulness. Indeed, our CAGTPOW pilot project was able to illustrate the sense of wellbeing generated by MAGs. An analysis of over 1,350 visitors to CAGTPOW during 2020–2021 showed that 80% had "no or little anxiety" and 75% felt happy (see Diagram 11.1)[17].

The findings suggest that Art Galleries have the potential to contribute to healthier cities.

Does that mean in future MAGs can build a business case for funding from a national health budget? In order to achieve some form of resource allocation from the health sector, the health benefit will have to be supported by scientific study. But, it should be noted that, in the United Kingdom, social prescribing as a form of health care is growing rapidly and, by 2023/2024, over two million people will be benefiting from such arrangements[18]. Social prescribing is a form of personalised healthcare "focusing on 'what matters to me' and taking a holistic approach to people's health and wellbeing. This health process can connect people to community groups and statutory services for practical and emotional support"[19]. Some examples and evidence are provided in section 1.8.

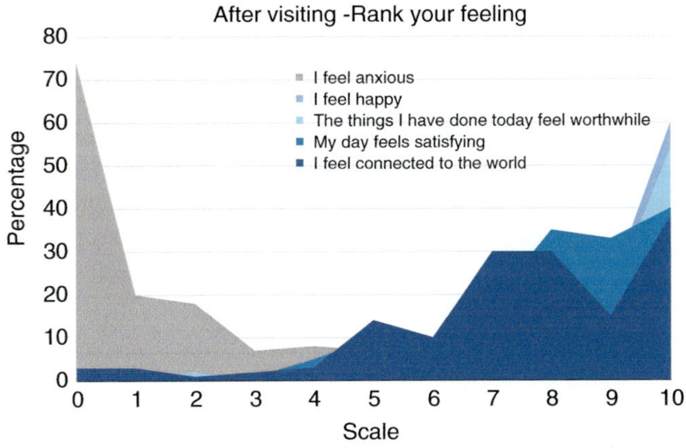

Diagram 11.1 Christchurch Art Gallery Te Puna O Waiwhetū, New Zealand and Happiness.

Brain Capital versus Digital Disruption—The Dilemma of Brain-friendly Museums

Refocussing holistically on people's health and wellbeing coincides with advances in brain science giving us improved tools for understanding how a brain works. Once upon a time, these instruments were crude but, as the futurist Ray Kurzweil observes, modern scanning technology has improved spatial and temporal resolution, price-performance, and bandwidth allowing us to accumulate data on the activity of the brain (Kurzweil, 2006).

The rapid development of neuroscience and its application beyond neural mechanisms to understand the human psyche and nature has led to what Francisco Mora labels a "neuroculture" where understanding the brain improves the nature of our society (Huston & Nadal, 2015). Already, economists see the potential of *Brain Capital.* The OECD in its exploration of new economic challenges has showcased a *Brain Capital Grand Strategy* where productivity in society is strengthened through the acquiring the skills to optimise brain health (Smith et al., 2021).

This strategic endeavour to structure and track investments that protect brain health and produce brain skills would appear to bring an additional dimension of value to MAGs, facilitating their role as engines for SMART and healthy cities; and human flourishing.

However, the neuroculture is occurring at the same time as the digital revolution where artificial intelligence is making machines capable of mind work (Agar, 2019). A challenge, therefore, facing *brain-friendly museums* is reconciling digital disruption (which values optimisation and automation of tasks), and with it the increased likelihood of losses of livelihoods and jobs, whilst acknowledging (big) data and technology can create opportunities and generate pathways to enhance wellbeing for individuals, communities, and cities. How can these two competing interests between what is labelled as the *digital economy* and the *social economy* be reconciled? Agar see this as a challenge and proposes defining a boundary between the two types of economy based on value: efficiency should be driven by the digital and *humanness* should be the defining marker for work assigned to human beings (Agar, 2019). So, Agar suggests a division of labour between the brain-friendly component of a museum and the digital dimension.

There is scope for something more compelling: a hybrid approach where the digital dimension allows MAGs to better understand the impact of their resources, identifying not just how to use resources efficiently but also strategically to generate and enhance wellbeing of its stakeholders. The humanness or brain-friendly component is in designing and creating the process, and developing strategies to access new capacity, dimensions, and resources to realise the vision. In short, building brain-friendly museums is about expanding the boundaries of possibilities and opportunities. Afterall, a healthy brain is nurtured by context in which humans interact at all levels socially, economically, physically, culturally, and environmentally (Smith et al., 2021).

Conclusion: MAGs Are Wealth Generators of the Future

The OECD has come up with a more comprehensive approach to measuring national performance—"wellbeing". Wellbeing measures not just jobs and income but uses other indicators such as social connections, environment, civil engagement, education, time-life balance, safety, etc., to comprehensively measure impact and societal progress. From the perspective of MAGs, the OECD framework allows new dimensions to recreate themselves and generate value beyond the relatively crude performance indicators existing in the arts and culture sector today. In the process, we have a foundation for human flourishing, extending from the institutions into the community, city, and nation. Capturing the value of the diverse, positive benefits of museums for wellbeing (as quoted by Falk in the introductory chapter, section 1.8) has significant implications for not only fostering long-term wealth for museums themselves but also at a macro level to improve the health and resilience of cities. And, if brain-friendly museums can harness brain science to develop brain capital, we have potential to build SMART Cities that are *commonweal* generators to compensate for the constraints of a net-zero carbon emission economy.

Notes

1 To understand the constraints of such an economic environment read: see the Club of Rome Report: *The Limits to Growth*.
2 Gross Domestic Product—GDP—is perceived as a measure of prosperity, and an indicator to determine whether a country and their citizens are successful or failing. See: Masood, E. (2021). *GDP: The World's Most Powerful Formula and Why It Must Now Change*. London: Icon Books.
3 The Global Footprint Network estimates Earth Overshoot Day, the day each year in which our planet falls into a resource deficit due to over exploitation of resources measured by dwindling resources and increases in atmospheric carbon dioxide. In 2021, the date was July 29. https://www.footprintnetwork.org/our-work/earth-overshoot-day/
4 https://www.oecd.org/statistics/better-life-initiative.htm
5 The first New Zealand *Wellbeing Budget* placed priority on mental health, reducing child poverty and domestic violence, supporting Māori and Pasifika culture as well as supporting the economy and productivity. Minister of Finance, https://www.treasury.govt.nz/publications/wellbeing-budget/wellbeing-budget-2019.
6 https://www.oecd.org/statistics/measuring-well-being-and-progress.html.
7 This is not to say that wellbeing is not being discussed within the context of MAGs. See Falk, J.H. (2021). *The Value of Museums: Enhancing Societal Well-Being*. Lanham, MD: Rowman & Littlefield.
8 The author of this chapter, Robert Sadleir, is a Director of QWB Lab Ltd.
9 As stated the proxy question to measure wellbeing was: "My day feels very satisfying". The responses were then mapped/modelled to activities. The data did not consider respondents income. Nor were we able to understand from the survey data available why there was a significant increase in wellbeing from visiting the café. It may be also be that the CAGTPOW café at the time of the survey was a hybrid café restaurant.
10 OECD Regions at a Glance, 2016.
11 https://www.labcwarranty.co.uk/blog/are-britain-s-houses-getting-smaller-new-data/, accessed 21 January 2022.

12 VOIP—Voice Over Internet Protocol.
13 Adopting a wellbeing management systems approach is beneficial for manifold reasons—not least the complexity of the system can be determined by each organisation. See: Sadleir, R. (2021). Designing a human rights management standard. In J. Gomez & R. Ramcharan (Eds.), *Business and Human Rights in Asia: Duty of the State to Protect* (pp. 247–248). London, New York and Shanghai: Palgrave Macmillan Singapore.
14 https://www.theguardian.com/music/2016/jun/25/erik-satie-vexations-furniture-music, accessed 22 January 2022.
15 https://www.open.edu/openlearn/history-the-arts/history/heritage/le-corbusier, accessed 22 January 2022.
16 This is the International Standards Organisation (ISO) interpretation of a SMART city see ISO standard: *ISO 37122:2019 – Sustainable cities and communities*.
17 These findings were from the analysis of over 1,350 audience surveys taken after a visit to CAGTPOW during 2020–2021. After a visit, 80% of those surveyed had no or little anxiety (based on a scoring from 0 to 10 where 0 to 2 was considered low) and 75% felt happy (where happy was defined as a scoring between 8 and 10).
18 https://www.england.nhs.uk/personalisedcare/social-prescribing/
19 Ibidem.

References

Agar, N. (2019). *How to be Human in the Digital Economy*. London: MIT Press.

Arnsten, A., Mazure, C., & Sinha, R. (2021). This is your Brain in Meltdown, *Scientific American*, 306, 48–53.

Bidgood, J. (2017, 11 March). How to Get the Brain to Like Art. *The New York Times*, https://www.nytimes.com/2017/03/11/arts/how-to-get-the-brain-to-like-art.html

Cormen, T.H., Leiserson, C.E., Rivest, R.L., & Stein, C. (2009). *Introduction to Algorithms*. Cambridge, MA: MIT Press.

Cossins, D. (2020, 12 December). Here's Looking at You. *New Scientist*. https://www.newscientist.com/article/mg17022902-100-heres-looking-at-you/

Cossins, D. (2021, 16 June). The Essential Guide to the Algorithms that Run Your Life. *New Scientist*. https://www.newscientist.com/article/mg25033390-200-the-essential-guide-to-the-algorithms-that-run-your-life/#ixzz7KW6vmwHs

Eagleman, D. (2015). *The Brain: The Story of You*. Edinburgh: Canongate Books.

Falk, J.H. (2021). *The Value of Museums: Enhancing Societal Well-Being*. Lanham, MD: Rowman & Littlefield.

Hardman, I. (2021). *The Natural Health Service*. London: Atlantic Books.

Hopkins, R. (2008). *The Transition Handbook: From Oil Dependency to Local Resilience*. White River Junction, Vt.: Chelsea Green Books.

https://www.business.govt.nz/risks-and-operations/health-and-safety/mental-health-workplace/

https://www.england.nhs.uk/personalisedcare/social-prescribing

https://www.footprintnetwork.org/our-work/earth-overshoot-day/

https://www.labcwarranty.co.uk/blog/are-britain-s-houses-getting-smaller-new-data/

https://www.oecd.org/naec/brain-capital/

https://www.oecd.org/statistics/measuring-well-being-and-progress.htm

https://www.open.edu/openlearn/history-the-arts/history/heritage/le-corbusier

https://www.theguardian.com/music/2016/jun/25/erik-satie-vexations-furniture-music

https://www.theguardian.com/science/2021/aug/15/the-hidden-sense-shaping-your-wellbeing-interoception

https://www.treasury.govt.nz/publications/wellbeing-budget/wellbeing-budget-2019
https://www.iso.org/standard/69050.html

Huston, J.P., & Nadal, M. (2015). *Art, Aesthetics and the Brain.* Oxford: Oxford University Press.

Kurzweil, R. (2006). *The Singularity Is Near: When Humans Transcend Biology.* New York: Penguin Books.

Kvalsvig, A. (2018). *Wellbeing and Mental Distress in Aotearoa New Zealand: Snapshot 2016.* Wellington: Health Promotion Agency.

Lee, M., Kubzansky, L., & VanderWeele, T. (2021). *Measuring Well-being: Interdisciplinary Perspectives from the Social Sciences and the Humanities.* Oxford: Oxford University Press.

Masood, E. (2021). *GDP: The World'S Most Powerful Formula and Why It Must Now Change.* London: Icon Books.

Max-Neef, M. (1991). *Human Scale Development: Conception, Application and Reflections.* New York: The Apex Press.

New Scientist. (2017). *How Your Brain Works: Inside the Most Complicated Object in the Known Universe.* London: John Murray Learning.

Romei, V. (2021, 14 September). Global House Prices Rise at Fastest Pace since 2005, report says. *Financial Times.* https://www.ft.com/content/0a2b8ed2-55bc-44b9-82e4-a325291154d6

Sadleir, R. (2021). Designing a Human Rights Management Standard. In J. Gomez, & R. Ramcharan (Eds.), *Business and Human Rights in Asia: Duty of the State to Protect* (pp. 247–248). London, New York and Shanghai: Palgrave Macmillan Singapore.

Smith, E., Ali, D., Wilkerson, B., Dawson, W.D., Sobowale, K., Reynolds, C., Berk, M., Lavretsky, H., Jeste, D., Chee, H., Soares, J.C., Aragam, G., Wainer, Z., Manji, H. K., Licinio, J., Lo, A.W., Storch, E., Fu, E., Leboyer, M., Tarnanas, I., Ibanez, A., Manes, F., Caddick, S., Fillit, H., Abbott, R., Robertson, I.H., Chapman, S.B., Au, R., Altimus, C.M., Hynes, W., Brannelly, P., Cummings, J., & Eyre, H.A. (2021). A brain capital grand strategy: Toward economic reimagination. *Mol Psychiatry*, 26, 3–22.

Tuttle, C. (1891). A study in economic theory. *The Annals of the American Academy of Political and Social Science*, 1, 615–634. https://www.jstor.org/stable/1008953

West, G. (2018). *Scale: The Universal Laws of Life and Death in Organisms, Cities, and Companies.* London: Weidenfield & Nicolson.

Winner, E. (2019). *How Art Works.* Oxford: Oxford University Press.

12 The Museum's Mind

A Genetic Code for Cultural Exhibitions[1,2]

Maurizio Forte and Eva Pietroni

Introduction

In Bateson's cybernetics, the process to perceive information is based on the relations we create between us, the environment, and our feedback (Bateson, 1972) (mutual interaction with the environment). A museum and a cultural exhibition are represented by an information context; therefore, in this sense, it is possible to consider a museum like an ecosystem, an informative environment constituted by inter-relations. All these relations constitute the genetic code of the museum because, through alphabetic connections ("syntagma"—Antinucci, 2004), they become cultural transmitters. It means that this informative ecosystem represents a map in cybernetic sense; apart from the original plans and exhibition projects of the museum curators, architects, communication designers, etc., this ecosystem lives according to its cultural relations.

According to Francesco Antinucci (2004) "one should create a museum where the artefacts are not paradigmatic elements but they can be put in syntagmatic relation, so that they are not signs to analyse, but communicating signs". The communication system of a cultural exhibition depends on all the possible ecological net-relations; this system represents the *museum's mind,* namely, the faculty to process and transmit knowledge and information.

In this paper, we will try to suggest a new approach for studying and describing the *museum's mind* and, finally, to create a virtual reality system dedicated to the simulation of possible different *museum's minds* (new artificial living museums). In testing the faculty to create new *museum's minds,* additional and diverse cultural relation will be investigated. We define the first investigation on the museum cultural ontologies "anamnesis" (Figure 12.1).

On the basis of this anamnesis, we are able to create an artificial cybernetic environment of simulation (VR) aimed to reconstruct the *museum's mind,* that is, the communication system for a cultural transmission.

Museum's Communication

According to Bateson's (1972): "without context there is no communication" and "the map is not the territory"[3]. Namely, the map is the code/alphabet for

DOI: 10.4324/9781003304531-12

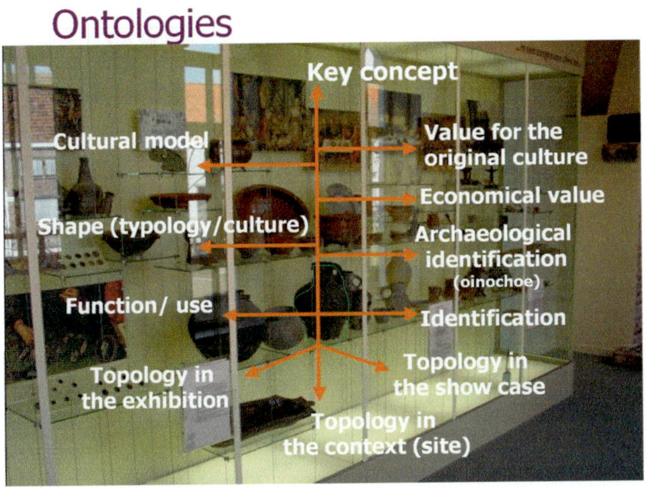

Figure 12.1 Example of Museum Showcase Showing Possible Relations of an Archaeological Artefact (Anamnesis).

interpreting information while the context represents the communication system. According to this scenario, the museum is a map or a territory? It is a territory (not-coded) because it removes and de-contextualises artefacts and items from the original context, but it is also a map because it re-creates a new context/alphabet in the topology/ontology of the exhibition (Forte et al., 2002). We have to emphasise that each original context is autopoietic and self-organised (Maturana & Varela, 1980) (in this sense, all the artefacts would have their understandable maps) but the "musealised" objects lose their previous communicating signs for acquiring new shapes of cultural transmission. If the code/map is wrong, we do not have any kind of cultural learning, feedback, or perception, so we can see only taxonomies but not "syntagma".

The more the information enhances connectivity, the more the symbolic associations grow up, and so the possibility for visitors to assimilate and elaborate cultural contents. The creation of an informative network increases the faculty of communication of each single cultural item/artefact. Therefore, in order to allow a correct comprehension of its meaning, we have to create the opportunity for the visitors to interpret this code. To make an object readable means to integrate its shape to perceive it according to correct spatial proportions; subsequently, the object has to be reintegrated in its original context. The final theoretical aim is to understand contents and contexts of cultural transmission of any artefact: what kind of cultural message did ancient people perceive from the object? What do we know about their mind? What kind of message did the author or the exhibitors want to transmit? What kind of relations there are between contemporary and ancient minds? How does a "sign" communicate through different cultures and times?

A Methodological Approach to Create a "genetic code" of the Museum

We have to imagine the communication process like a cone where at the top we find the object/artefact and, in the successive levels (towards the base), all the relations correlated with its context (psychological, social, philosophical, historical, symbolic, and so on). In order to explain and to identify these relations, one needs to show the key informative concepts in the museum's space and, starting from this basis, to create a communication system.

The first phase to construct an integrated project of museum communication is the anamnesis (Figure 12.1). We have mentioned earlier that the museum is a map, so it is necessary to understand how this map has been conceived and constructed. To do so, we will have to: analyse the typology of the objects in order to understand why they have been disposed in that particular order; understand how they are interpreted; and consider if their position is functional to their meaning. Subsequently, we can identify categories of evaluation that can help us build a sort of genetic code of the museum and see if objects become readable, contextualised, and thematised, according to different kinds of relations (Figures 12.1 and 12.2). We define a genetic code to the process of evolution of the cybernetic relations of all the artefacts in the space-time.

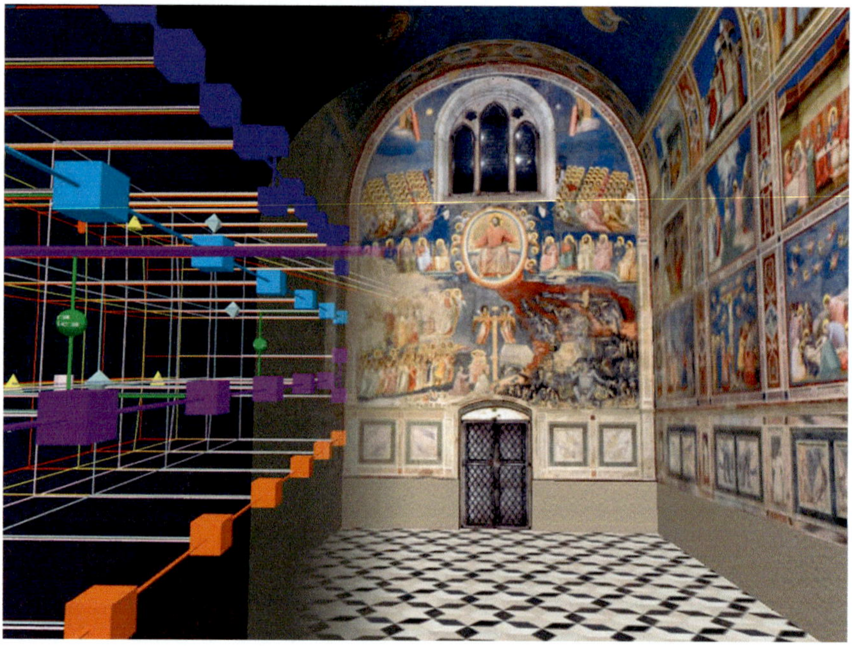

Figure 12.2 Cybermap of the Virtual Museum of the Scrovegni Chapel (CNR-ITABC, 2003).

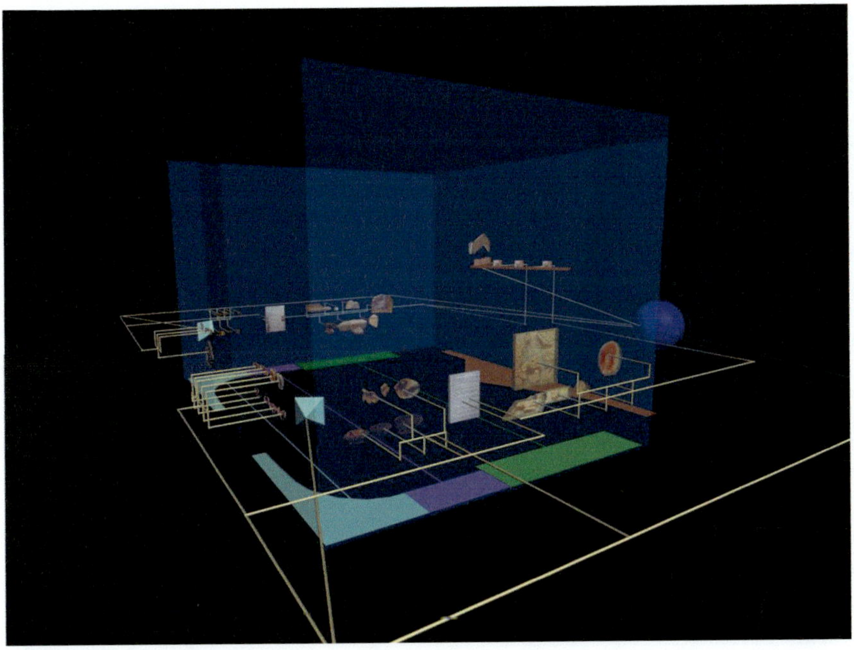

Figure 12.3 An Initial Experiment of Cybermap of the Etruscan Archaeological Museum of Castiglion Fiorentino (Room of the Temple).

At the end of this interpretative process, we should be able to reconstruct networks of relations between information in and out of the museum (Figure 12.2). On this basis, we will be able to recreate an integrated project of communication, according to the concept that the museum is an ecosystem (Figures 12.3 and 12.4).

The Virtual *Museum's Mind*

The VR application we are developing is aimed to visualise in three dimensions a museum cybermap (Figures 12.3 and 12.4).

The map is a symbolic environment, a cognitive space, where contents are represented through abstract codes: simple geometries will suggest objects; different colours can be associated to particular properties of items according to their similarities, affinities, or correspondences. At the beginning, the spatial organisation of the cybermap represents the actual topology of the exhibition: objects are grouped and placed in the virtual space according to their real disposition in the rooms and in the showcases. In addition, it is possible to switch to other different relations, creating new maps according to the type of analogies to highlight (e.g., typologies, use, context, material, theme, and so on). The cybermap is the metaphor of the space-map of the museum: the plan

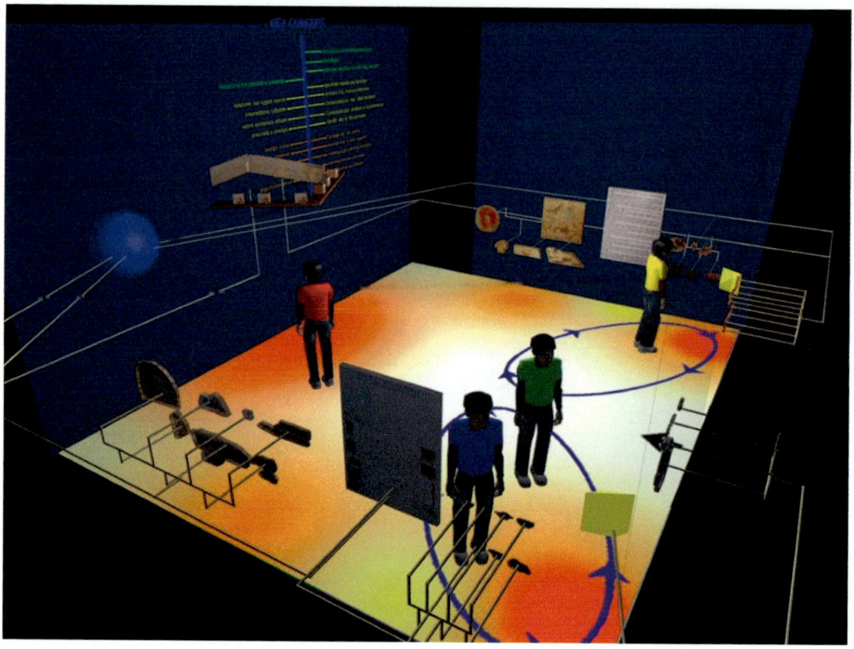

Figure 12.4 Cybermap of the Temple Room (Museum of Castiglion Fiorentino): Gradient of cOlors Represent Different Levels of Attraction. Red Areas Are the Most Attractive, in Correspondence with the Video Installations (Storytelling Attractors), and with the Reconstruction of the Temple's Roof. The Relations are of Circular Type around Video Installations, because Their Communication Is Possible Any Time, Unlike the Fruition of Exhibited Objects (Museum Path).

of each room is extruded; and the walls become transparent and represent "branches" of the spatial relations within the environment. Real places of the territorial context are shown by other simple geometries and colours, according to the identity of places (sacral, civic, collective, commercial, and domestic areas; Figure 12.3). In interacting with the cyber map, we can move in real time through the objects, in the virtual space. When we stop in front of an object, we begin to "focalise" the object, penetrating progressively into the hierarchical levels of description and content. For instance, the whole integrated shape will emerge from the fragment, the context will emerge from the integrated shape, and finally the key cultural concept will embrace all the sub-levels of information. Objects/artefacts are connected by vectors visualising all the possible relations between the museum, the territory, and other sites or contexts. The final result is a network of interactive vectors/relations connecting the inside and the outside, the actual exhibition, hierarchical maps, taxonomic maps, and other possible different contexts of relations (Figures 12.3 and 12.4). In this way, one can edit spaces, move geometries, and create new links and concepts; in short, it will be possible to create a new museum alphabet with its genetic code.

A possible solution to draw and visualise relations among objects can be to organise a sort of "metrics" of analogies. Because the cultural items have different kinds of analogies, typology, shape, chronology, use, value, material, original context, symbolic content, etc., it is possible to evaluate the degree of adherence to each type of analogy, assigning a value between 0 and 1 (0 = no adherence, 1 = adherence). Every analogy is a property described by three parameters, assigned to Cartesian axis x, y, and z. For instance, the property "shape" can be described by parameters of width (x), height (y), and concavity (z). The adherence to these parameters will give a specific position on the Cartesian axis and in the 3D space. Objects with identical values of adherence will have the same position in the 3D space, according to identifiable shapes (e.g., to an "oinochoe", a "plate", an "olla", and so on). If a property needs more than three parameters to be described, a space with "n" dimensions should be introduced. Finally, the system will configure automatically the cyber map, according to the type of requested relations: so, distances and positions of objects in the space will be very precise, because they are calculated by mathematical metrics. When the cyber map will change its configuration, according to the new metrics, the software engine will automatically access to its index in order to select those images matching that concept. The cyber map will look like an intelligent creature, an expert system representing the *museum's mind*, able to change, step by step, according to our movement and interaction inside this symbolic space (Annunziato & Pierucci, 2006).

Conclusions

In a cybernetic frame, the museum is an ecosystem, a context of cultural relations representing its *mind*, its genetic code. In order to understand how a museum communicates, it is fundamental to identify all the cultural relations of exhibited artefacts; these relations are created apart from museum curators and designers' intentions, because they represent genetic cultural transmission codes. Each artefact communicates according to its topology, ontology, and concept, in short, by all the correlations we are able to identify. In its original context, it was autopoietic, so its communicating sign was understandable and transmittable, but, in a museum context (a new map and a new territory), currently, it is out of frame, deprived of its relational context.

Therefore, our preliminary research has been directed in two directions: museum anamnesis and virtual museum mind. In the museum anamnesis, we have investigated the current relations produced by museum exhibitions, by creating a virtual cybermap, able to visualise and show in real time the key cultural relations. Then, we have conceived the virtual *museum's mind*, namely an artificial environment, a new cybermap representing possible relations organised by "metrics" of analogies. This virtual simulation will permit to measure and to evaluate the level of cultural matching between artefacts relations, their original context, the old "map" (once autopoietic), and the new "map" (museum exhibition and communication system). As first preliminary case studies, we have chosen the Scrovegni Chapel Project (Forte et al., 2002) (Figure 12.2) and the archaeological museum of Castiglion Fiorentino (Figures 12.3 and 12.4).

Following this approach, in the next future, we estimate to complete the cybermap system in order to construct flexible VR software for museum exhibitions, both for a cognitive anamnesis of what is existing (evaluating phase) and for a virtual simulation of new exhibitions. In this way, it will be possible to test, in artificial but living environments, the faculty to produce additional forms of cultural transmission based on the eco-relations and neural networks. Could we answer, one day, the question: how is the museum's mind?

Notes

1 Originally published in: https://www.academia.edu/203797/The_Museum_s_Mind_A_Genetic_Code_for_Cultural_Exhibitions_Maurizio_Forte_Eva_Pietroni copyright owned by the authors.
2 This paper summarises also some results of our didactic experiences made during the Master "Management of culture and art" (Rovereto, Italy, July, 2005). A special thank is due to Dr. Mauro Annunziato for his important contribution to this discussion.
3 *Mind and Nature: A Necessary Unit.* (1979). New York: Dutton.

References

Annunziato, M., & Pierucci, P. (2006). Emergenza e biodiversità della forma: l'estetica dello scambio tra vita reale ed artificiale. In *Proceedings of the Second Italian Workshop of Artificial Life*, Rome, 2–5 March.

Antinucci, F. (2004). *Comunicare il museo*. Roma-Bari: Edizioni Laterza.

Bateson, G. (1972). *Steps to Ecology of Mind*. San Francisco: Chandler Press.

Forte, M., Pietroni, E., & Rufa, C. (2002). Musealising the Virtual: The Virtual Reality Project of the Scrovegni Chapel of Padua. In VSMM 2002, Proceedings of *The Eighth International Conference on Virtual Systems And Multimedia — "Creative And Digital Culture"*. Gyeonggju, Korea, 25–27 September 2002, 43–52.

Maturana, H., & Varela, F. (1980). Autopoiesis and cognition: The realization of the living. In R.S. Cohen, & M.W. Wartofsky (Eds.), *Boston Studies in the Philosophy of Science* (vol. 42). Dordrecht: D. Reidel Publishing Co.

13 Virtual Reality and Neuroarchaeology

Visual Perception and Cognition of an Archaeological Excavation

Maurizio Forte, Leonard E. White, Kate Straneva, and Sean Woytowitz

Introduction

The definition of neuroarchaeology was originally suggested by Colin Renfrew and Lambros Malafouris (Renfrew & Malafouris, 2008) as a new research field at the intersection of archaeology, cognitive science, and neuroscience.

However, this original background is actually related to a more theoretical debate rather than a heuristic search for new methods of investigation and experimental activities. In this chapter, we will consider neuroarchaeology as a specific research and experimental field applying the methods of digital videography and cognitive neuroscience, such as eye-tracking systems, virtual reality, and EEG devices, to better understand the embodied sensorimotor and neurocognitive experiences of persons engaging with archaeological artefacts and sites. The digital case study creates a virtual scenario where specific neuroscientific experiments can be placed and, in the future, be compared with empirical situations in the field.

More in detail, the main research question of this study is: do naive observers and experienced archaeologists observe a digital recreation of an archaeological excavation using the same oculomotor strategies for visual engagement? Secondary questions include: do they share the same learning curve? Are they attracted by the same shapes, colours, textures, or visual patterns? How do they approach a virtual/visual walkthrough of the trench?

An archaeological excavation in progress is a very chaotic and complex stage where data and information are based on strata, layers, monumental structures, and archaeological material. It is very difficult in this context to connect and memorise spatial information and to mentally visualise reconstructed buildings and architectures. This cognitive activity requires a bottom-up and top-down approach: bottom-up is based on the recognition of meaningful structures and archaeological data in the field; top-down is based on the reconstructive process and mental comparison of these data with graphic images, models, and other classified case studies. The combination of bottom-up and top-down approach builds our interpretation.

DOI: 10.4324/9781003304531-13

Spatial Embodiment, Memory, and Sensorimotor Skills

Spatial embodiment refers to the grounding of cognitive processes in the operations of our sensory and motor systems (Barsalou, 2008; Davis et al., 2021). This view argues that cognitive processes are not amodal—meaning that they are not disconnected or unrelated to the means by which the brain receives and processes information from our sensory systems and constructs a schema of the embodied self in relation to the sensory environment around us (Forte & Gallese, 2014). Rather, this perspective argues that the embodiment of our sensations in the contingent systems of the body and brain are the basis for representing and understanding the meaning of spaces, places, and objects in that environment. Moreover, the construction of that body schema from proprioceptive signals (proprioception; from the Latin, *proprius*, "one's own" or "individual", and *capio* or *capere*, meaning "to take" or "to grasp") and exteroceptive (special sensory) signals provide the substratum for sensorimotor integration and the means for motor simulation. Together, sensorimotor integration and motor simulation builds a mimetic understanding of observed or potential action in context. Such simulation creates meaning through the association of present embodied experience with stored representation of episodic and implicit memory, such as the explicit remembrances of prior experience and the emotions and feelings associated with such memories (Forte & Gallese, 2014; Gallese & Cuccio, 2017; Williams et al., 2020). For expert practitioners in archaeology, the operations of such neurocognitive processes underlying embodied consciousness would be expected to be shaped by specific sensorimotor experience essential for the development of instrumental skills and the acquisition, assimilation, and integration of specialized knowledge. Collectively, these processes and experience constitute expertise in the discipline.

Vulci: A Virtual Excavation

Vulci (Viterbo Province, Italy) was one of the most important Etruscan city-states in the 1st millennium BCE and became a Roman city in 280 BCE. The habitation site had over 1,500 years of continuous life and a very large funerary area around the volcanic plateau. Duke University leads a multi-years plan of archaeological excavations in the Southern part of the volcanic plateau, the so-called Western Forum; initially Etruscan, then a Roman part of the city.

This partial view of an urban society requires broader contextualisation addressing the city's formation, plans, and spatial organisation; the relationships among domestic, public, and religious architecture; and the religious and political connections between urban and suburban sanctuaries, temples, and funerary monuments. The study of waterscapes in 3D is the key to answer these research questions. Vulci was formed in proximity to an important river, the Fiora, and its fluvial port. The complexity of underground water systems, cisterns, pipes, tunnels, and channels at different depths in Vulci can be correctly visualised and studied only in a 3D virtual simulation. In fact, the geolocation of underground water systems at different depths, as well as associated ground monuments, reveals a complex waterscape.

This 3D data recording is extremely accurate for the reconstruction of all the chronological phases of the site. Each layer is the reference context for all the archaeological objects, fauna, and other residuals found within it. The 3D geolocation and shape of each element reconstructs water paths, volumes, and clusters of the same infrastructure, which was serving the entire city. Related to this, the Duke research team documented for the first time in Southern Etruria a very large (about 40 cubic meters) intact cistern, stratigraphically excavated and documented in 3D, including all the correlated tunnels, occluded shafts, well curbstone, and feeding conduits. In the southern part of the plateau, Duke's team mapped an additional six cisterns and two wells. This means that all the archaeological stratigraphy and architectural elements were documented in three dimensions, by means of laser scanning, geophysical prospections, and digital photogrammetry. All these digital assets constitute an important 3D database for virtually reconstructing all the main phases of archaeological excavation and visualising them in VR headsets. This simulation is used in the field and in the lab for the archaeological training of diggers and other specialists.

Eye-tracking: A Form of Cognitive Experience Measurement

In an attempt to explore the space between archaeology and cognitive science in order to better understand the mind–environment relationship, we chose to begin our investigations by recording the patterns of eye movements expressed by viewers as they engaged with the digital reconstructions of the Vulci site. Eye-tracking has long been a major component of psychological and neuroscientific research, as it has provided psychologists with the means to draw links between visual sensation and cognition. While eye-tracking devices were relatively rudimentary at their conception, over a century of development and improvement has led to the creation of advanced eye-tracking technologies that can help address a broad range of questions related to both physiology and the perception process (Wade, 2010). With an increase in applications of eye-tracking technology, it is important to not only consider our observations of neurological processes in the lab but also in the natural environment, as this can provide necessary insight into how we interact with our surroundings. Liu et al. (2019), for instance, made use of eye-tracking technology to analyse audio-visual interactions in the forest landscape, therefore, peering behind the curtain to understand our interactive relationship with nature. Also, Stevenson et al. (2019) used eye-tracking devices to analyse the restorative effects of the natural environment on children's cognitive processes. There is a clear precedent and need for a greater understanding of how natural sensation affects our cognition, and analysing the eye-movement patterns that mediate visual interactions with the environment appears to be an efficient step towards this goal.

Eye movement control has previously been divided into four primary subdivisions: saccadic, smooth pursuit, vergence, and vestibulo-ocular (Robinson, 1968). Smooth pursuit involves conjugate eye movements that track a moving object in the field of view. Vergence movements are dis-conjugate eye movements in the horizontal direction allowing for binocular fixation when the target of fixation shifts from a distant to a near object, or vice versa. Vestibulo-ocular eye movements are generated by the vestibular systems, which comprises positional and rotational and linear acceleration mechanisms originating in the inner ear that are transducing the movements and position of the head. These systems work with the visual system to stabilise fixation and prevent blurring of vision when the head moves. Lastly, saccades are rapid, ballistic eye movements that change the point of fixation, which are essential for inspecting a scene, a landscape, or an object (Robinson, 1968). Thus, of the basic patterns of eye movements, saccades are those of greatest relevance for our pilot studies as they provide opportunity for documenting and analysing the means by which viewers engaged with visual objects and imagery–real or digital.

As research on the oculomotor system has developed, neuroscientists have gained a better understanding of which brain regions are responsible for which patterns of eye movements. Vergence movements appear to be controlled through communication between the occipital lobe, parietal lobe, and frontal eye field, with the primary visual cortex of the occipital lobe being responsible for the tuning of fixations and higher-order visual cortex initiating the vergence movement (Searle & Rowe, 2016). Saccades and smooth pursuits both appear to be controlled in part by the frontal eye field, parietal eye field, supplementary eye field, superior colliculus and cerebellar vermis, with sub-regions that appear to be dedicated to each type of eye movement (Tian & Lynch, 1996). Though their control may be spread out throughout the brain, saccades are generally recognised as being under the control of the superior colliculus and the frontal eye field (Purves et al., 2001). Saccades themselves have been the subjects of many recent studies within the field of neuroscience, providing beneficial insight into how eye-tracking data can be interpreted. In a study by Abrams et al. (1989), it was discovered that there is a near-linear relationship between saccadic velocity and accuracy, with distance from an intended target having greater variability as the target moved further from the initial line of vision. Additionally, a study conducted with drivers identified that lower saccadic velocity is linked to mental fatigue (Stasi et al., 2012). Knowledge of the relationships between these brain regions and of the nature of saccadic eye movements provides context to the analysis of eye-tracking data, especially analyses that are situated in free-viewing circumstances.

Methods: Web-based Eye-tracking

An account was made on the GazeRecorder online platform (https://gazerecorder.com/) and the recorded videos of the archaeological VR experience were linked to a project within GazeRecorder. This software then allowed us to send two links to the participants which, when clicked on, would begin short eye-tracking calibrations before presenting the videos. The VR simulation of the archaeological excavations in Vulci was entirely developed in Unity 3D and accessible in desktop applications and in Oculus Rift and Vive Cosmos headsets. Each video lasted 60 seconds.

The design for the VR world included a nearly flat archaeological site with limited spatial dimensions, and all space beyond these boundaries was empty (as seen in Figure 13.1). Ambient noise was added to the experience, as this has been shown to make VR experiences more immersive.

Due to the nature of web-based eye-tracking and the GazeRecorder software, there were certain limitations that needed to be addressed during data collection. Primarily, based on pre-assessment analysis of GazeRecorder's functionality, it was determined that the most accurate results could be obtained with maximum natural lighting directly on the face (as opposed to artificial lighting), with glasses taken off, and with the eyes approximately 0.5 m from the webcam. Participants were asked to follow these guidelines as much as possible. Participants were also asked to keep their focus on their screens for the duration of the experience, as we found that turning one's head more than approximately 45° in any direction permanently disrupted GazeRecorder's calibration.

When the experience was complete, we were able to analyse the participants' experiences via heatmaps of visual gaze that were laid over the videos they were presented (Figure 13.1). These heatmaps use the colour green to indicate the direction of observation, blue to indicate saccadic movement to another green region, and yellow or red to indicate areas of persistent gaze (with the fixation in red regions being of the greatest intensity). It is important

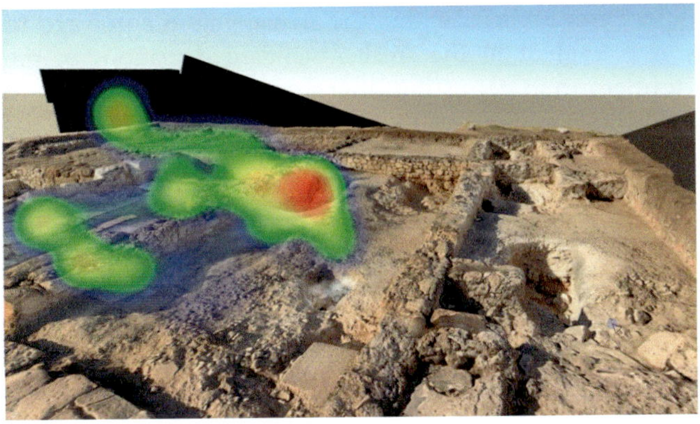

Figure 13.1 Sample Heatmap on the VR Environment. This Heatmap Data was Generated from Ten Seconds of Visual Engagement with the Virtual Environment.

to note that the participants experienced the environments through videos with ambient noise as opposed to still images. This inherently changes the experience, as it is more immersive, provides a greater sense of depth, allows participants to view different aspects of the environments from different angles, and provides a shorter period of time with the edges of the environments still in view. In addition to the heatmaps, CSV files were exported from GazeRecorder that documented x–y position of gaze every at every location of fixation, which typically shifted after 50 msec with the notable exception of sporadic fixations on features of interest that could last up to 900 msec.

For this pilot study, samples of convenience were obtained through the personal and professional networks of the authors with the goal of obtaining data from 20 expert archaeologists and 20 novice observers on each of three videos prepared to present surface observations of the Vulci site. Not all observers completed the web-based eye-tracking protocol on all three videos. The perspective of observation was designed in Unity 3D to simulate the view of a human observer walking the site.

Preliminary Results

Quantitative analyses were conducted to determine the average number of visual fixations as well as the timestamps in the videos when participants fixated features of interest. Figure 13.2 presents histograms of the average number of fixations for both groups of participants on each of the three videos. The results of this phase of our analysis were inconsistent across the three videos. In Study 1 (the first video), there were no differences between observer groups. Novice observers tended towards greater numbers of fixation in Study 2 compared to the archaeologists. The opposite trend was observed with Study 3 (the third video). Despite these inconsistencies in average number of fixations across videos, we did observe more consistencies within the archaeologists compared to the novice observers as is evident in the smaller standard deviations of the measurements in the former group versus the latter.

Although the data on average number of fixations was inconsistent across the three videos between the groups of observers, there were much more consistent differences between groups when we analysed the time of fixation. To do so, GazeRecorder software provided a measure of "gap", which is defined as the amount of time between changes in the direction of gaze. Thus, the average gap time is a measure of the average duration of fixations on features in the video. This analysis revealed consistencies across all videos, with archaeologists exhibiting longer durations of visual fixation during engagement with each of three videos compared with the novice observers (Figure 13.3).

Given these quantitative findings regarding oculomotor behaviour during visual engagement with the videos, we next pursued qualitative analyses to determine what aspects of the scenes presented in the videos engaged the observers, as indicated by periods of visual fixation. Figure 13.4 shows representative heatmaps generated from four, 0.5 s segments of visual

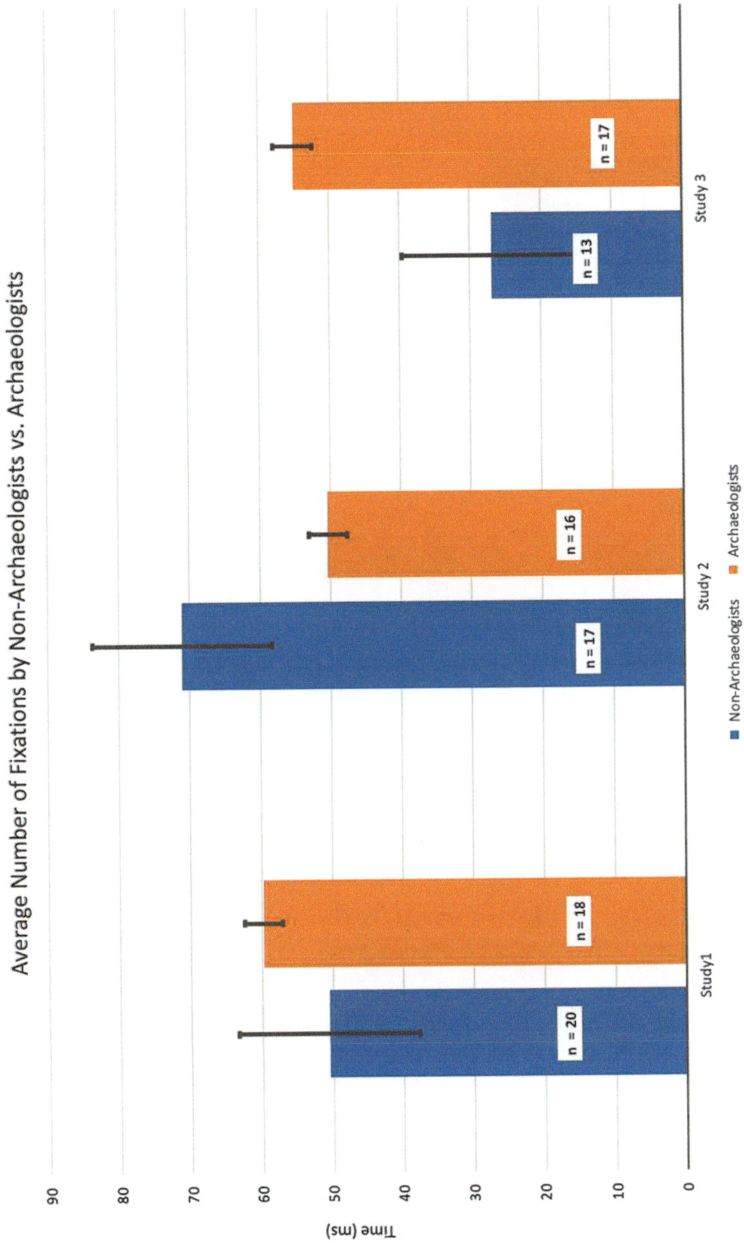

Figure 13.2 Average Number of Fixations by Novice Observers (Non-Archaeologists) and Expert Archaeologists (Bars Represent Standard Deviations).

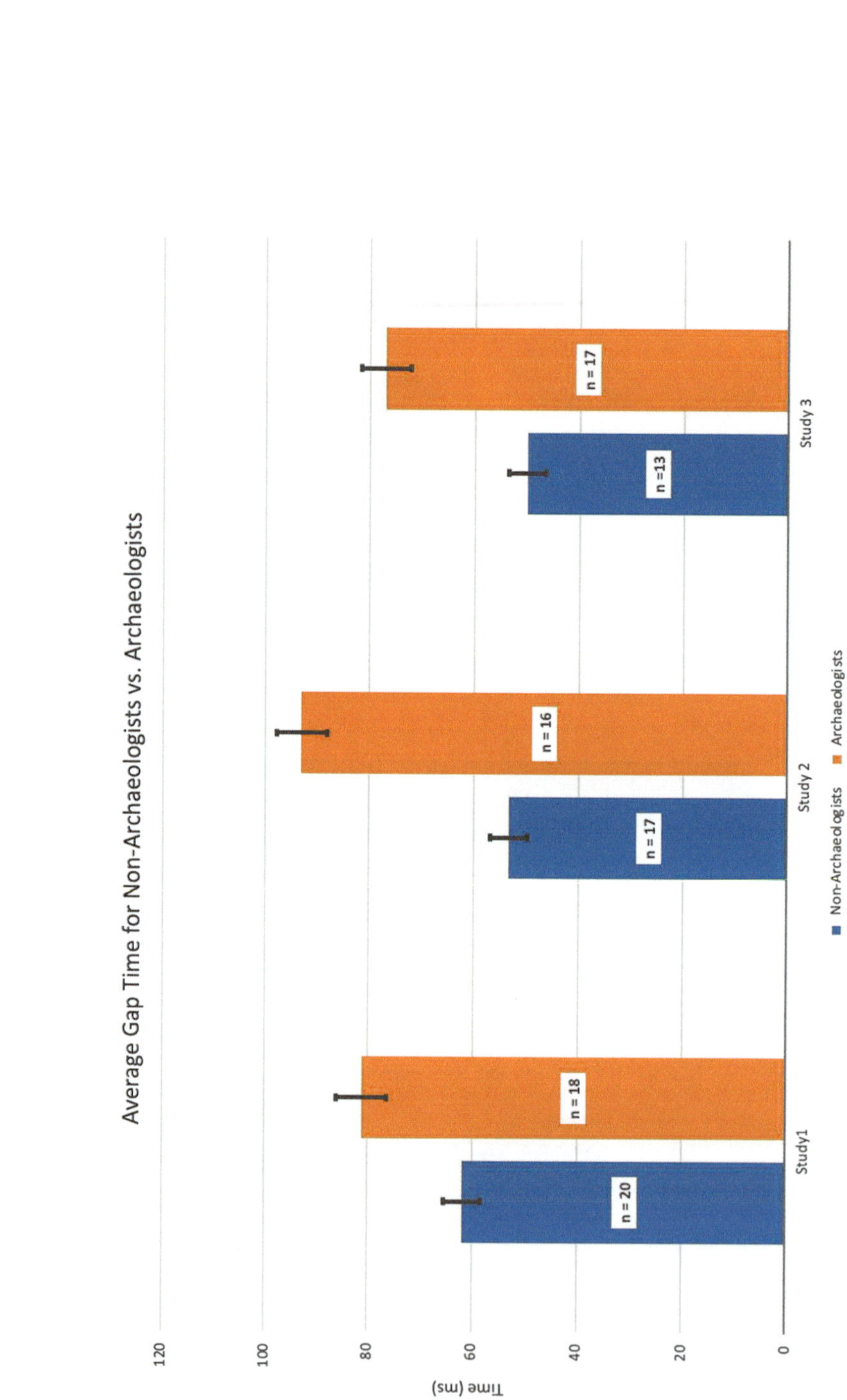

Figure 13.3 Average Gap Time for Novice Observers (Non-Archaeologists) and Expert Archaeologists (Bars Represent Standard Deviations).

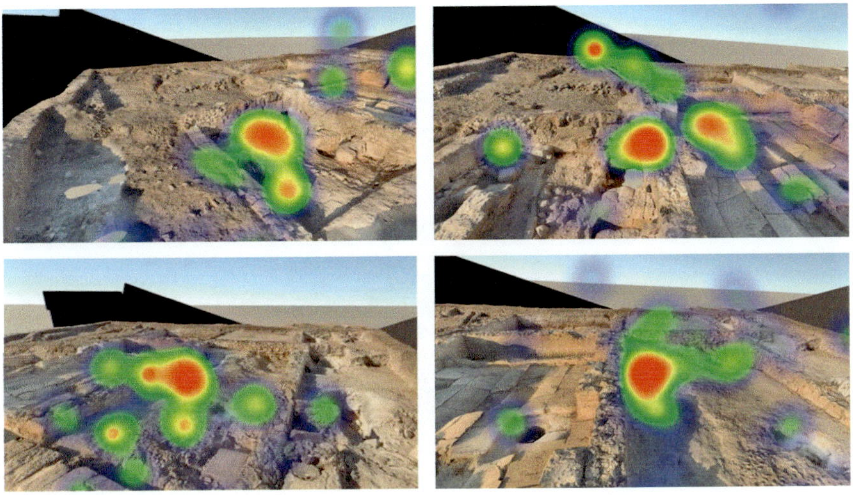

Figure 13.4 Four Heatmaps from the Composite Dataset of All Novice (Non-Archaeologist) Observers. Each Panel Represents 0.5 s of Free Viewing Collected across All Observers in this Group.

engagement in the novice (non-archaeologist) group. As is evident in these representative heatmaps (and observed elsewhere in the dataset), the visual gaze of novice observers is often drawn towards holes, dark or shadowed recesses, and apparently fragmented artefacts. Fixations were often temporally clustered together, but these clusters were typically separated by epochs of more frequent saccadic behaviour, consistent with the shorter mean gap time for this cohort.

Figure 13.5 shows representative heatmaps generated from four, 0.5s segments of visual engagement in the group of expert archaeologists. Overall, expert observers appeared to show less uniformity within the group, as is evident by the relatively diminished presence of red in the heatmaps of the experts compared to the heatmaps of the novices (cf. Figure 13.4). Thus, fewer locations within the visual scenes attracted the attention of the expert observers compared to the novices. However, there were selected locations that tended to draw the visual gaze of the experts. Archaeologists tended to spend more fixation time on foreground features and on a greater number of artefacts that were well-lit in the virtual environment. Moreover, they spent more time scanning ahead to the objects that were soon to come into the central field of view as the video panned across and into the virtual environment.

Conclusions and Future Perspectives

This pilot study is part of a new research program established at Duke University on neuroscientific applications in archaeology and virtual reality.

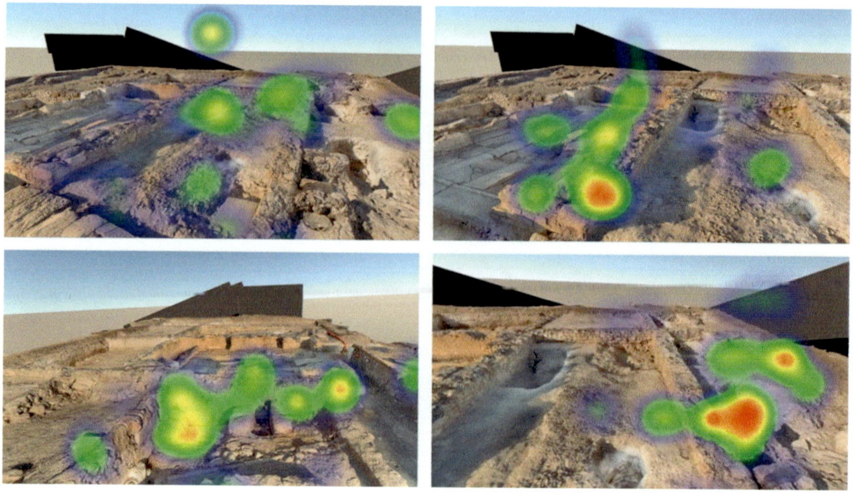

Figure 13.5 Four Heatmaps from the Composite Dataset of All Expert (Archaeologist) Observers. Each Panel Represents 0.5 s of Free Viewing Collected across All Observers in this Group.

Consequently, as work in progress, these interpretations are just a preliminary step to more articulated quantitative and qualitative analyses this team will conduct in the near future. In this project, because of the COVID-19 restrictions, most of these experiments were conducted remotely and on the web (by web-cam eye-tracking). It was not possible to access and utilise more ideal controlled environments for research, such as the Dig@Lab at Duke University (https://diglab.duke.edu/).

In general, eye-tracking is mainly based on conscious engagement with visual environments and artefacts assessed through quantitative measurements and qualitative descriptions of free-viewing behaviour, most of which is happening in real-time without explicit, top-down direction of oculomotor behaviour. Thus, observers are free to allow various features of an object or a scene capture their attention and elicit saccade eye movements and visual fixations. Nevertheless, the observer is generally unaware of the kinematics of the movements, such as the metrics of saccadic eye movements or the dwell time on features of interest. Thus, for the purposes of understanding how observers (novices or experts) engage with real or virtual environments, the eye-tracking record is absolutely significant for the analysis of observation and visual interaction. Dwell time, visual path, and fixations can show not only possible regions or points of interest, but also the modalities of visual attraction. Our next steps in this analysis will be to more systematically categorise those features of the Vulci site that attract and sustain the interest of the observers. We also aim to complement our studies of oculomotor engagement with EEG-based studies of cognitive mechanisms of engagement. This next phase of our neuroarchaeological investigations will require more complex analyses and specific research questions that are appropriate for this methodology. For example, we would seek to determine which features of an archaeological site engage various modes of cognitive processing that are reflected in specific spectral profiles of EEG activity. One might hypothesise that expert observers will have increased power in gamma frequency bands when inspecting features of archaeological significance, compared to novice observers. Secondarily, one might hypothesise further that EEG power would shift in systematic and predictable frequency patterns are experts actively explore a virtual recreation of an archaeological site, such as Vulci.

Successful integration of virtual reality, eye-tracking, and EEG methodologies provides a tractable approach for cognitive and neurobiological studies of spatial embodiment in archaeological experience. In our pilot study, the two groups of observers showed strong interest in the identification of archaeological data; but they tended to show different approaches in their visual engagement with the simulations. The group of novice, non-archaeologists tended to show an overall appreciation of the excavation without a detailed understanding of significant elements. On the contrary, the group of archaeologists showed greater skill in feature-tracking with a particular focus on clusters of archaeological material and architectural characterisations.

In conclusion, despite the demonstrably different observational skills of archaeologists and non-archaeologists, these preliminary results suggest differences between groups in visual and spatial embodiment—even in virtual simulations of archaeological experiences. The accuracy of the 3D embodiment in virtual headsets is determined by the correctness of scale and sense of presence in VR; we assume that these factors can improve the quality of the experience. Future experiments in VR and on-site by EEG and eye-tracking could be used also to evaluate training and spatial learning for archaeologists, heritage experts, and then the general public.

References

Abrams, R.A., Meyer, D.E., & Kornblum, S. (1989). Speed and accuracy of saccadic eye movements: Characteristics of impulse variability in the oculomotor system. *Journal of Experimental Psychology: Human Perception and Performance*, 15, 529–543.

Barsalou, L.W. (2008). Grounded cognition. *Annual Review of Psychology*, 59, 617–645.

Davis, J.D., Coulson, S., Arnold, A.J., & Winkielman, P. (2021). Dynamic grounding of concepts: Implications for emotion and social cognition. In M.D. Robinson, & L.E. Thomas (Eds.), *Handbook of Embodied Psychology* (pp. 23–42). Switzerland: Springer.

Forte, M., & Gallese, V. (2014). *Embodiment and 3D Archaeology: A Neolithic House at Çatalhöyük*, in *Breaking Barriers*. In Proceedings of the 47th Annual Chacmool Archaeological Conference, 7–9 November 2014, edited by Robyn Crook, Kim Edwards and Colleen Hughes Chacmool 2015. The Chacmool Archaeological Association of the University of Calgary, 2014, pp. 35–55.

Gallese, V., & Cuccio, V. (2017). The paradigmatic body. Embodied simulation, intersubjectivity and the bodily self. In T. Metzinger, & J. Windt (Eds.), *Open Mind*. Cambridge, Massachusetts: The MIT Press.

Liu, Y., Hu, M., & Zhao, B. (2019). Audio-visual interactive evaluation of the forest landscape based on eye-tracking experiments. *Urban Forestry & Urban Greening*, 46, 126476.

Purves, D., Augustine, G.J., Fitzpatrick, D., Katz, L.C., LaMantia, A., McNamara, J. O., & Williams, S.M. (2001). Neural control of saccadic eye movements. In *Neuroscience* (2nd edition). Sunderland (MA): Sinauer Associates.

Robinson, D.A. (1968). The oculomotor control system: A review. *Proceedings of the IEEE*, 56, 1032–1049.

Renfrew, C., & Malafouris, L. (2008). Steps to a "neuroarchaeology" of mind, Part 1, Introduction. *Cambridge Archaeological Journal*, 18, 381–385.

Searle, A., & Rowe, F.J. (2016). Vergence neural pathways: A systematic narrative. Literature review. *Neuro-Ophthalmology*, 40, 209–218.

Stasi, L.L.D., Renner, R., Catena, A., Cañas, J.J., Velichkovsky, B.M., & Pannasch, S. (2012). Towards a driver fatigue test based on the saccadic main sequence: A partial validation by subjective report data. *Transportation Research Part C: Emerging Technologies*, 21(1), 122–133.

Stevenson, M.P., Dewhurst, R., Schilhab, T., & Bentsen, P. (2019). Cognitive restoration in children following exposure to nature: Evidence From the attention network task and mobile eye tracking. *Frontiers in Psychology*, 10, 42.

Tian, J.R., & Lynch, J.C. (1996). Corticocortical input to the smooth and saccadic eye movement subregions of the frontal eye field in Cebus monkeys. *Journal of Neurophysiology*, 76, 2754–2771.

Wade, N.J. (2010). Pioneers of eye movement research. *I-Perception*, 1, 33–68.

Williams, J.H.G., Huggins, C.F., Zupan, B., & Willis, M., Van Rheenen, T.E., Sato, W., Palermo, R., Ortner, C., Krippl, M., Kret, M., Dickson, J.M., Li, C.R., & Lowe, L.A. (2020). Sensorimotor control framework for understanding emotional communication and regulation. *Neuroscience & Biobehavioral Reviews*, 112, 503–518.

An End That Is a Beginning

Annalisa Banzi

A few words to conclude this book and start experimenting what has been suggested here. All types of museums are invited to take advantage of the newly developed BFM approach by exploring innovative ways to design visitors' experiences.

I am currently creating the first BFM project with a mixed group of experts. It is focused on emotions, which is the first topic addressed in this book and a very urgent matter to consider in the global pandemic panorama we are experiencing. Stress and anxiety have dramatically increased and museums can play an important role in offering relaxing activities that give relief from these afflictions. Decreasing negative mental states improves our mental wellbeing and the quality of life. According to psychologists and psychiatrists, a person can be completely cured from anxiety. There are well-proven techniques that can be learned which effectively deal with this emotion and stress. The BFM project explores five methods. Some of them are famous (e.g., mindfulness and art therapy), others are experimental techniques, such as the one that combines the stimuli of the cultural heritage with those of nature. The three-year research study will be carried out in Milan (Italy) and will involve a fine arts museum and a natural history museum. It aims to demonstrate that these strategies can be applied to various types of museum objects. This initiative is addressed to people affected by different levels of non-pathological anxiety, who want to engage themselves in cultural experiences that can relieve their emotional tension, and thus improve their wellbeing. The objective is not to attempt to diagnose or treat visitors who have anxiety problems. The overall goal is to provide a calm and safe space where people:

- feel less anxious by improving their wellbeing during their museum experience
- can be more aware of what stress and anxiety are, and how they affect an individual
- have the chance to learn and practice some techniques to relieve the mental pain while looking at and learning about museum objects
- familiarise with a museum and become regular visitors

The project is intended to be a practical aid to museums interested in wellbeing-related activities. For this reason, it proposes more than one strategy in order to give museums the chance to choose the most appropriate method for them. In this regard, the selected strategies, once tested, will be presented and evaluated not in competitive terms but in a descriptive way as a guide for their application.

There are two other main objectives to be achieved. The first is to develop practices similar to those available in Canada and United Kingdom, enabling family physicians to prescribe museum visits. The second is to share the proven procedures and information collected with interested museums. This could also promote an exchange of experimental data between museums and research centres.

In the near future, it would also be worthwhile to resume experiments on memory (e.g., priming—chapter 4 of this book) and to design others on the cognitive processes introduced here. The first chapter suggests procedures which can be considered as advice on how to start experimenting with these phenomena in museums.

This book does not deal with museum staff. However, the BFM approach considers museum personnel as a key element in developing rewarding visitor experiences. This statement might sound trivial, but actually it is not. There are various issues to consider such as the wellbeing of the staff, how the environment in which they work influences them, and their capacity to work as a team. Further publications will address this topic in depth.

The BFM approach is under development and an on-going project. Each of the proposed contributions (chapters 9–13) may help to define it better. Let's develop brain-friendly museums together!

Index

For Product Safety Concerns and Information please contact our EU representative GPSR@taylorandfrancis.com Taylor & Francis Verlag GmbH, Kaufingerstraße 24, 80331 München, Germany